New Talent Design 2002

The International Annual of Student Design and Communication Arts
Das internationale Jahrbuch über Kommunikationsdesign von Studenten
Le répertoire international de projets d'expression visuelle d'étudiants

CEO & Creative Director: B. Martin Pedersen

Publisher: Doug Wolske

Editors: Michael Porciello, Andrea Birnbaum
and Heinke Jenssen

Art Director: Lauren Slutsky
Design & Production: Joseph Liotta
and Nicole Recchia

Published by Graphis Inc.

This book is dedicated to the
memory of Horst Busecke
(1931-2001)

Opposite: Watercolor by Teresa Holder, Oklahoma State University

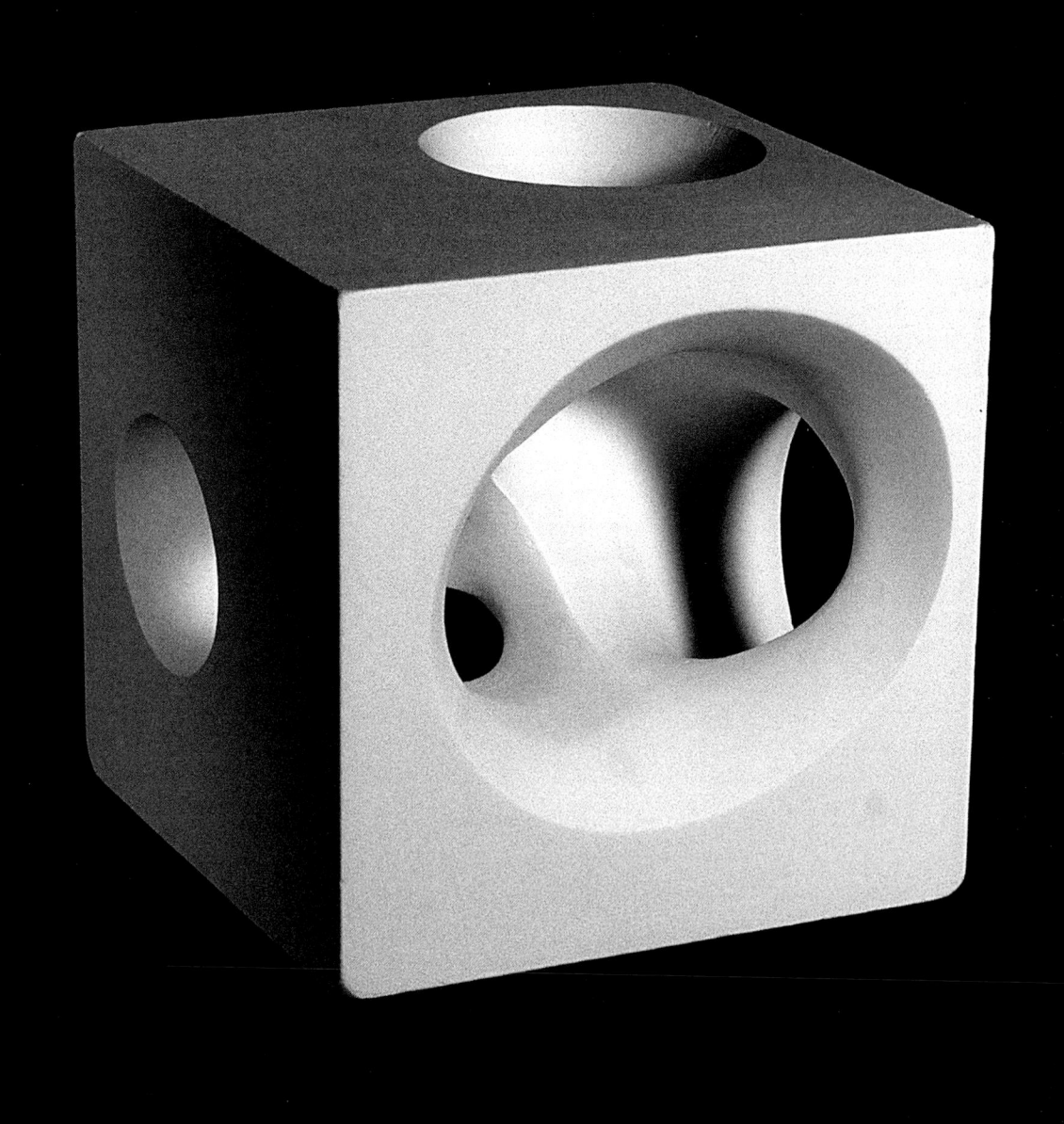

Contents Inhalt Sommaire

Commentary Kommentar, Commentaire 6

Advertising, Werbung, Publicité 12
Annual Reports, Jahresberichte, Rapports annuels 68
Books, Bücher, Livres 70
Brochures, Broschüren, Brochures 80
Calendars, Kalender, Calendriers 82
Corporate Identity 84
Currency, Banknoten, Billets de banque 93
Editorial, Publikationen, Publication 94
Games, Spiele, Jeux 110
Illustration, Illustrationen 114
Letterhead, Briefschaften, Papiers à lettres 128
Logos, Logos, Logos 132
Music CDs, Musik-CDs, CD 136
Packaging, Packungen, Packaging 148
Paper Promotion, Papierhersteller, Fabricants de papier 181
Photography, Photographie 182
Poster, Plakate, Affiches 192
Products, Produkte, Produits 210
Promotion, Promotionen, Promotions 220
Shopping bags, Tragtaschen, Sacs 222
Stamps, Briefmarken, Timbres 227
Typography, Typographie 228
Websites 230
Other Diverses, Divers 234

Captions and Credits, Legenden und Künstlerangaben, Légendes et artistes 236
Index, Verzeichnisse 248
Schools and Universities, Schulen und Universitäten, Ecoles et Universités 250

Remarks: We extend our heartfelt thanks to contributors throughout the world who have made it possible to publish a wide and international spectrum of the best work in this field. Entry instructions for all Graphis Books may be requested from: **Graphis Inc.**, 307 Fifth Avenue, Tenth Floor, New York, NY 10016, or visit our Web site at www.graphis.com. *Anmerkungen:*

Unser Dank gilt den Einsendern aus aller Welt, die es uns ermöglicht haben, ein breites, internationales Spektrum der besten Arbeiten zu veröffentlichen. Teilnahmebedingungen für die Graphis-Bücher sind erhältlich bei: **Graphis Inc.**, 307 Fifth Avenue, Tenth Floor, New York, NY 10016. Besuchen Sie uns im World Wide Web, www.graphis.com. *Remerciements:*

Nous remercions les participants du monde entier qui ont rendu possible la publication de cet ouvrage offrant un panorama complet des meilleurs travaux. Les modalités d'inscription peuvent être obtenues auprès de: **Graphis Inc.**, 307 Fifth Avenue, Tenth Floor, New York, NY 10016. Rendez-nous visite sur notre site web www.graphis.com. © Copyright under universal copy-

right convention copyright © 2001 by Graphis Inc., 307 Fifth Avenue, Tenth Floor, New York, NY 10016. Jacket and book design copyright © 2002 by Graphis, Inc. No part of this book may be reproduced in any form without written permission of the publisher. Distributed in North America by Publishers Group West. Printed in Korea.
ISBN: 1-931241-05-8

Opposite: "Convexity Problem" by Ryan Bruce, Pratt Institute

OCULUS

Published by the American Institute of Architects New York Chapter, Volume 62, Number 1, September 1999

AN EYE ON NEW YORK ARCHITECTURE

- 6 — The Newest Penn Station
- 7 — Kolatan/MacDonald at Artists Space
- 8 — New Books on Houses
- 10 — Alexander Gorlin on The Un-private House at MoMA

Home, Sweet Home?
New Houses and Housing by New York Architects

Commentary Kommentar Commentaire

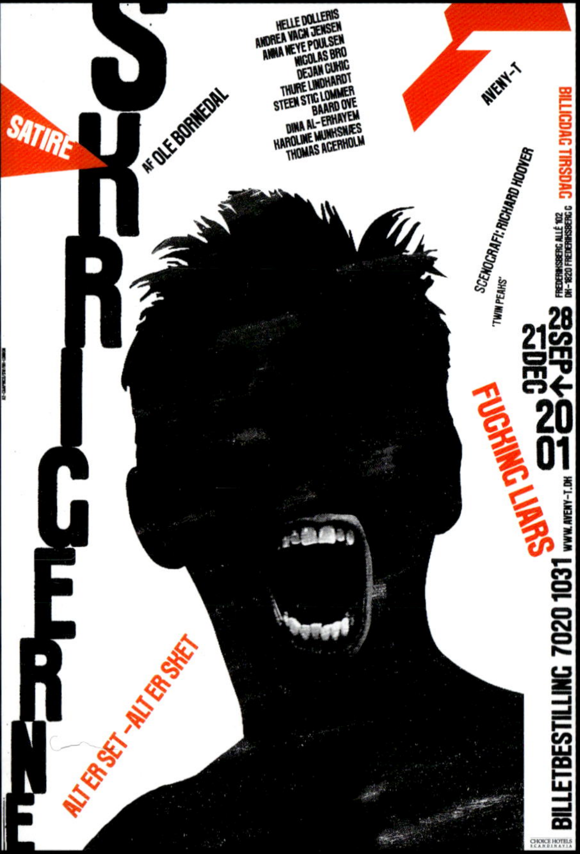
SKRIGERNE
SATIRE
AF OLE BORNEDAL
HELLE DOLLERIS
ANDREA VAGN JENSEN
ANNA NEYE POULSEN
NICOLAS BRO
DEJAN CUKIC
THURE LINDHARDT
STEEN STIG LOMMER
BAARD OVE
DINA AL-ERHAYEM
KAROLINE MUNKSNÆS
THOMAS ACERHOLM
AVENY-T
BILLIGDAG TIRSDAG
FREDERIKSBERG ALLÉ 102
DK-1820 FREDERIKSBERG C
SCENOGRAFI: RICHARD HOOVER
'TWIN PEAKS'
28 SEP → 21 DEC 2001
FUCKING LIARS
WWW.AVENY-T.DK
BILLETBESTILLING 7020 1031
ALT ER SET - ALT ER SKET
CHOICE HOTELS SCANDINAVIA

AVENY-T
FORESTILLINGER
SHE LOVES YOU
2001 2002
SKRIGERNE
NATTEVAGTEN
BOBLERNE I BÆKKEN
BORNEDAL
WERDELIN
SCHAUFUSS
AVENY-T
FREDERIKSBERG ALLÉ 102
DK-1820 FREDERIKSBERG C
T +45 7020 1031
F +45 3323 3765
W WWW.AVENY-T.DK
E INFO@AVENY-T.DK

For this year's New Talent Annual, Graphis offered several young designers—graduates of some of the schools that regularly contribute to the annual—an opportunity to share their thoughts on a design education and the professional field. Here's what they had to say:

Henrik Kubel
Royal College of Art, London, 2000
Immediately after graduating from the Royal College of Art last year, Henrik Kubel and Scott Williams formed A2-GRAPHICS/SW/HK, a design firm that is set apart from many others because they create their own typefaces for each of their projects. From the start they were amazed by how eager the world seemed to embrace new designs, and by how well received they were by the industry. In the past year they've received a Distinctive Merit Award from the ADCNY, a Silver Cube, 5 Merit Awards in the Poster category and one Silver Award from the D&AD student awards for applied graphics. The have been featured in the Graphis Poster Annual, *Creative Review, Baseline Magazine,* the *Communication Arts USA Design Annual* and D&AD 2001 Annual. Last December they were selected for "Creative Futures" a yearly event showing young promising talent in the field of communications hosted by The Industry and Creative Review in London. They've just finished a major book project for the Victoria and Albert Museum, and an identity program for a new theatre in Copenhagen.

Who has inspired you most in your professional life?
I believe that my greatest inspiration is the people that I work with, and very much the collaboration with the client, the communication itself. Art and typography, wood type and letterpress, have been a great inspiration for many years. It would be hard to mention any designers over others, but James Victore, Henryk Tomaszewski, Paul Rand and Paula Scher represent, for me, some of the finest people in the industry.

Do you have any advice for current students?
Work hard, very hard. Be true to your self—and to the client. Make connections within the industry, especially the "old guard." Be open, share your knowledge. And last: never be afraid to go back to school.

Laura Crookston
The Portfolio Center, Atlanta, 1999
Since December 2000 Laura Crookston has been working in the gift division of Chronicle Books, the department that creationes and produces the company's gift products—items like journals, stationery, post cards, gift boxes and address books. Laura considers herself fortunate to have the opportunity to design in a variety of formats, each with its own challenges. As part of a team of three—designer, editor and production—she designs and art directs the project and coordinates artwork that is assigned out of house. "This has given me the opportunity to work with many talented designers and design firms in San Francisco as well as New York and other cities," she explains. Overall, the job allows Laura to enjoy creative freedom while working as part of a team, not to mention an extraordinary amount of control for someone who's only worked in the field for 2 1/2 years.

Who has inspired you most in your professional life?
My peers. I had the opportunity to study with and work with some very talented people who have inspired me to push myself and grow as a designer and an individual. It is very inspiring to see the accomplishments of those people as we move forward with our respective careers. Hank Richardson, my advisor and now dean of students at The Portfolio Center in Atlanta has also been an influential part of my career to date. He has encouraged me to do more than I thought I was capable of, pushing me as an individual and a designer. Even more than two years after graduating, Hank has been a great advisor and friend to me.

Do you have any advice for current students?
Practical experience is very important for current students and recent grads. If possible, students should try to an get internship while still in school. This practical knowledge will give a recent grad more leverage when trying to find their first job. Outside inspiration whether it is in another art field or just observation of the world in general should also be a very important aspect of a designer's education and career.

Carla Figueroa
Art Center College of Design, San Francisco
Carla Figueroa recently started her own company, cfigdesign, after working for the Design Office of the Art Center College of Design and several other companies in the Los Angeles area. Throughout her career, Figueroa's professional designs have earned recognition from her peers. The "Open House" catalogue for the Williamson Gallery, which she designed with Darin Beaman at the Art Center Design Office, won an *ID* 43rd Design Annual Distinction Award as well as the L.A. Winners Award by The Architectural Foundation of Los Angeles. Figueroa also teaches Experimental Typography at Art Center College of Design. She was recently recognized by the graduating students in the Graphics department and was named one of the "Great Teachers of the Graphics Design Department."

Who has inspired you most in your professional life?
I was lucky to have many great teachers while studying Graphic Design. Sharon Aki was the most influential

Opening page: OCULUS magazine covers by Maggie West and Pentagram. Opposite: Posters for Aveny-T by Henrik Kubel and Scott Williams at A2-GRAPHICS/SW/HK. This page: Promotional bag for REAL SIMPLE magazine by Laura Crookston and The Valentine Group teacher during my foundation courses. She introduced me to the core of Graphics, showing me how to start walking in this field. Denise Gonzales Crisp was my teacher while she was completing her Master Degree. That created a special atmosphere in the classroom since she exposed us to things she was experimenting with. She pushed my limits through the projects she assigned and introduced me to contemporary designers and design writing.

Do you have any advice for current students?
Always observe what is around you for inspiration. Take in the culture around you and expose yourself to as many different cultures as possible. Being a worldly person will make you a more conscious designer. Among all your future possibilities select the ones that really interest you. Do them with your heart, but at the same time remember that you are in the real world, so always follow the legal procedures, have your proofs signed, your contracts signed, no matter how small the project is or who your client is. This is not school any more.

Sophie Thomas and Kristine Matthews
Royal College of Art, London, 1997
Sophie Thomas and Kristine Matthews, founders of the design firm thomas.matthews, began working together while studying at the Royal College of Art School of Communication. They describe their design as "graphic interpretation that helps to humanize environments and makes people stop and think," and a guiding principle in their work is "maximum graphic impact with minimum environmental impact." Upon entering the professional world they were fortunate (and pleasantly surprised) to receive commissions for large-scale public design projects without yet earning a reputation or years of experience. When their "No Shop," a temporary storefront environment to promote "International No Shop Day," opened in 1997, there were 10 television crews waiting at 6 a.m. to film it. In 2000 they were among the *I.D.* 40, the top forty international designers under the age of 40.

Who has inspired you most in your professional life?
We are greatly inspired by the work of Tibor Kalman. His work was humorous, original and idea-driven but he never compromised on his beliefs. When you see his work and you understand the concept you think "Ahh, I wish I had done that!" We are also big fans of Saul Bass and Cornelia Parker.

Do you have any advice for current students?
Don't sell yourself to the design devil. Be original and strong in your concepts. Originality always stands out. Take responsibility for your design work. Be aware of the power you hold as a designer and use it well.

Maggie West
The Portfolio Center, Atlanta, 1997
Maggie West is currently the Creative Director at *Town & Country* magazine. Prior to that she worked at Pentagram, where she was a member of the team responsible for the logo and identity program of AirTrain, the light rail system being constructed by the Port Authority of New York and New Jersey to connect John F. Kennedy Airport to New York's mass transit system. "As construction on AirTrain launched," West explains, "my work appeared on billboards, the sides of busses and in subway cars. It was praised in *The New York Times* and celebrated in a ceremony chaired by the Governor. It was incredible to feel, for the first time, like a contributor at such a high level."

Who has inspired you most in your professional life?
I arrived at the Portfolio Center with an undergraduate degree in English Literature. Unsure of my decision to go to design school, I sat down with Hank Richardson, the Chair of the Design Department at the time. He spent an hour describing what a person with my perspective could accomplish as a designer. I left the "pep talk" with a list of reading material and a feeling of empowerment. Ever since, he has given me a "pep talk" and list of reading material for each turn in my career.

Do you have any advice for current students?
I am always surprised by the power of good presentation. Logic, confidence and good communication skills can be as important as brilliant design.
Know your audience. Do research. Each project is unique; solve the problem at hand. Use design as a tool to communicate. Feel passionate about the message you are relaying. Don't forget what inspires you, particularly interests outside of work. Give praise and credit when due. Never take yourself too seriously. Trust your gut.

This page: Products and Shopping bags for EarthShop by Sophie Thomas and Kristine Matthews at thomas.matthews. Opposite: Spreads from TOWN & COUNTRY *magazine by Maggie West and* TOWN & COUNTRY *magazine.*

Oh So Chic

AN INTERNATIONAL BEAUTY MEETS HER MATCH: THE WORLD'S MOST BEAUTIFUL COUTURE CLOTHES. PHOTOGRAPHS BY LORENZO AGIUS STYLED BY GRETCHEN GUNLOCKE

The Spanish actress and model Ines Sastre is not yet thirty, and already she has had some pretty amazing men in her life. As a UNICEF ambassador, she once interviewed the Dalai Lama on the subject of underprivileged children. Last year she made her singing debut with Luciano Pavarotti at the San Remo Festival in Italy. This September she was tapped to play a round of golf with world-class professional golfers in France for the Lancôme Trophy. (She's the face of Lancôme's Trésor perfume and a 20 handicap.) When she's not swinging a club for the cosmetics giant, she is one of the company's four main models, along with Italy's Cristina Reali, Belgium's Marie Gillain and America's Uma Thurman.) Currently Ines stars with Gerard Depardieu in the French thriller Videcq, which has just opened in Europe and will soon come to the United States. Based on the true story of Eugène-François Videcq, a 19th-century criminal who became Paris's police chief, it proves what a scene-stealer she is. (It won't be her first appearance in America, however; in 1990, at sixteen, she was photographed by the legendary Norman Parkinson as the quintessential Spanish beauty for the cover of Town & Country.) "Everyone tells me that Videcq is the film that will change my life," says the actress, who, apart from a small role in the 1995 remake of Sabrina, has appeared only in Spanish and French movies. But when your life includes male friends such as hers, frequent safaris — an anthropology student, she's been to Africa nearly forty times — and invitations like ours to dress up in the best of the season's haute couture clothes, who needs a change?

Put yourself on a pedestal, from top: Yellow satin Falona mule ($518), lizard Gibello heel ($755), pale-green alligator Carolyne slingback ($1,725) and lavender alligator crisscross Calliano mule ($975), all available at Manolo Blahnik, NYC. Select styles also available at Bergdorf Goodman, NYC, and Neiman Marcus.

Unschooled fantasy: Ines revels in the comforts of Christian Dior Haute Couture's gray silk taffeta skirt, South Sea pearl Clover ring, EMI logo tag from Chanel Fine Jewelry.) Opposite: An embroidered black lace haute couture dress by Valentino, one of Ines's favorite designers. Pearl and diamond Contrast earrings. For couturier and jewelry information, see page 266.

THE GREATEST SHOES ON EARTH
MANOLO BLAHNIK

WHO WANTS TO WEAR MANOLO BLAHNIKS? WHO doesn't? By now, everyone does, because everyone — even women who don't own a single pair, poor things! — knows that these legendary shoes, made by the Spanish-born, London-based designer of the same name, can spice up the simplest shift, the most pedestrian blue jeans. "Sex in a shoe," everyone says, including the men who buy Manolos for their wives and girlfriends.

But you — as a true devotee, you know it's much more than that. The softest leather, the whimsical colors, the most ingenious designs and the briefest whisper of a sole — that's really Manolo. You also know that they're rare, and pricey, too (from $400 to $2,400 a pair), and that they come in a range of looks, from flats to 90-, 70-, 90- and Marilyn Monroe-making 105-millimeter heels. You probably also realize the importance of toe cleavage, or the "décolleté of your shoe," as George Malkemus, president of Blahnik's American operation, delicately puts it. And you certainly know the private ritual of storing your treasures in their felt drawstring bags to protect them.

In fact, you can no doubt discuss the many other fine points of Manolos as adroitly as any Hollywood actress or New York fashionista.

But just so he absolutely sure...

Did you know that the slim heel Audrey Hepburn favored is called a Loon heel, and that in her home, Blahnik's version of it is called the Sabrina? Or that in London the same design is known as the Princess or kitten heel?

Did you know that only thirty to sixty pairs of Manolos are produced (which is, in Blahnik's world, means handstitched) a day at four family-owned factories?

Or that Blahnik himself, who normally divides his time between his headquarters in London and his home in Bath, England, spends four months a year at the factories, whose every location in northern Italy are a closely guarded secret?

Did you know that Blahnik's clientele runs all the way from grande dames — even very grande dames, like the late Jacqueline Kennedy Onassis and Pamela Harriman — to young diances (Tiffany Dubin, Marina Rust, Jane Lauder and her sister Aerin Lauder Zinterhofer) and on to divas and sexy stars like Sarah Jessica Parker, Jennifer Lopez, Heather Locklear and Foxy Brown? (That's quite a run, especially in heels!)

Did you know that Blahnik's latest knee-high alligator boots sold out this fall at Neiman Marcus at $13,000 a pair, as did three somewhat more moderate cousins at Bergdorf Goodman: alligator ankle boots for $4,500?

Sure, Manolos are expensive, but not after you learn what goes into them — and you probably don't know some of this: Blahnik's design and whimsy are straight from his heart, and after sketching out an idea that could come from anywhere — Africa, an English fern, macramé was big last season — the designer heads for one of his factories, where he carves his idea for the heel from a piece of wood. Then he does the same with the toe. Once the last is made from these two pieces, it is covered in masking tape, and Blahnik sketches his design directly onto it. The tape is carefully removed, and a pattern is taken from the sketched design. The material (it could be leather, silk, suede, feathers, whatever) is then cut and carefully tacked onto the last and allowed to set for two to three days (if the toe is pointy, for instance, it takes more time). Finally, the wafer-thin sole is mounted as the delicate shoe goes down the assembly line. The result: the prototype of a new Manolo, called the posta, from posare, which means "to try" in Italian (a fact we find utterly charming).

George Malkemus likens the individuality of Blahnik's whole shoemaking process to a chef making a soufflé. "The thing you cannot duplicate is the lightness of a Manolo Blahnik shoe — take one in your hand and lift it! If you have someone whip up a soufflé individually and bring it to your table, it's totally different than if they make a soufflé for 150 people."

BY PAMELA CLARKE KEOGH
PHOTOGRAPH BY GABRIELLA IMPERATORI-PENN
STYLED BY JULIE FLYNN

PORTRAITS IN BLACK AND WHITE

Spurning the florals and bright patterns that typically dominate spring collections, the major fashion houses have introduced a remarkable number of pieces in black and white this year. Ralph Lauren almost eschewed color altogether, while Yves Saint Laurent, Donna Karan and Valentino all used black and white for a substantial portion of their lines. Our look at the best of these offerings proves there is more to these classic "colors" than meets the eye.
Photographs by Anders Overgaard
Styled by Gretchen Gunlocke

Skin-care executive and former model Olivia Chantecaille once relied on color as an antidote to New York's all-black dress code. Thanks to offerings like this chevron-patterned dress from Ralph Lauren ($5,995), she has altered her stance. "Now that all of us have had time to play with color, black is coming back, but juxtaposed with its extreme, white," she says. Opposite: Chantecaille completes her outfit with a Leah C. Couture Millinery black-and-white horsehair sauce hat ($425). For shopping information, see page 232.

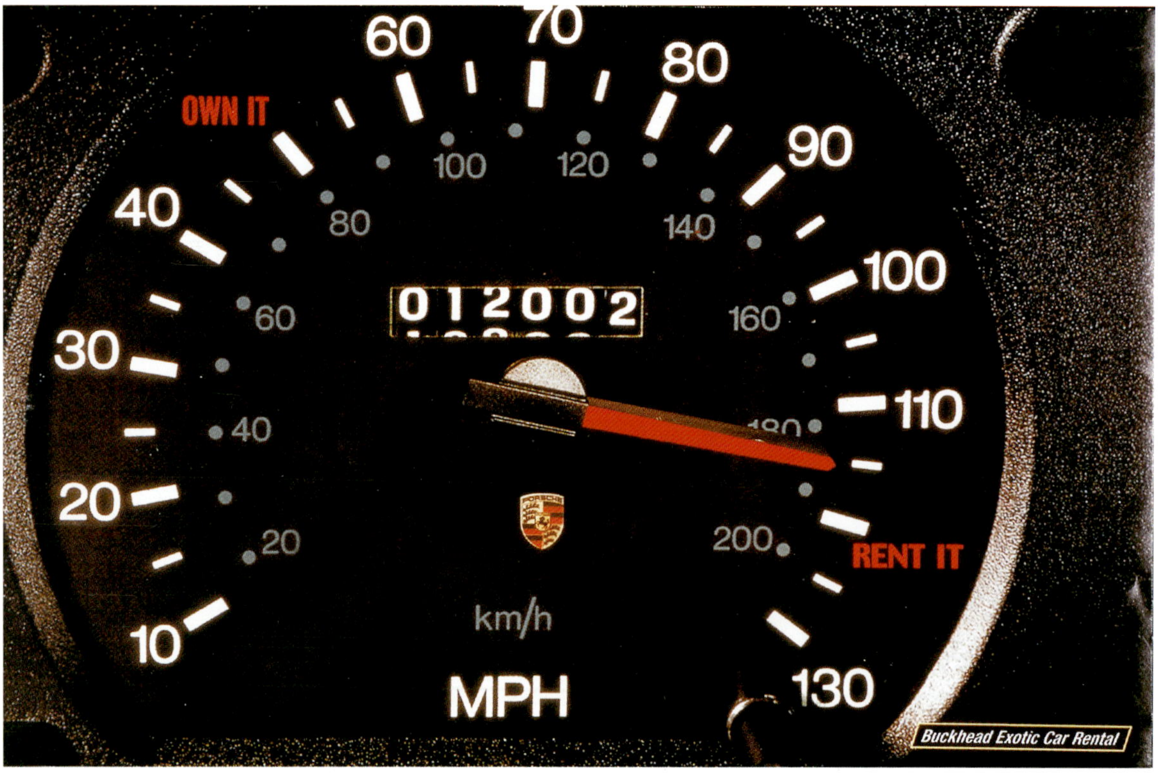

Tim Stier The Creative Circus

HUMMER

The horny hummer.

The helpful hummer.

The adventurous hummer.

*If you need a loan to afford one,
you might want to consider a nice economy car.
Like a BMW 7 Series.*

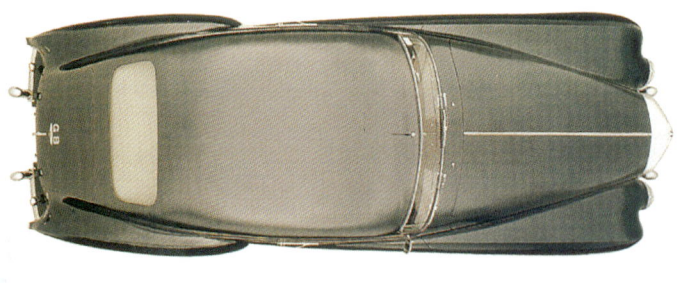

Rolls Royce

*Material posessions often reflect economic status.
Translation: If you got it flaunt it.*

Rolls Royce

Your chauffeur will appreciate the time off.

Rolls Royce

THE NEW
TOPLESS C70

VOLVO

ABSOLUT ART.

Michail Kiousis Vakalo School of Art & Design

ABSOLUT SPOT.

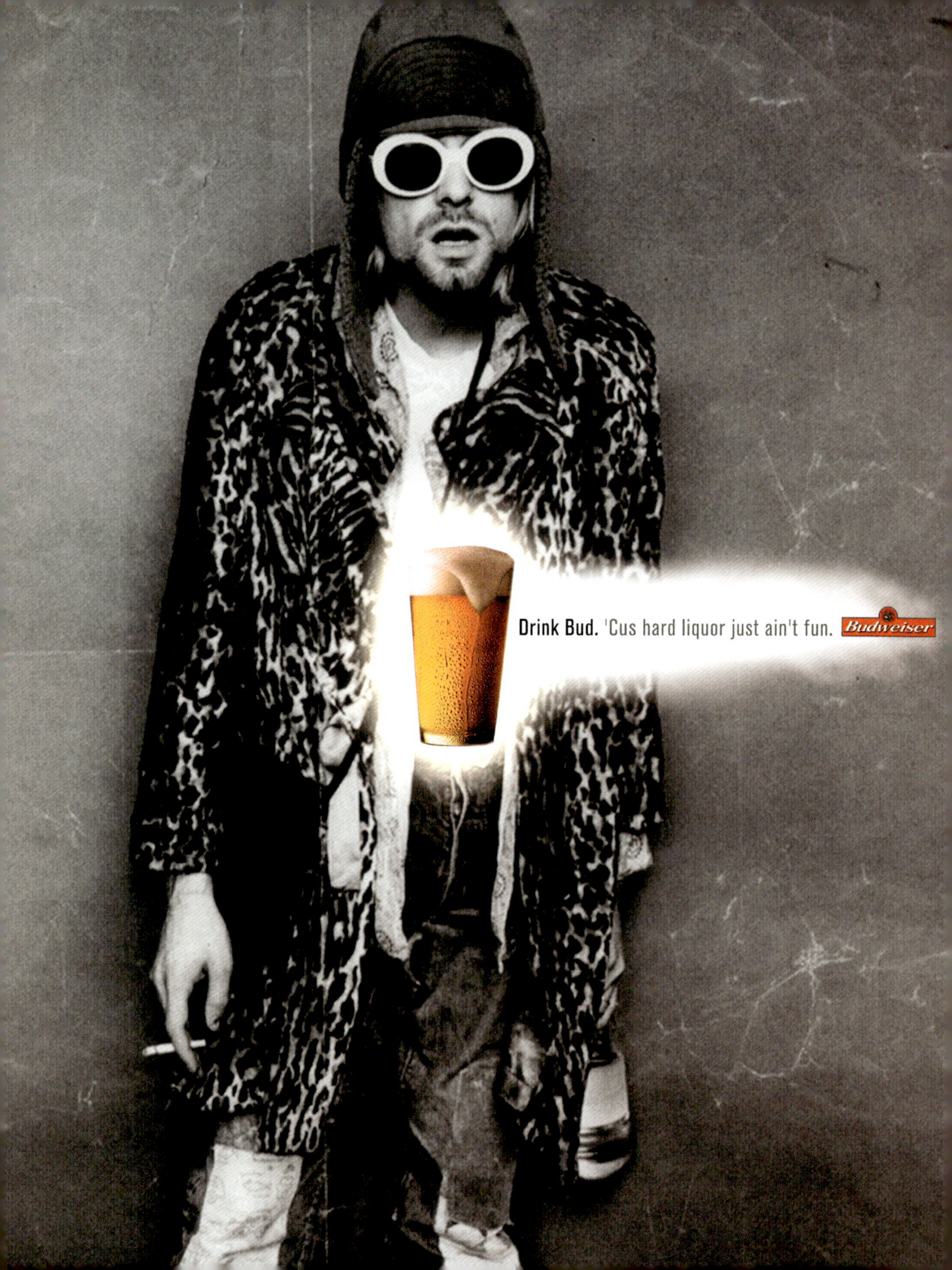
Drink Bud. 'Cus hard liquor just ain't fun.
Budweiser

Spread the Word **XEROX**

MAURICE GREENE
BULLET BOY
WORLD'S FASTEST MAN!
Faster than a speeding horse!
USA
TDK
1464
SEVILLA '99
Amazing!
See it to believe it!
Come watch some of the world's finest athletes compete for the World Record.
For more information on upcoming events log onto www.trackfield.com

Sergei Bubka the Human Spring
Able to leap giraffes with a single bound!
SHOCKING BUT TRUE
Come watch some of the world's finest athletes compete for the World Record.
For more information on upcoming events log onto www.trackfield.com

The CANNON ARMED WOMAN
PETRA FELKE
Outthrows 3x the length of a Brontosaurus with one shot!
NEVER BEEN done BEFORE
Come watch some of the world's finest athletes compete for the World Record.
For more information on upcoming events log onto www.trackfield.com

LOOK AROUND, SEE ANYONE WORTH BUMPING INTO?

matchmaker.com

MORE CHANCES AVAILABLE

Gone through everyone in the office?

matchmaker.com

More chances available.

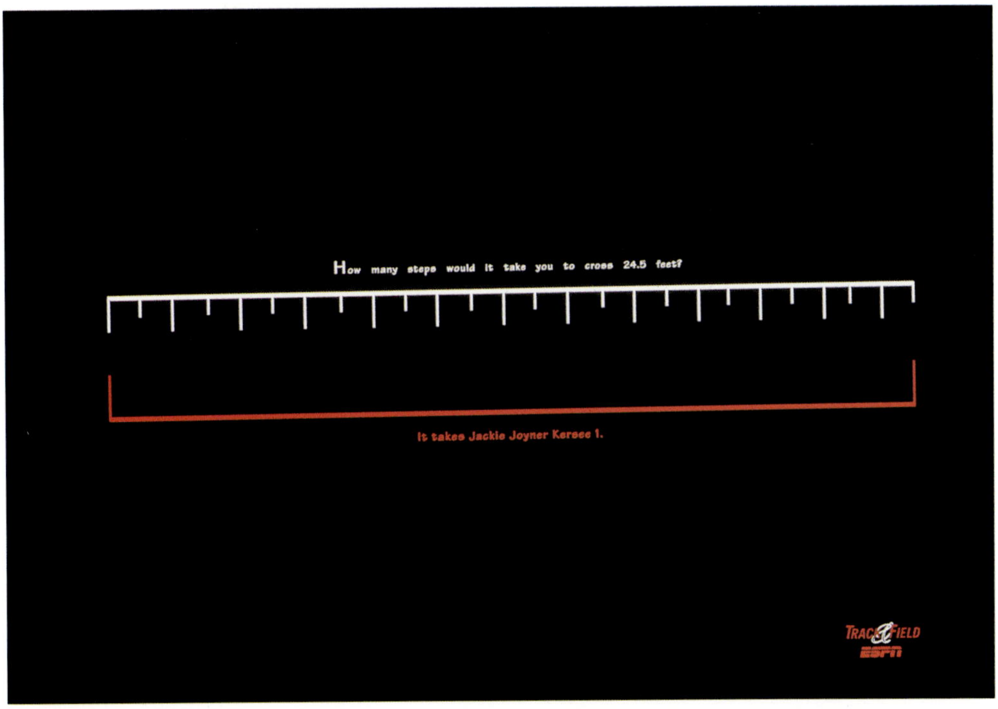

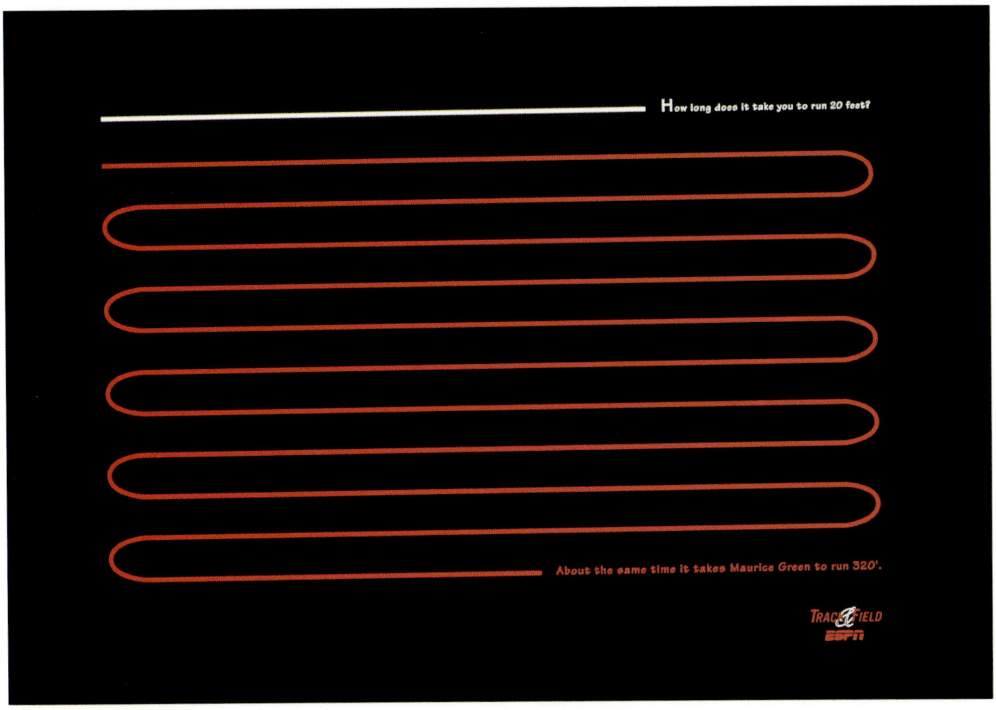

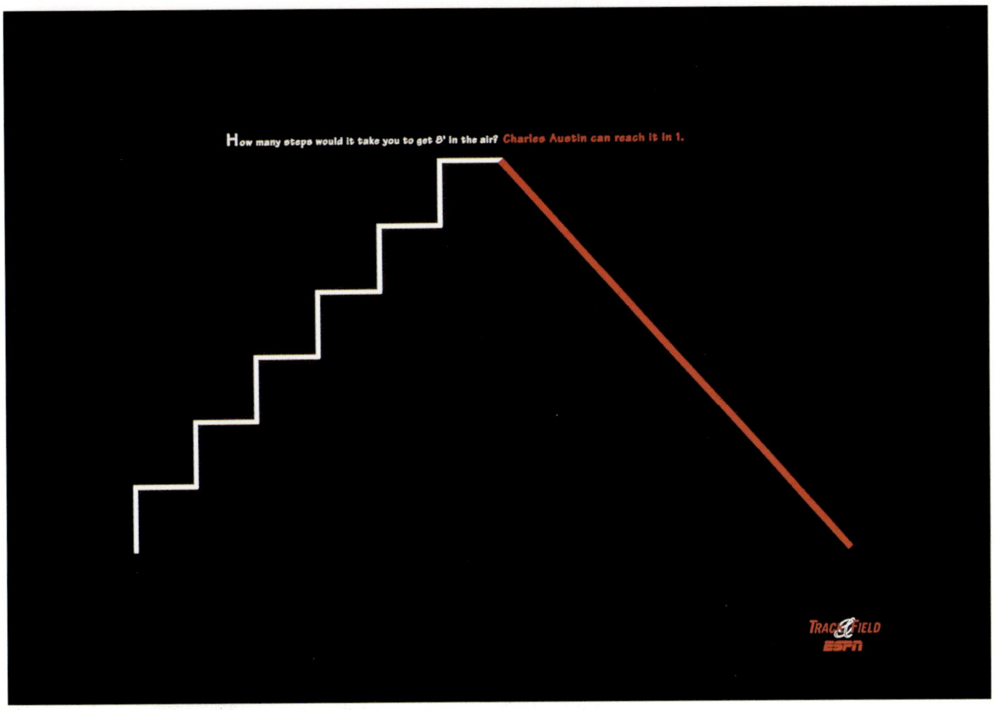

Michele Ernst School of Visual Arts

Would you? Could you? In a Tree?

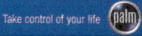

Would you? Could you? In the Rain?

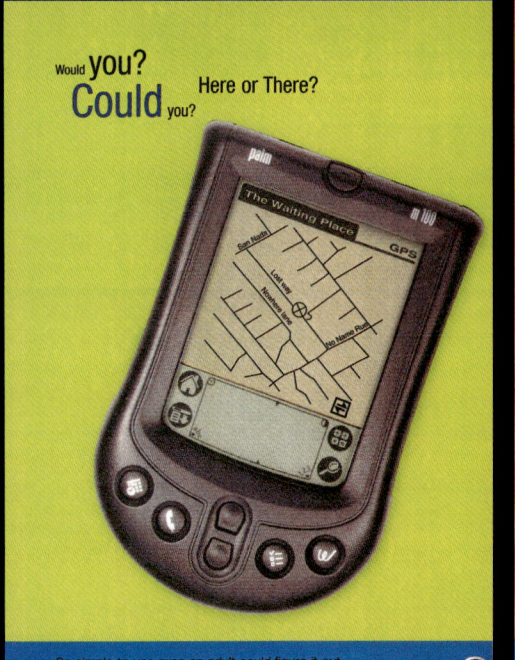

Would you? Could you? Here or There?

Would you? Could you? In the Dark?

So simple to use even an adult could figure it out. Take control of your life. palm

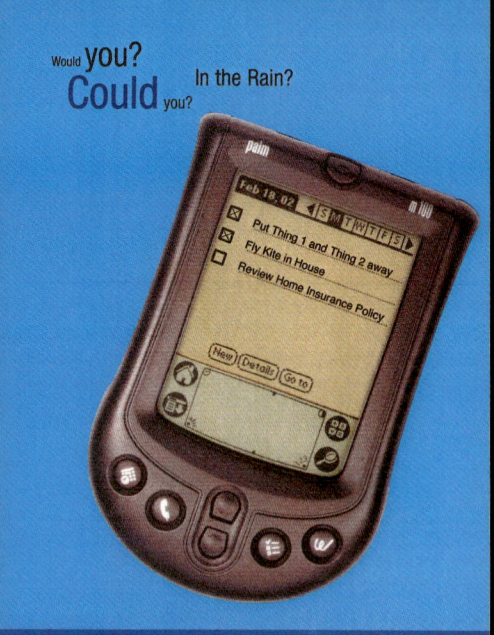

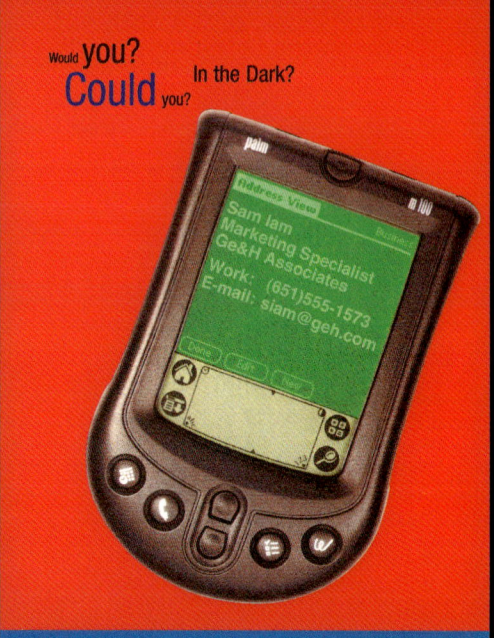

ROBOT EXPO 2001
AMERICAN INTERNATIONAL ROBOT EXPO 2001
THE AMERICAN INTERNATIONAL ROBOT EXPO 2001 IS THE LARGEST ROBOT EXPO SHOW IN THE OHIO STATE. NEARLY 500 MANUFACTURERS, DISTRIBUTORS, IMPORTERS AND SALES AGENTS FROM 30 COUNTRIES WILL SHOWCASE THEIR ROBOT AND ENTERTAINMENT PRODUCT HERE.
FEB 11-17, 2000
C O S I
2166 BURGOYNE Ct. COLUMBUS, OH 43220
614. 442. 1885
www.robot2001.com
ALL COPY RIGHT ARE RESERVED BY AMERICAN INTERNATIONAL ROBOT EXPO 2001

Mary Boyko School of Visual Arts

| Hooker | Call girl |

KIWI SHOE POLISH
Put your best foot forward.

| Janitor | Custodial Engineer |

KIWI SHOE POLISH
Put your best foot forward.

| Pimp | Entertainment Manager |

KIWI SHOE POLISH
Put your best foot forward.

(this spread) **Robin Milgrim** Miami Ad School

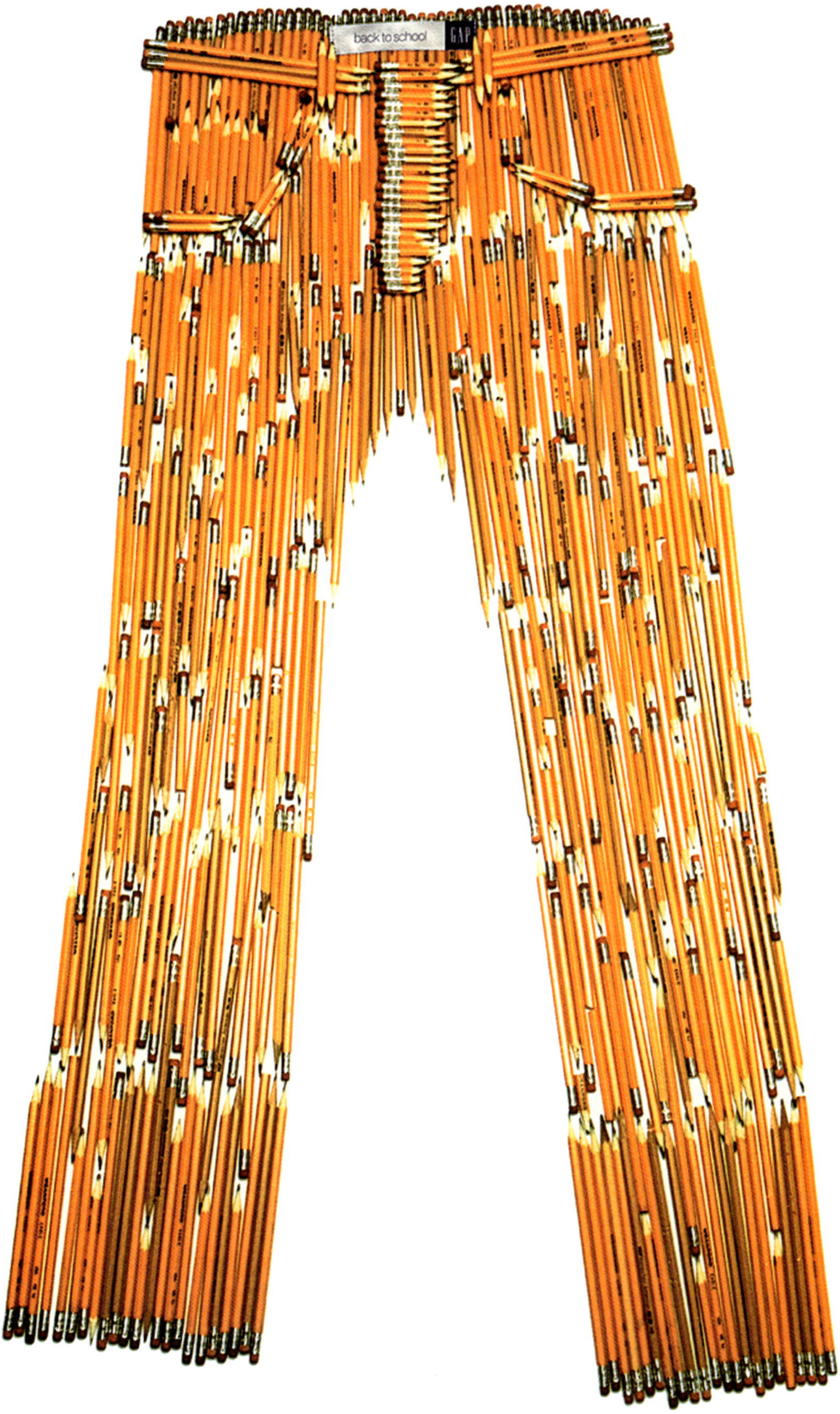
back to school
GAP

REMEMBER THE REASON YOUR TROPHY WIFE
MARRIED YOU IN THE FIRST PLACE.

If you still don't look good, blame your parents.

Sunglass Hut INTERNATIONAL

VASQUE BOOTS®
They're Tough

When you have to stay outside for a long time.   THE NORTH FACE

When you have to stay outside for a long time.   THE NORTH FACE

Chuck (Howlin' Cowboy) Bryant
now weighs 240lbs, wears spurs,
chaps, and wrestles steers in the rodeo.
The howling
came naturally,
the 240lbs
was hard earned muscle,
the rest is supplied by
Wrangler.
Wrangler was there when Chuck was 5. Wrangler was there when he became
a cowboy. No matter what stage of life you are in Wrangler will be there for you.
Wrangler

Little Debbie
Snack cakes

Your secret pleasure

Little Debbie
Snack cakes
Your secret pleasure

WRIGLEY'S
DOUBLEMINT
CHEWING GUM
WRIGLEY'S
DOUBLEMINT
CHEWING GUM

WRIGLEY'S
DOUBLEMINT
CHEWING GUM
WRIGLEY'S
DOUBLEMINT
CHEWING GUM

WRIGLEY'S
DOUBLEMINT
CHEWING GUM
WRIGLEY'S
DOUBLEMINT
CHEWING GUM

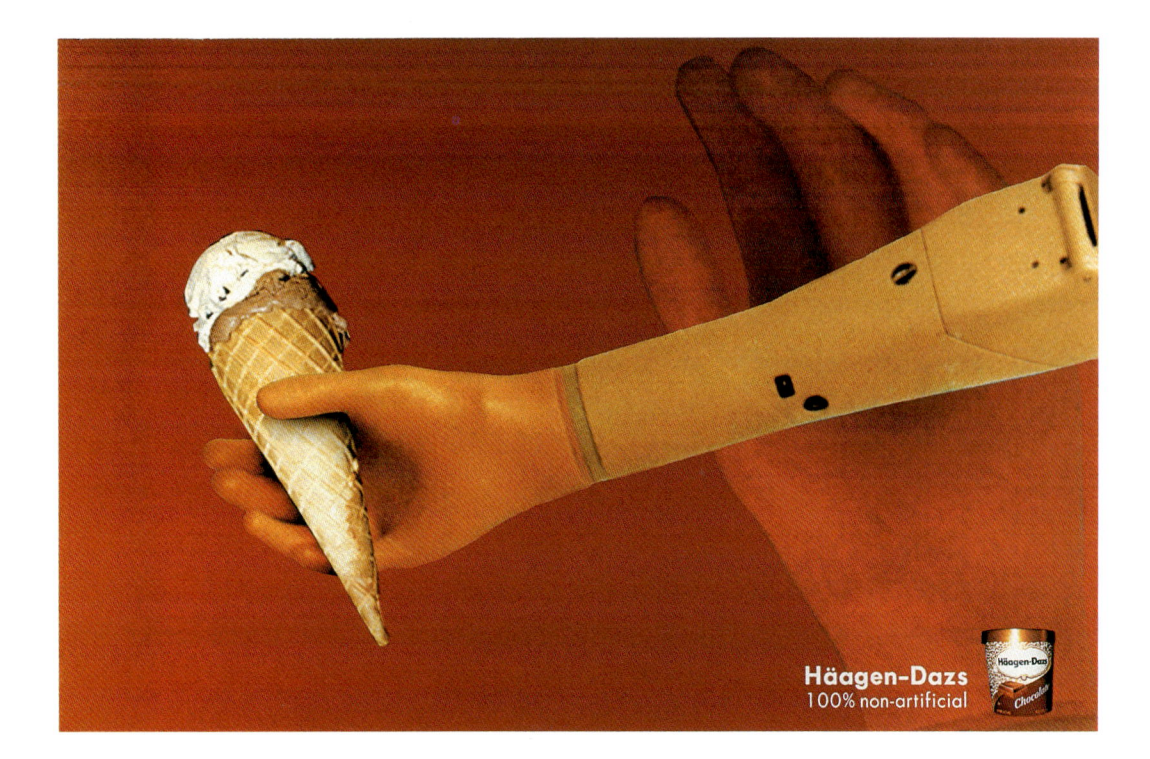

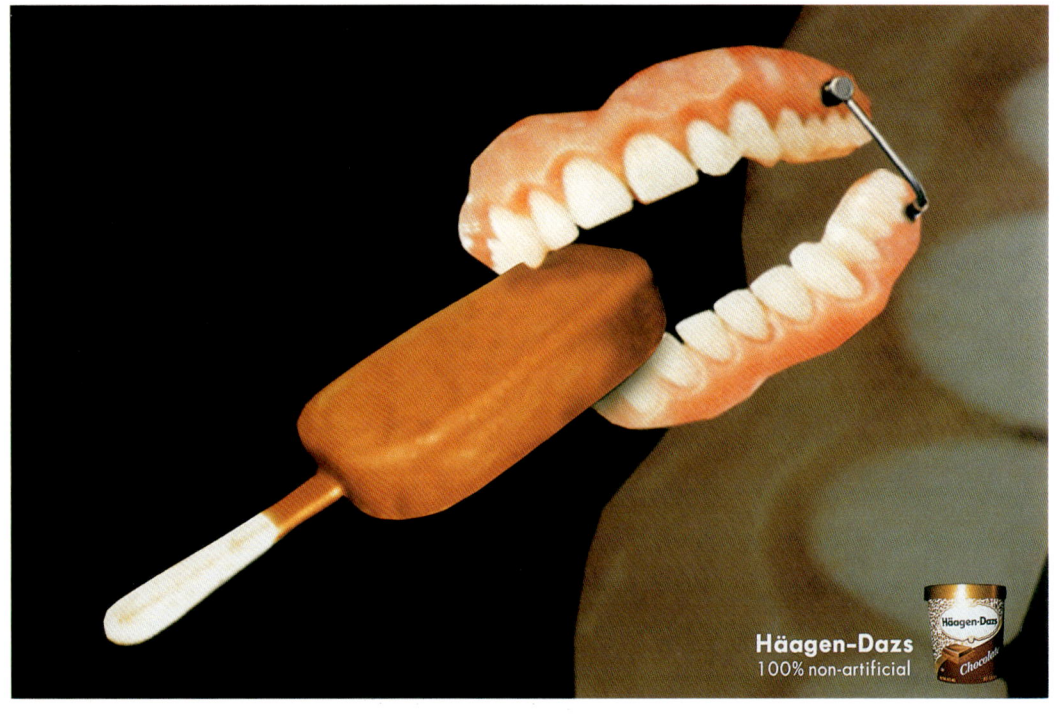

Häagen-Dazs
100% non-artificial

Häagen-Dazs
100% non-artificial

Häagen-Dazs
100% non-artificial

Tibor van Ginkel and **Stefan de Costa Gomez** School of Visual Arts

Oster

TABASCO© **Pepper Sauce**

do nothing

Barc-O-Lounger

do nothing

Barc-O-Lounger

do nothing

Barc-O-Lounger

Smith and Robin Milgrim Miami Ad School   Advertising: Food

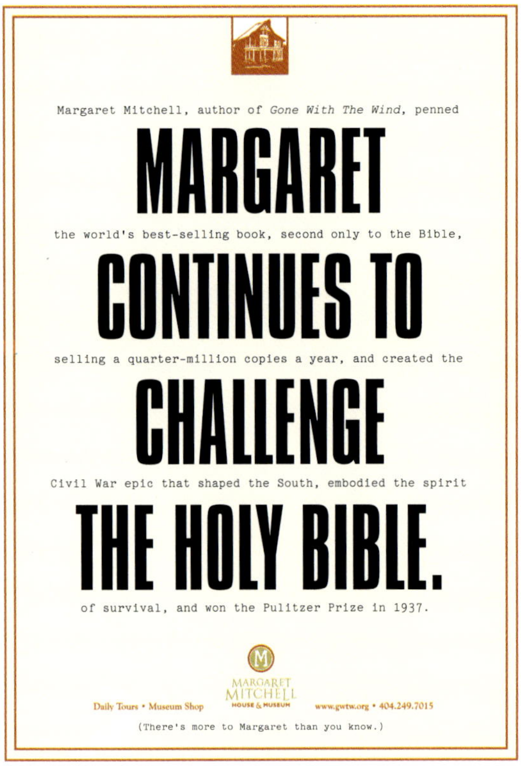

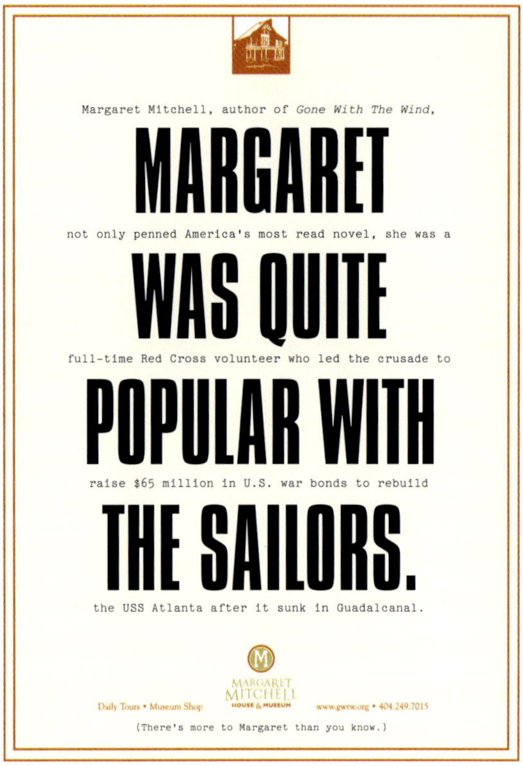

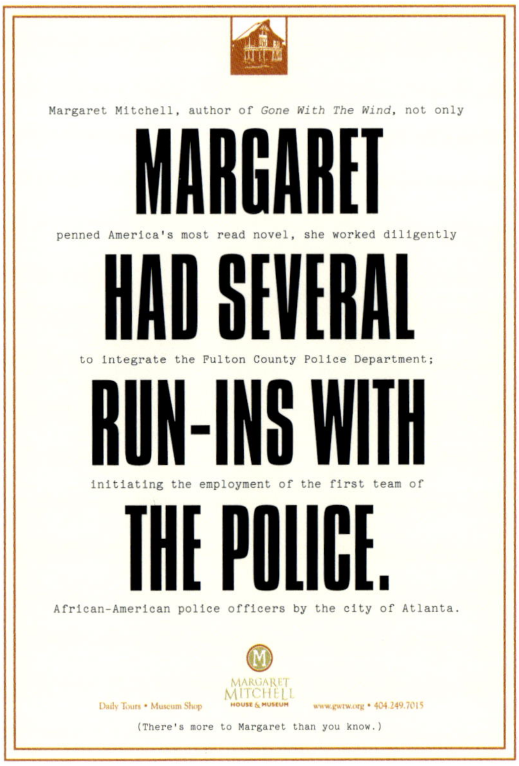

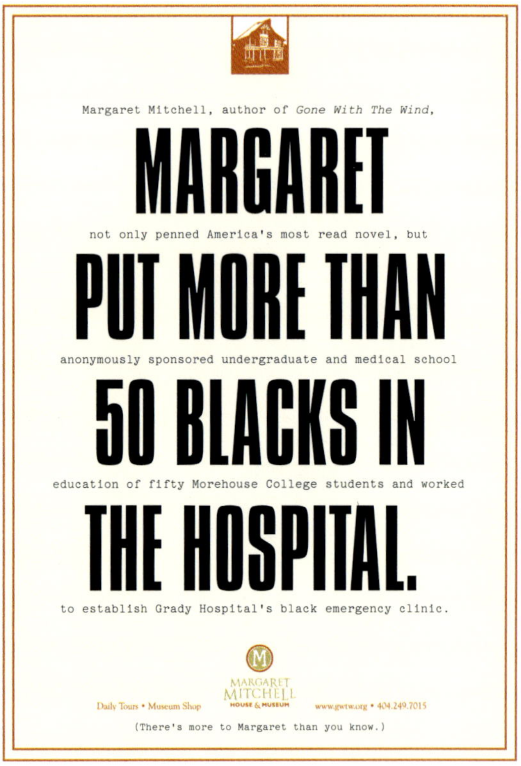

Poster 1 (top-left):

Margaret Mitchell, author of *Gone With The Wind*, penned

MARGARET

the world's best-selling book, second only to the Bible,

CONTINUES TO

selling a quarter-million copies a year, and created the

CHALLENGE

Civil War epic that shaped the South, embodied the spirit

THE HOLY BIBLE.

of survival, and won the Pulitzer Prize in 1937.

MARGARET MITCHELL HOUSE & MUSEUM
Daily Tours • Museum Shop   www.gwtw.org • 404.249.7015

(There's more to Margaret than you know.)

Poster 2 (top-right):

Margaret Mitchell, author of *Gone With The Wind*,

MARGARET

not only penned America's most read novel, she was a

WAS QUITE

full-time Red Cross volunteer who led the crusade to

POPULAR WITH

raise $65 million in U.S. war bonds to rebuild

THE SAILORS.

the USS Atlanta after it sunk in Guadalcanal.

MARGARET MITCHELL HOUSE & MUSEUM
Daily Tours • Museum Shop   www.gwtw.org • 404.249.7015

(There's more to Margaret than you know.)

Poster 3 (bottom-left):

Margaret Mitchell, author of *Gone With The Wind*, not only

MARGARET

penned America's most read novel, she worked diligently

HAD SEVERAL

to integrate the Fulton County Police Department;

RUN-INS WITH

initiating the employment of the first team of

THE POLICE.

African-American police officers by the city of Atlanta.

MARGARET MITCHELL HOUSE & MUSEUM
Daily Tours • Museum Shop   www.gwtw.org • 404.249.7015

(There's more to Margaret than you know.)

Poster 4 (bottom-right):

Margaret Mitchell, author of *Gone With The Wind*,

MARGARET

not only penned America's most read novel, but

PUT MORE THAN

anonymously sponsored undergraduate and medical school

50 BLACKS IN

education of fifty Morehouse College students and worked

THE HOSPITAL.

to establish Grady Hospital's black emergency clinic.

MARGARET MITCHELL HOUSE & MUSEUM
Daily Tours • Museum Shop   www.gwtw.org • 404.249.7015

(There's more to Margaret than you know.)

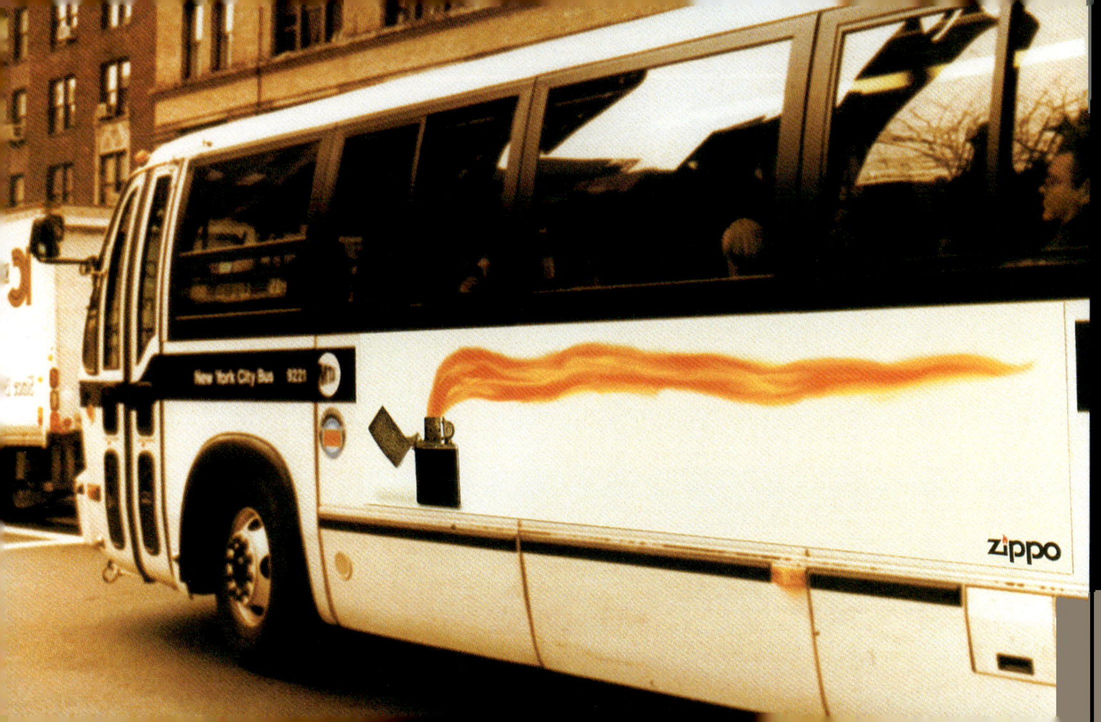
New York City Bus 9221
zippo

case# 3924

The only stains welcome on this table.

Benjamin Moore: Color for Life.

case# 1007

They'll come for the color.

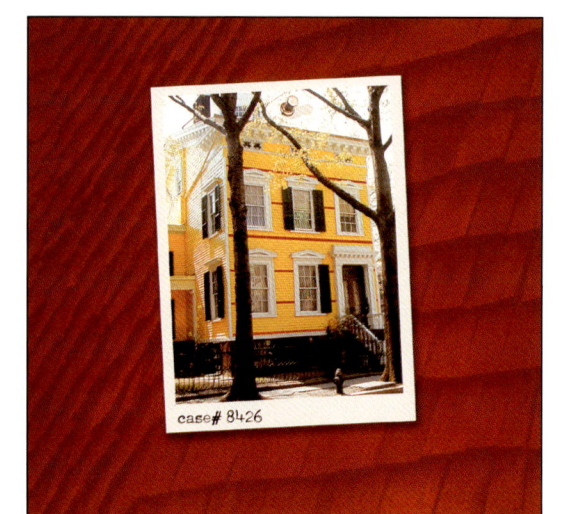

Benjamin Moore: Color for Life.

case# 8426

Introducing Benjamin Moore's new line of colors.
What hue do with them is your choice.

Benjamin Moore: Color for Life.

Avi Kravitz Pratt Institute

Crayola

Playtex

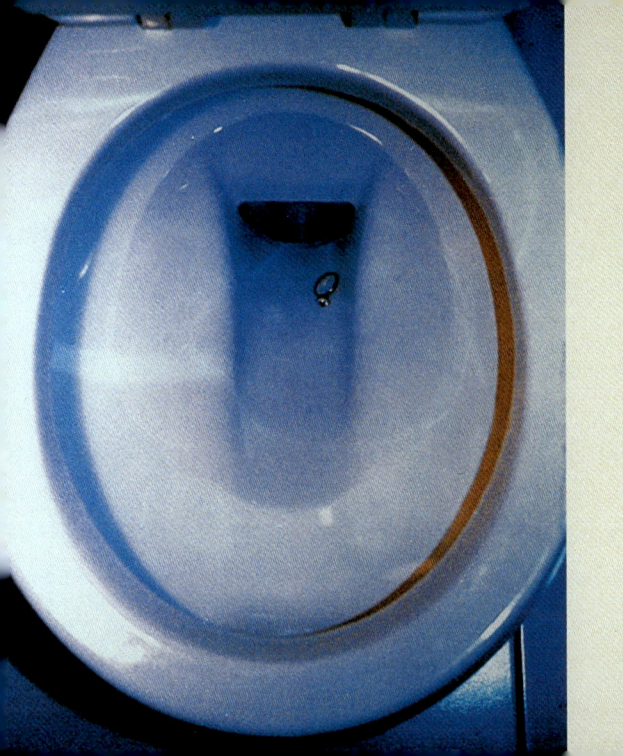

LEATHERMAN

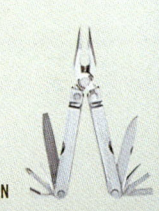

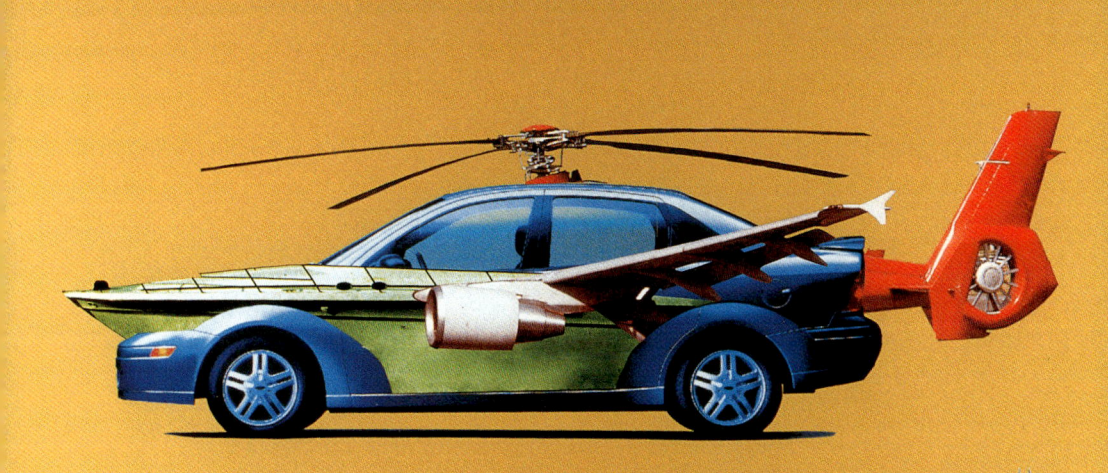

LEATHERMAN

Sveinn Ingimundarsen — School of Visual Arts

*Spending too much time tending one fire
can put the other one out.*

duraflame

OLD TOWN CANOE COMPANY
THE STILLWATER. ABLE TO CARRY 15 TIMES ITS OWN WEIGHT.
OLD TOWN, MAINE, U.S.A.

OLD TOWN CANOE COMPANY
THE TRIPPER. A CANOE BUILT FOR EXCEPTIONAL SPEED.
OLD TOWN, MAINE, U.S.A.

OLD TOWN CANOE COMPANY
THE PATHFINDER. A DEEPER HULL FOR MORE STORAGE SPACE.
OLD TOWN, MAINE, U.S.A.

ban
Anti-Perspirant
Deodorant
ROLL-ON
Regular Scent
At least you'll smell good during rush hour.

Sorry,
but we just
keep the bugs away.
OFF!
Perfect for the park and everywhere else.

Sorry,
but we just
keep the bugs away.
OFF!
SKINTASTIC
SUNSCREEN
Perfect for the beach and everywhere else.

Sorry,
but we just
keep the bugs away.
OFF!
Perfect for the woods and everywhere else.

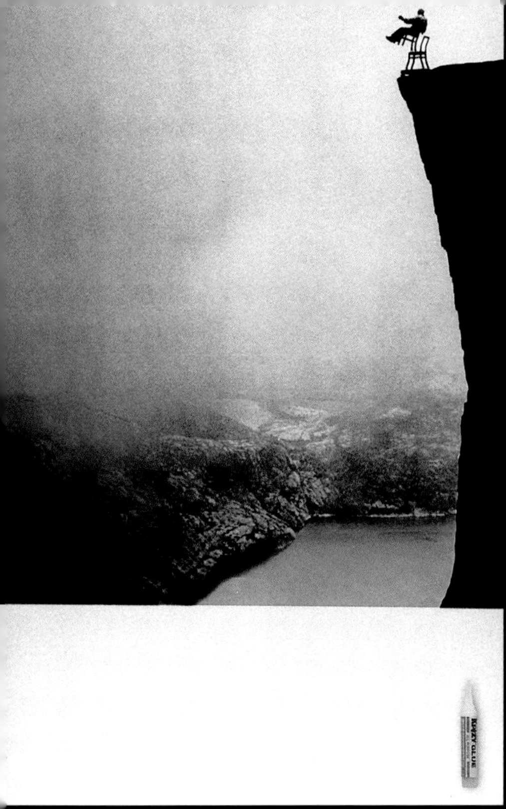

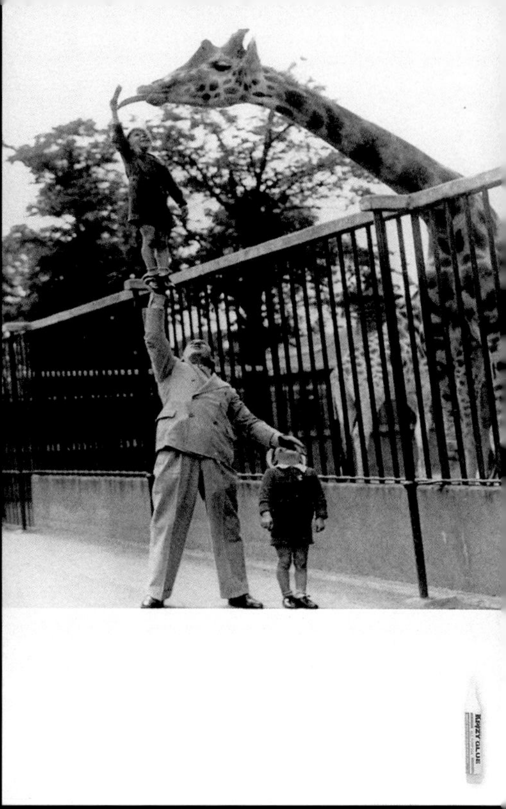

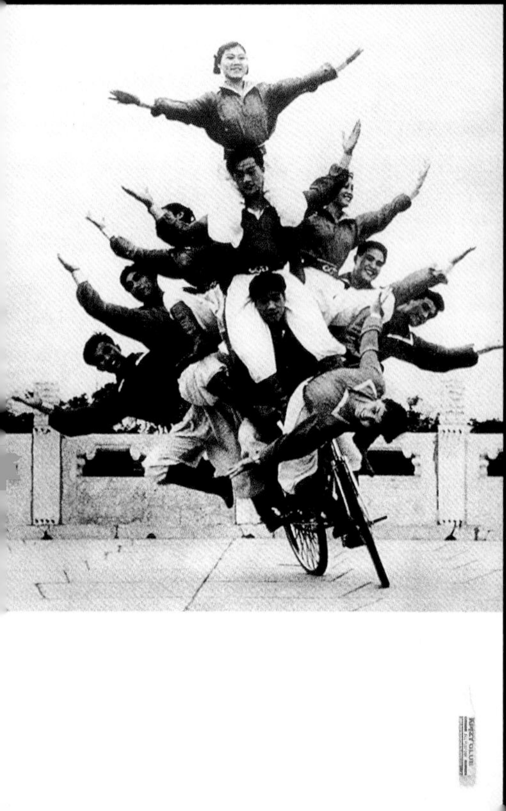

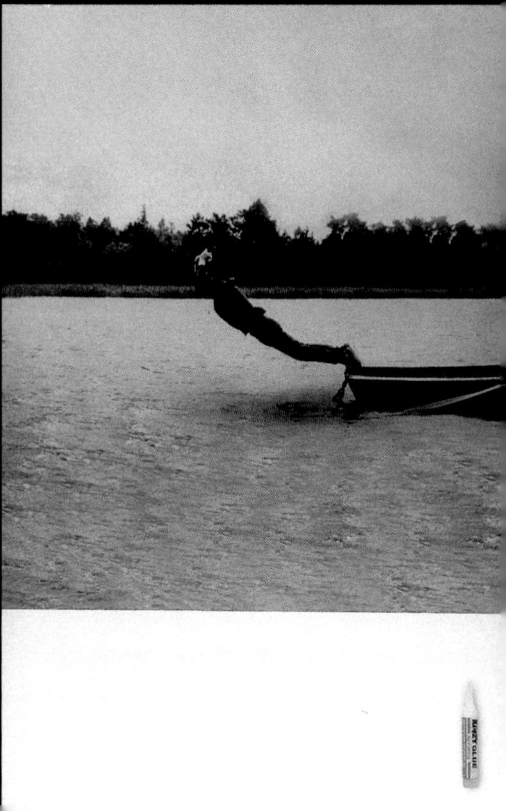

Advertising: Products 54, 55

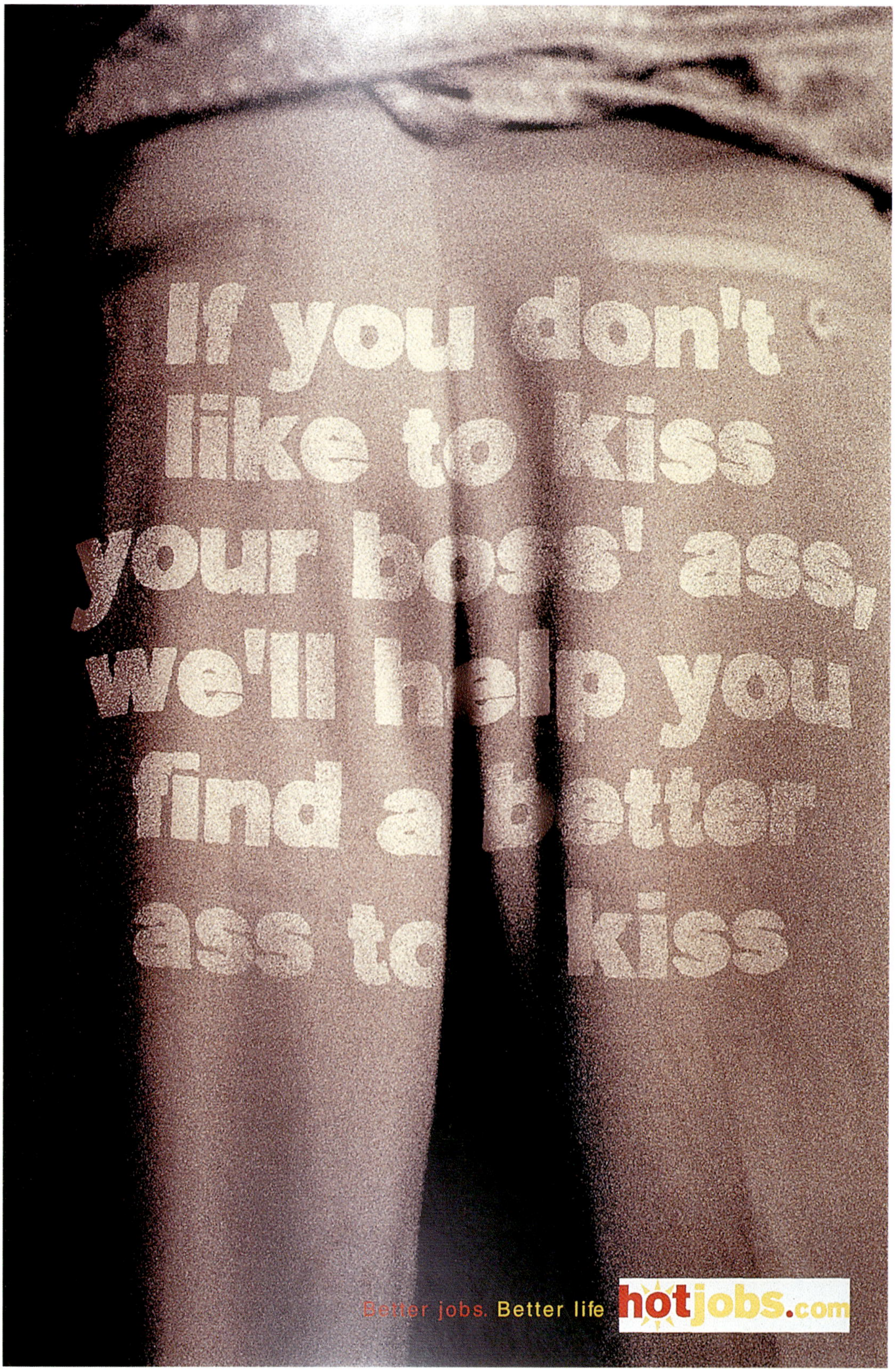

Ervin Serrano School of Visual Arts

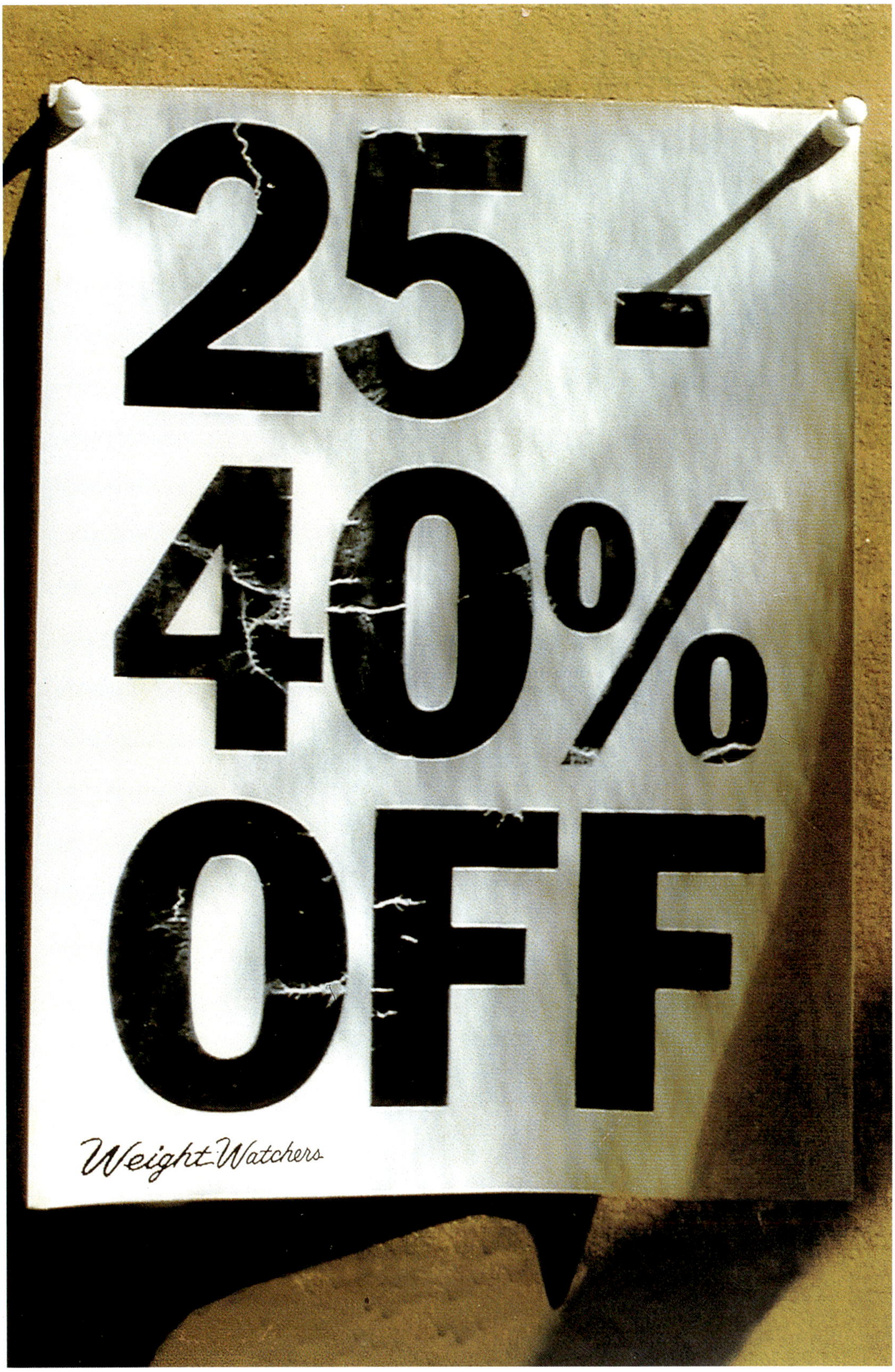
25-
40%
OFF
Weight Watchers

You gotta start somewhere.

Beginner classes offered. TIGER SCHULMANN'S KARATE

VALUED CUSTOMER SINCE 1993.

Electric Crayon Tattoos
2300 Stoneridge Drive Austin, Texas 78723
512-285-4355   800-626-3293

WE'RE JUST A BUNCH OF PRICKS!

Electric Crayon Tattoos
2300 Stoneridge Drive Austin, Texas 78723
512-285-4355   800-626-3293

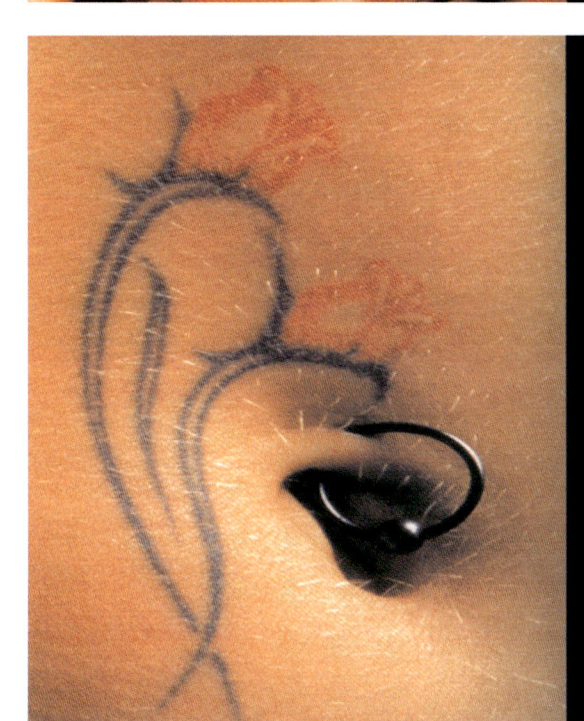

REMEMBER WHEN JUST BULLS WORE RINGS?

Electric Crayon Tattoos
2300 Stoneridge Drive Austin, Texas 78723
512-285-4355   800-626-3293

3.5 Million of our clients lost what they came here for.

Weight Watchers

Kristen Maloney School of Visual Arts

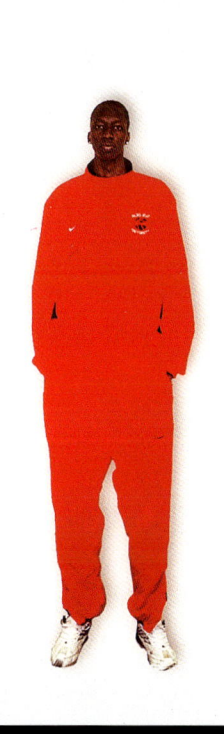

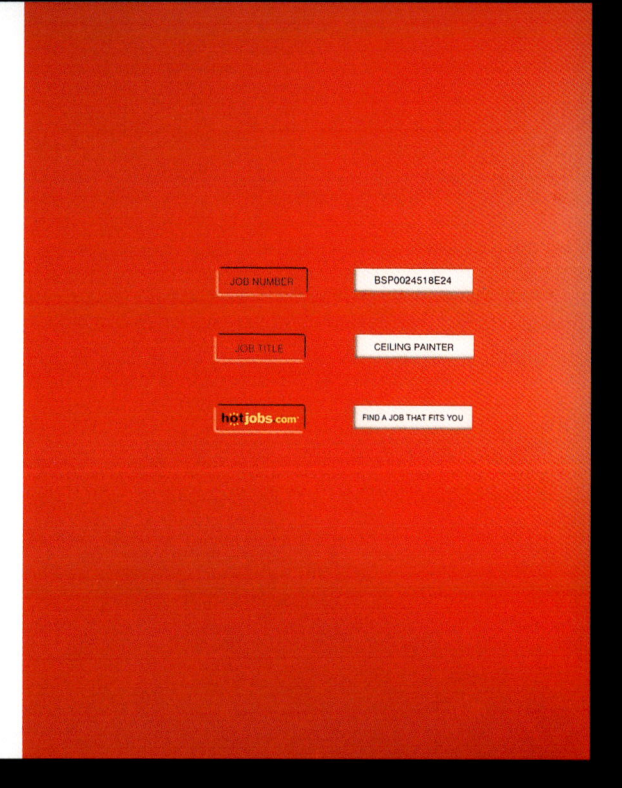

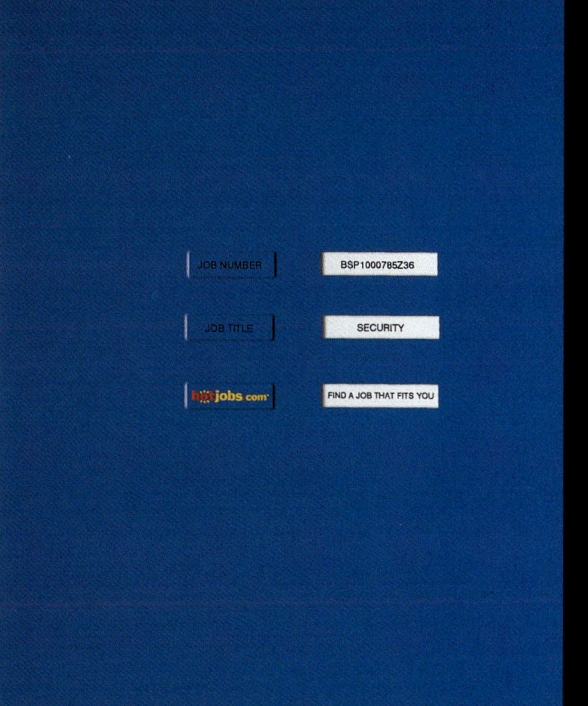

JOB NUMBER	BSP0024518E24
JOB TITLE	CEILING PAINTER
hotjobs.com	FIND A JOB THAT FITS YOU

JOB NUMBER	BSP1000785Z36
JOB TITLE	SECURITY
hotjobs.com	FIND A JOB THAT FITS YOU

U-HAUL SELFSTORAGE
Some people need more space.

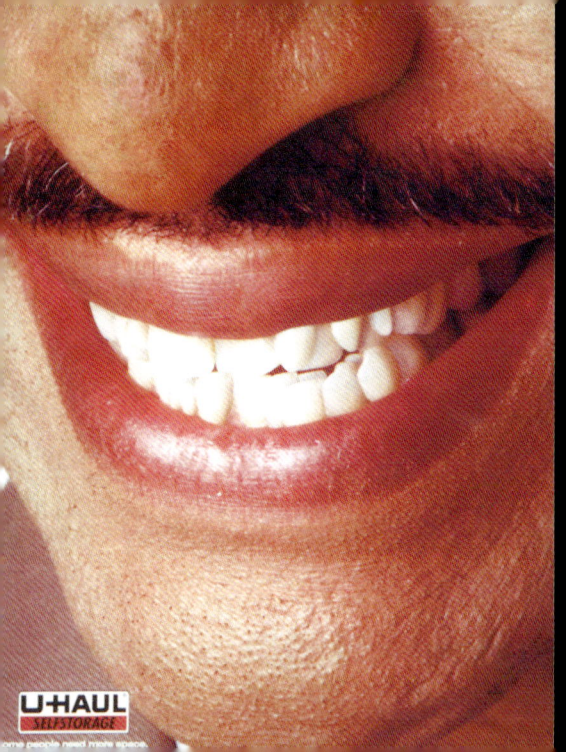

U-HAUL SELFSTORAGE
Some people need more space.

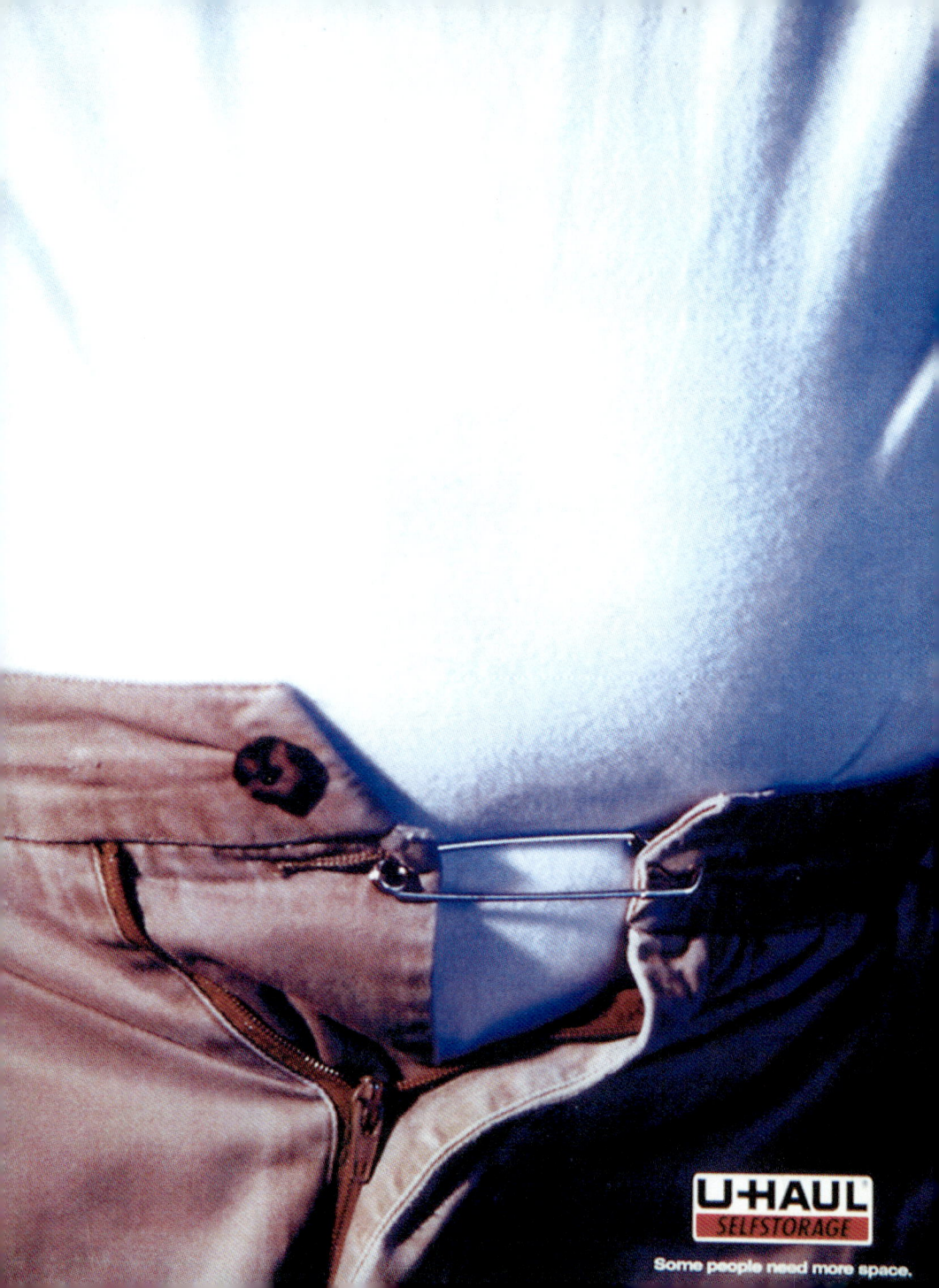

Increasing spin and
divorce rates everywhere.
Titleist
golf balls

Maximize your
DISTANCE
from the office.
Titleist

When speed is important.
But slowing down is essential.
Titleist

Dan Giachetti School of Visual Arts

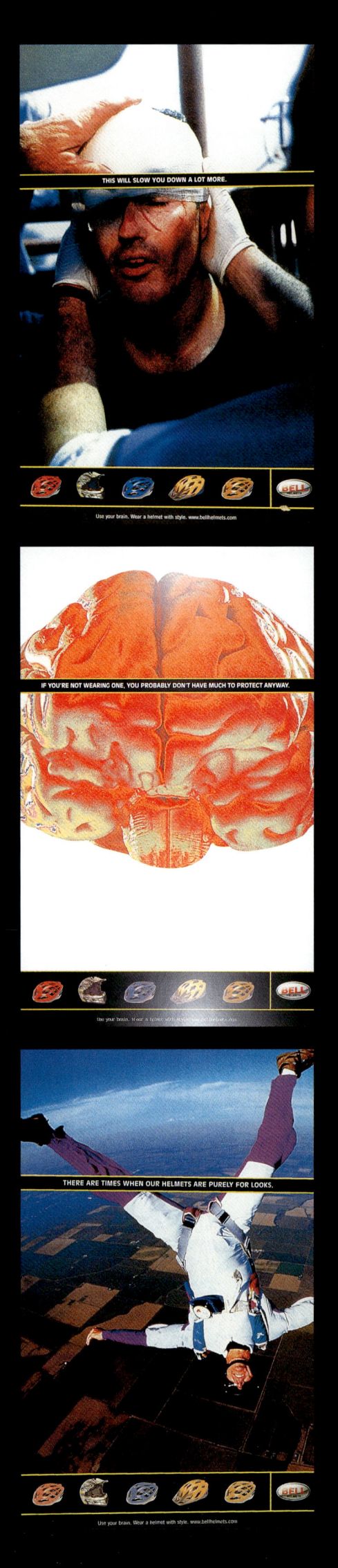

PARKING WILL BE
A BITCH
8AM-6PM
EXCEPT SUNDAY
DEPT OF TRANSPORTATION
MTA
New York City Subways *A Better Way to Get Around*

(top) **Enzo Granella** Academy of Art College (bottom) **Brian Blakely** Academy of Art College

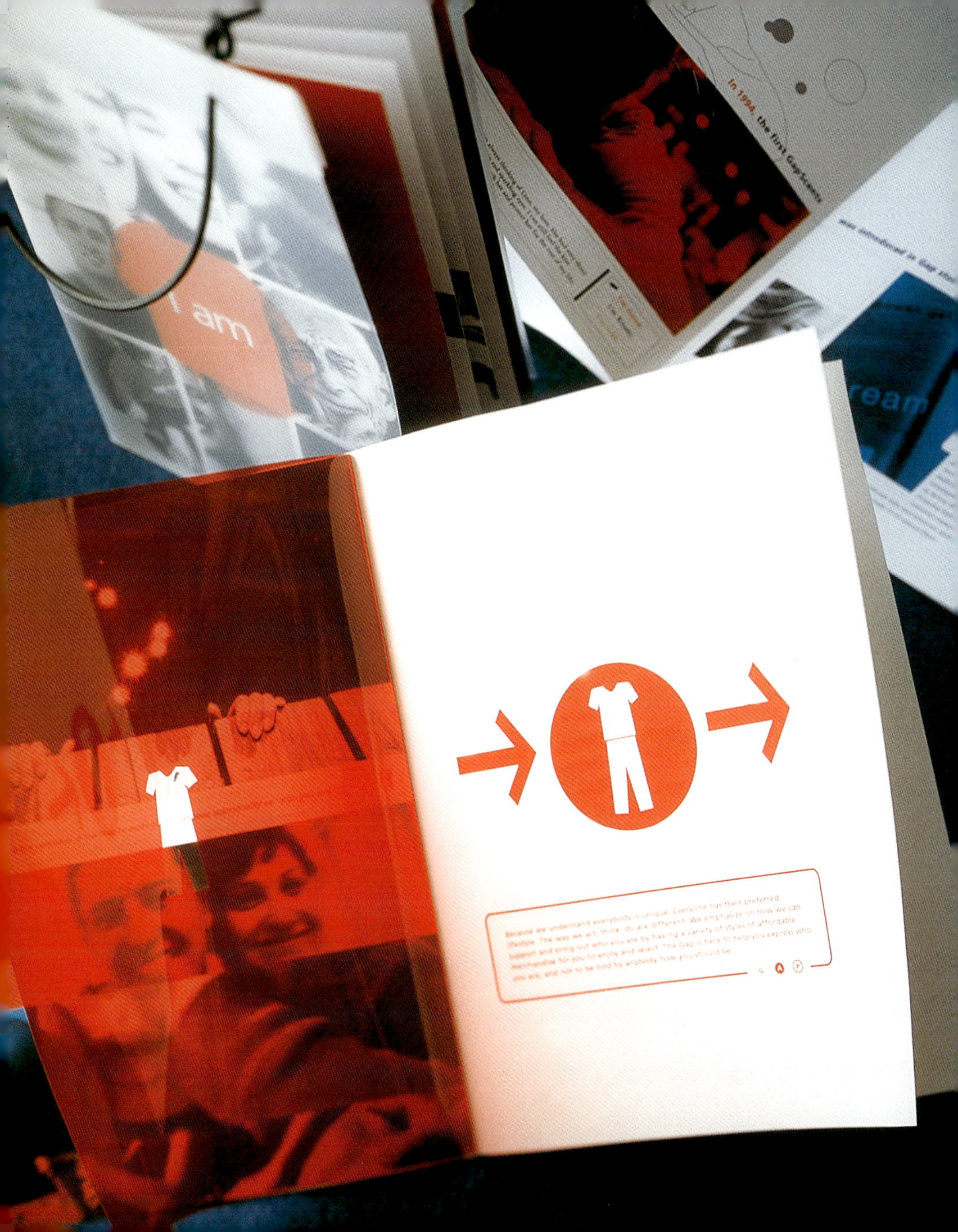
I am
In 1994, the first GapScents

Yelena Lysogorskaya School of Visual Arts

The Language of GUSTAV KLIMT

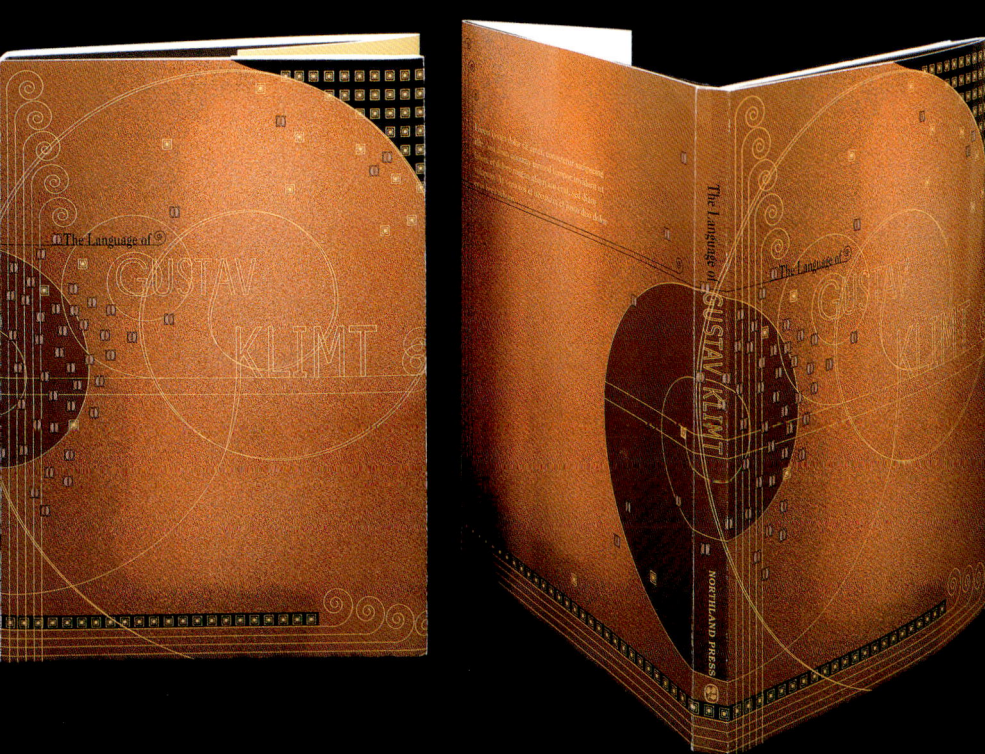

NORTHLAND PRESS

Recreate

Many cultures in history, including the Greeks, Egyptians, and Chinese have venerated a divine entity known as the Phoenix. It is said that at the end of the Phoenix's life it builds a nest of sticks and twigs, whereupon it sits when completed, and immolates itself.
The Phoenix is destroyed, but from its ashes a new phoenix is be born. This new Phoenix carries the wisdom and experience of its ancestors, but through the purification by fire it sheds its old, degenerated body.
A creative individual should go through a similar process after completing projects and other undertakings. In the process between beginning and ending an endeavor, we inevitably pick up feelings of frustration, anger, and disappointment. Carry away the experience and knowledge you gain from your efforts, but shed the weight gained by negative feelings; they can only hold you back.

The refreshment of one's body or mind; to create anew; to expose fresh life to; refresh mentally or physically.

[Latin recreare, to create anew: re- back, again + creare, to CRE-ATE.]

Recycle

The box represents one product of the recycling process. What was once a piece of paper, newspaper, or paper towel roll may easily be part of a newly created cardboard box. In today's market more and more of our paper products are derived from recycled stock; paper pulp from former paper pulp.
Recycling is entirely about transformation. You begin with something that has outlived its usefulness. It is then systematically broken down, and reformed into a new product. This works for everything from paper and glass, to concepts and ideas.
When an idea doesn't seem to work, don't simply discard it. Break it down into its components and remove that which is lacking or doesn't apply to the problem. Take the material left and form it into a new idea; give it a new purpose. Combine material from multiple concepts, and form new ideas from that. Recycle your thoughts and ideas, don't waste them.

To extract and reuse; to extract useful materials from; to start a different cycle in.

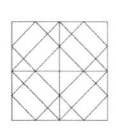

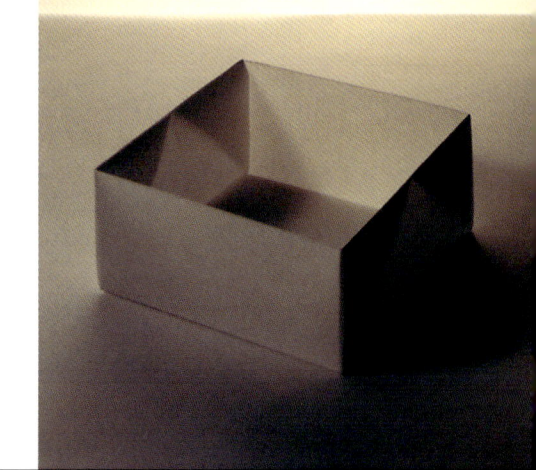

[French, from Late Latin cyclus, from Greek kuklos, circle.]

Regenerate

The fish represents Christ in many of the Christian religions of the western world. As the fish is a creature of water, it may also elude to baptism. Baptism is representative of the highest form of commitment mankind can make, that between a person and God.
Commitment is an important element in the field of design. On a daily basis designers make commitments to begin new projects, meet deadlines, etc... These commitments are obvious and easily made, but higher forms of engagement are often overlooked.
These are the commitments to one's self. Commit yourself to the best, don't settle for second. Do the best work you can, complete products that you can take pride in. The pressures associated with design fields can create negative feelings, and may result in a lack of true commitment from the designer to their work, clients, and self. Halfhearted or sub-par work is not fulfilling, and will ultimately lead to a lack of satisfaction from your profession. Commit yourself to quality.

To reform spiritually or morally; to undergo spiritual conversion or rebirth.

[Latin regenerare, to reproduce : re-, again + generare, to beget, GENERATE.]

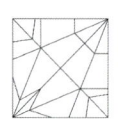

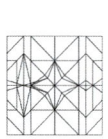

Reincarnate

The butterfly is a universal symbol of transformation. Butterflies represent reincarnation; as they enter a cocoon and then emerge in their new bodies.
Our conceptions of form, function, and style embody our thoughts and feelings about design. Just as our physical body undergoes change, so does our mental body. An inspiration or revelation may cause our perceptions of our surroundings and ideas to change.
We must know when to reincarnate the way in which we function as designers. To know when a new style or new direction needs to be taken is the beginning of this passage. Reincarnation is a process that should end with a new frame of conceptions.
Pay attention to what is and is not working for you, and know when the time has come to evolve into new bodies of thought and reason.

To be reborn in another body.

[Late Latin incarnare, to make flesh: re-, back, again + in (Latin causative) + caro, flesh.]

Rejuventate

Ponce de Leon's quest was to drink of life when he set out to discover the Fountain of Youth. The search for regained youth has been constant throughout human history. From Ponce de Leon's dream, to the ancient Norse belief in the goddess Idun tending to the tree bearing apples of youth, man has sought to restore vigor and energy to everyday life. Ideally we'd like to be a combination of our physical youth and age acquired experience. Designers must avoid trends and gimmicks. They are dated, and adventurish grow old. Good design does not age, and investing good design into anything will give it new life and longevity.

To restore the youthful vigor or appearance of
[From RE- + Latin juvenis, a youth.]

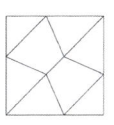

Renew

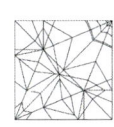

The rooster is a well recognized symbol of dawn in the western world. He heralds the coming of the new day through his call. Dawn is a time of renewal and transition. The sun begins its shift again at dawn, taking over for the stars and moon. This time of transition from dark to light is accomplished through many steps of changing color, brightness, and contrast.
Design is replete with transition. Transition is often an uncomfortable process for people to undertake, and they usually end up resenting it at one time or another. Transition can be as smooth a process as dawn, but one must come to terms with it. Appreciate the steps it takes, appreciate the points of transformation, and even appreciate the discomfort it causes. Transition assures us of our vitality. If it doesn't cause any discomfort, then we likely aren't gaining anything from it. It's easy to lose sight of the value of discomfort.

To make as if new again; restore. To take up again; resume. To repeat so as to reaffirm.
[Middle English newe, Old English nīwe. Related to neos (Greek), novus (Latin).]

Replenish

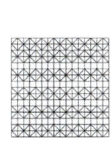

The pinecone is but one symbol of Mother Nature. Pinecones spread their seeds to replenish and spread its species. Nature is perhaps the best example of replenishment, as it is constantly refreshing itself through widespread systems of birth and death, governed by the seasons. We must discover the ways in which we can replant ideas and motivation within ourselves. These methods could be as simple as a trip to the bookstore or a walk in the park. Go to the movies or a museum. Attend a concert or symphony. Inspiration is all around us in its potential form. By paying more attention to the things that affect and influence us, we make the process of replenishment easier and more fulfilling. Expose yourself to the things that inspire you.

To fill or make complete again; add a new supply or stock to.
[Middle English replenishen, from Old French replenir : re, again + plenir, to fill, from plein, full, from Latin plenus.]

Resurge

The hourglass is a physical representation of time. Time has been a concern of mankind since its conception. It is an important factor in everyday life, playing a role in the majority of our interests.
Today mainstream society is concerned with bigger, better and faster. Finding time to do all of the things we want to do becomes more and more difficult. The expense of this pace is often burnout. Sometimes ideas and concepts just seem to die in the face of our revival attempts. Another kind of death can occur within the designer; This is the demise of motivation. Burnout can occur despite our greatest efforts to curb it. When all avenues for active resurgence have been exhausted, the final saving grace may simply be time. We are so used to forcing elements in our lives one way or another, but leaving them at rest may be the key to resurgence. Give yourself time to rest. Make time to do the things you want to do, not just the things you have to do.

To rise again; be resurrected.
[Latin resurgere : re-, again + surgere, SURGE.]

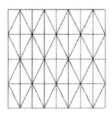

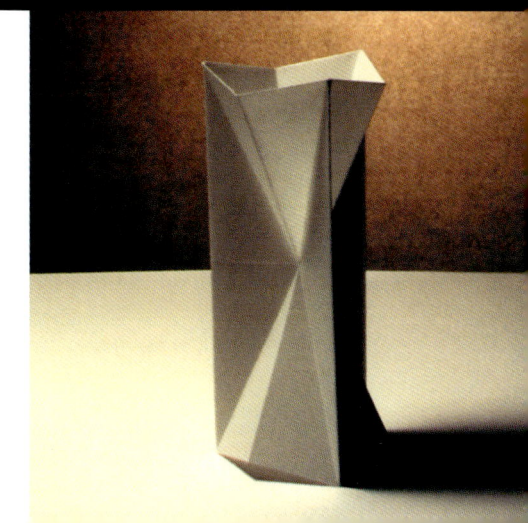

MOOD CHANGE

WHAT CAN YOU DO TO CREATE YOUR
HOUSE TO RADIATE COLORFUL LOOK

There are thinkers who claim that if the modern age began with the discovery of America, it also ended in America. This is said to have occurred in the year 1969, when America sent the first man to the moon. From this

By BILL STEELE   photograph JAMES WOJCIK

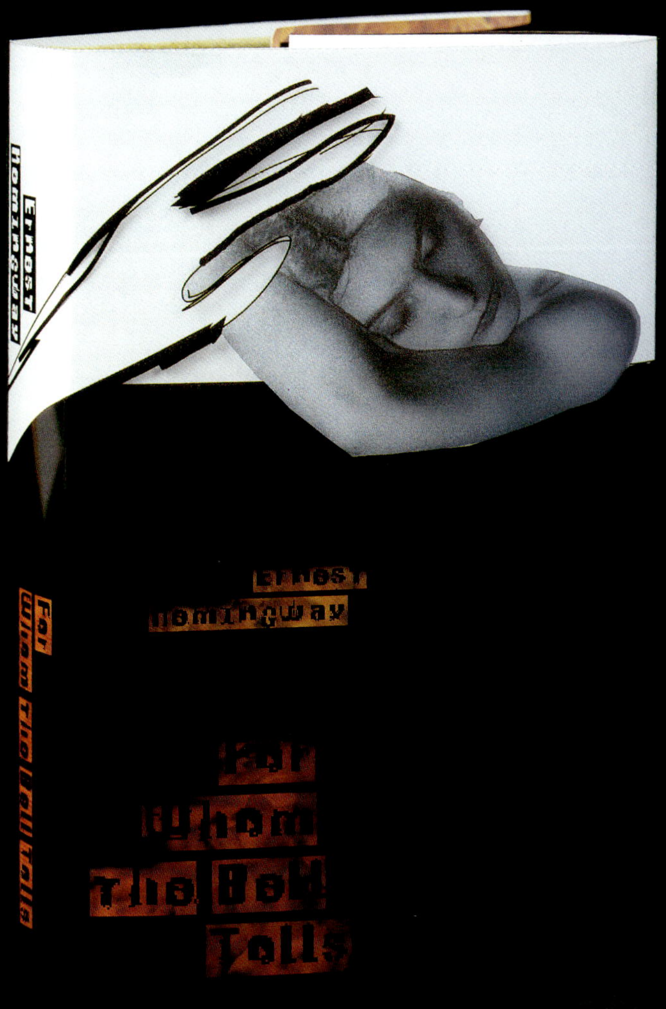

Robyn Wiles Northern Illinois University

Helen Yentus School of Visual Arts

GOLD
FISH

RAYMOND CHANDLER

Minhee Park School of Visual Arts

(top) **Min Kyong Lew** School of Visual Arts (bottom) **Gill Autrey** Portfolio Center

Shok Goik Khor Academy of Art College

>RECHARGABILITY

Cellular phones are supposed to be about freedom; that's why our rechargable batteries last the longest. Now when you set sail for even a three-hour tour, you won't end up stranded.

NOKIA >2001

>LONG DISTANCE

Whether you're closing big deals or just want to call home to report your latest adventures, Nokia offers a service plan to meet your individual needs. And the best long distance rates in the galaxy.

>CLIENT INFORMATION

Make a list, check it twice, find out who's naughty and nice. With the revolutionary new Nokia 9110, you'll have access to up-to-the-minute information on clients, whatever the season.

>NAUGHTY!

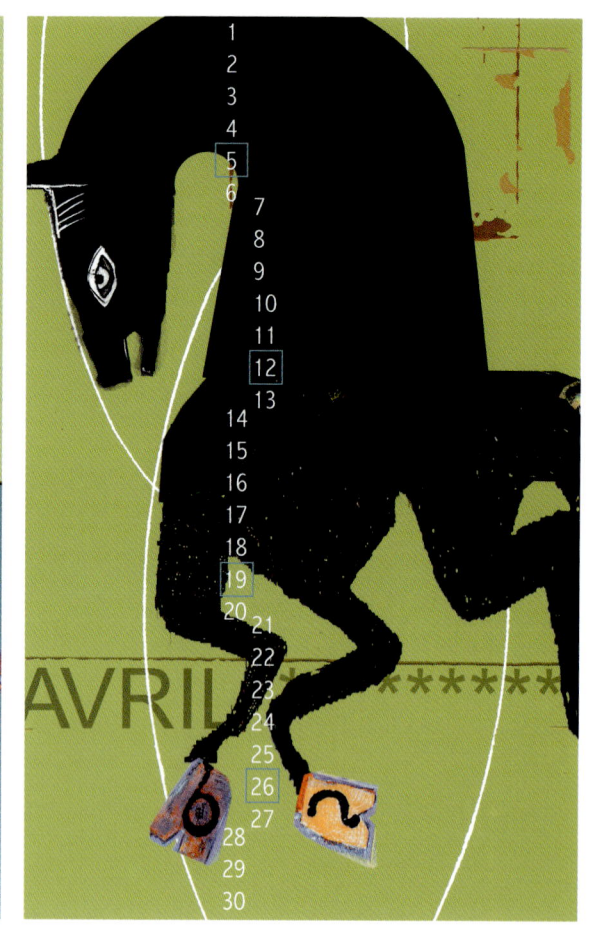

Sonia Léontieff Université du Québec à Montréal

JANUARY
FEBRUARY
MARCH
APRIL
MAY
JUNE
JULY
AUGUST
SEPTEMBER
OCTOBER
NOVEMBER
DECEMBER

POULTRY FARMACEUTICALS
DELIVERS
CALL
FAT CHICK
weight gain powder

POULTRY
Farmaceuticals
Providing Outstanding Products Since 1947
We will supply your poultry's medicinal needs
for even the most exotic of birds.
Reliable, friendly service and
a product unbeatable in
quality and price is
our first concern.
Visit your local supplier today to begin your personally designed order or call 1-800-643-8267

Omar Mrva School of Visual Arts

VERCESI HARDWARE
common
NAILS
$3.50
NET WT. 16ozs. (1LB.)
common
NAILS
1 3/4"

VERCESI HARDWARE
V E R C E S I   H A R D W A R E

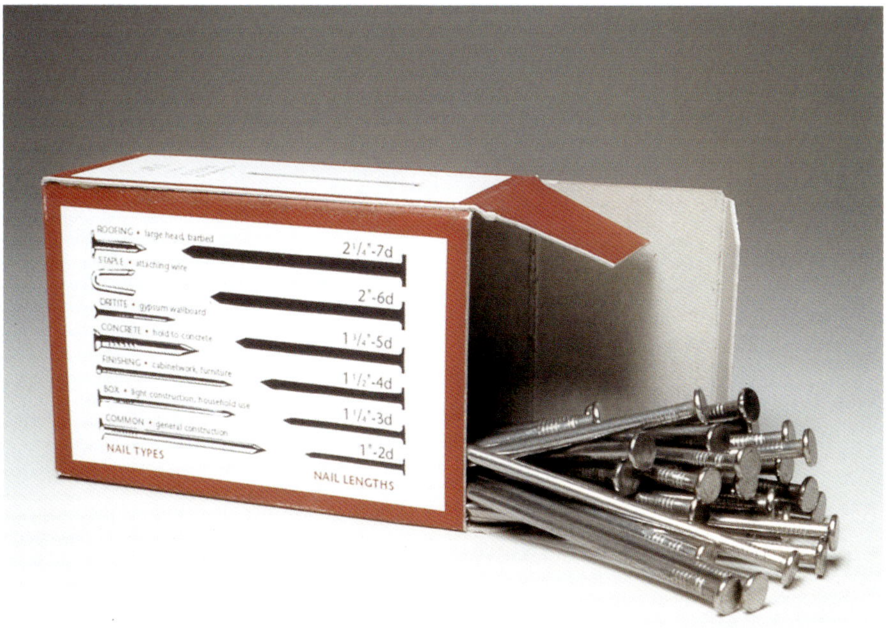
ROOFING • large head, barbed
STAPLE • attaching wire
CONCRETE • hold to concrete
FINISHING • cabinetwork, furniture
BOX • light construction, household use
COMMON • general construction
NAIL TYPES
2 1/4"-7d
2"-6d
1 3/4"-5d
1 1/2"-4d
1 1/4"-3d
1"-2d
NAIL LENGTHS

(this spread) **Tai Tran** School of Visual Arts

Corporate Ide

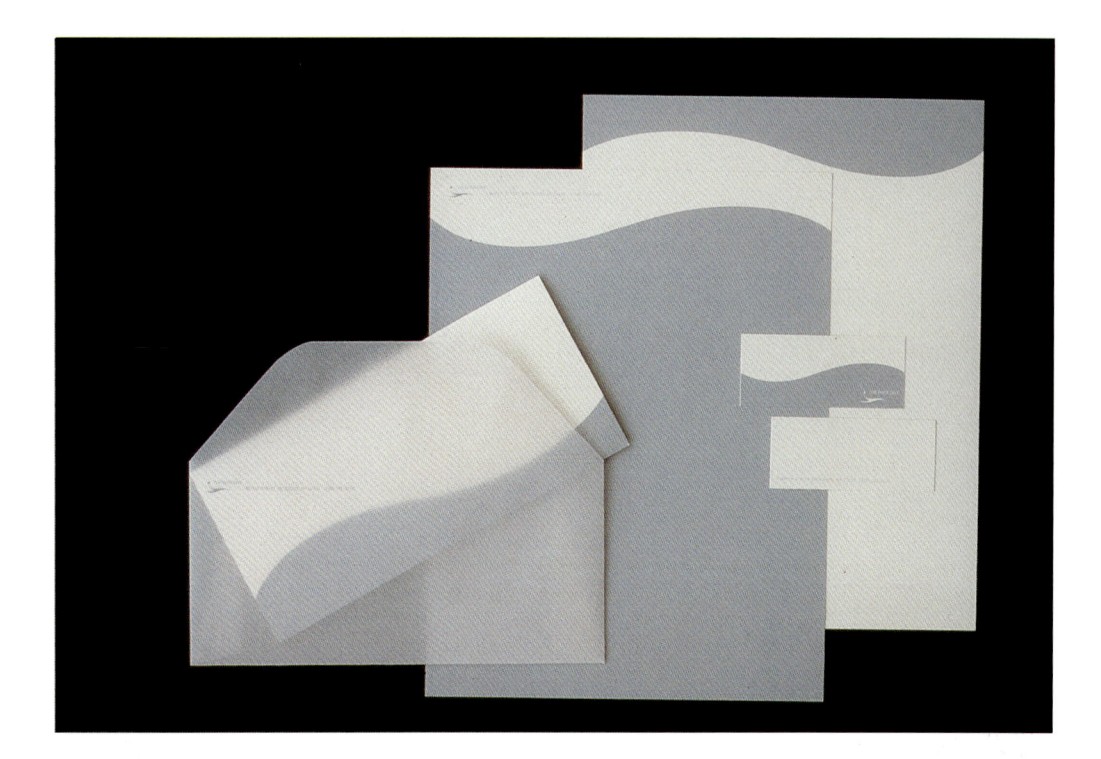

(this spread) **Spencer Bagley** School of Visual Arts

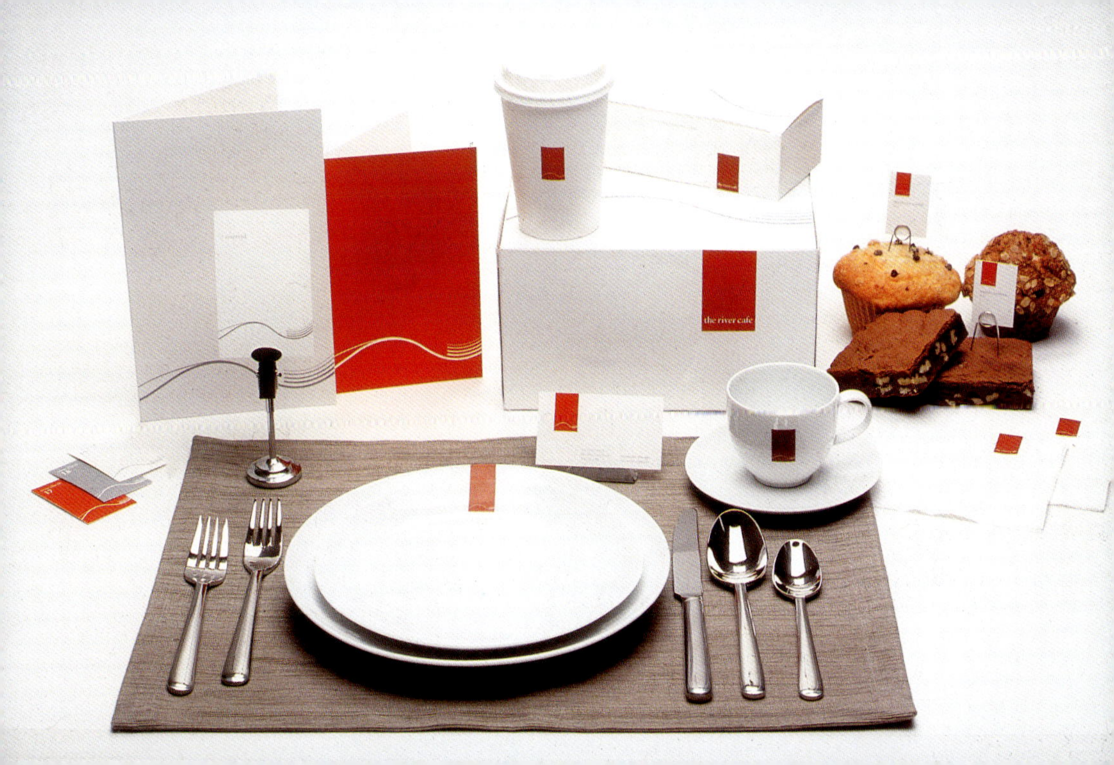
the river cafe

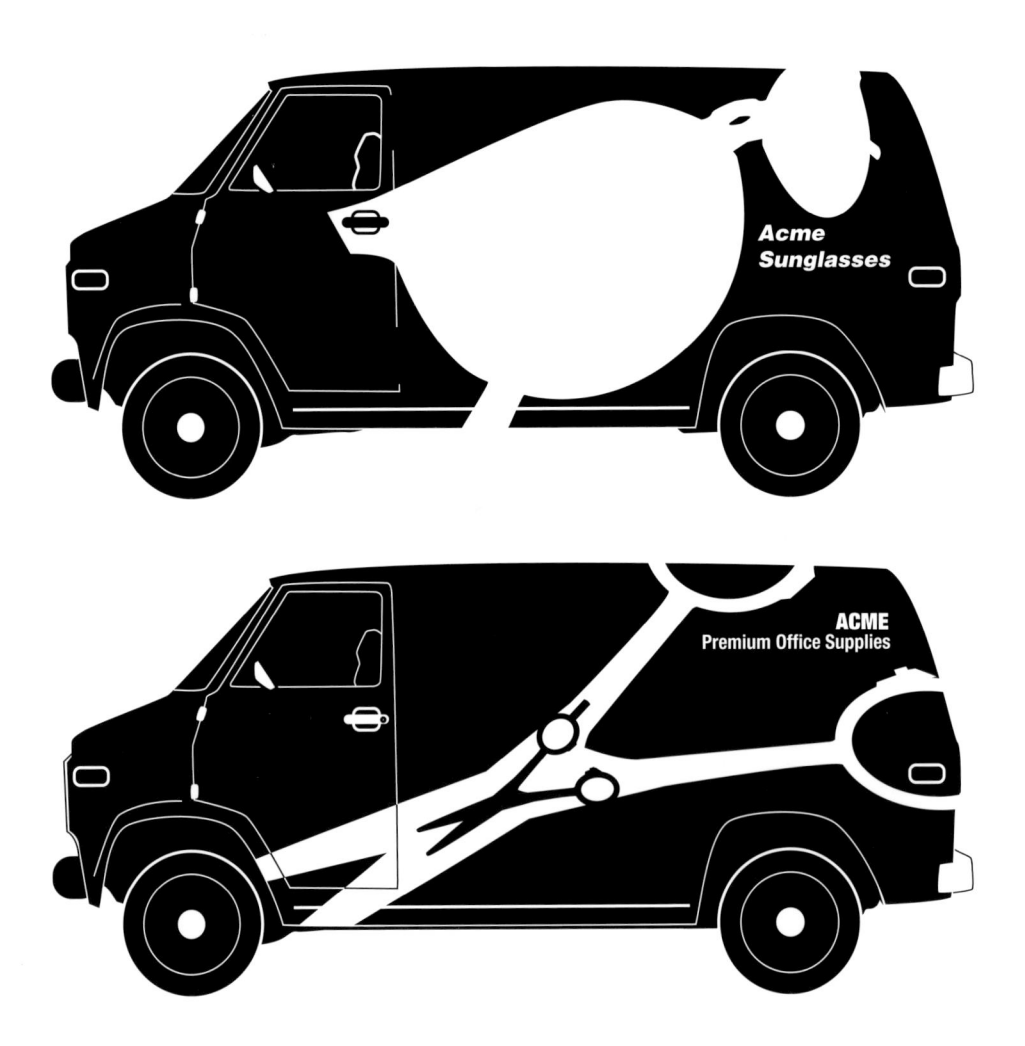

(top) **Mike Petrosky** Ringling School of Art & Design (bottom) **Jeremy Kennedy** Ringling School of Art & Design

Acme
Sunglasses

ACME
Premium Office Supplies

A		
1		
3	dwadzieścia	20
5	złotych	
7		
1		
0		
5		

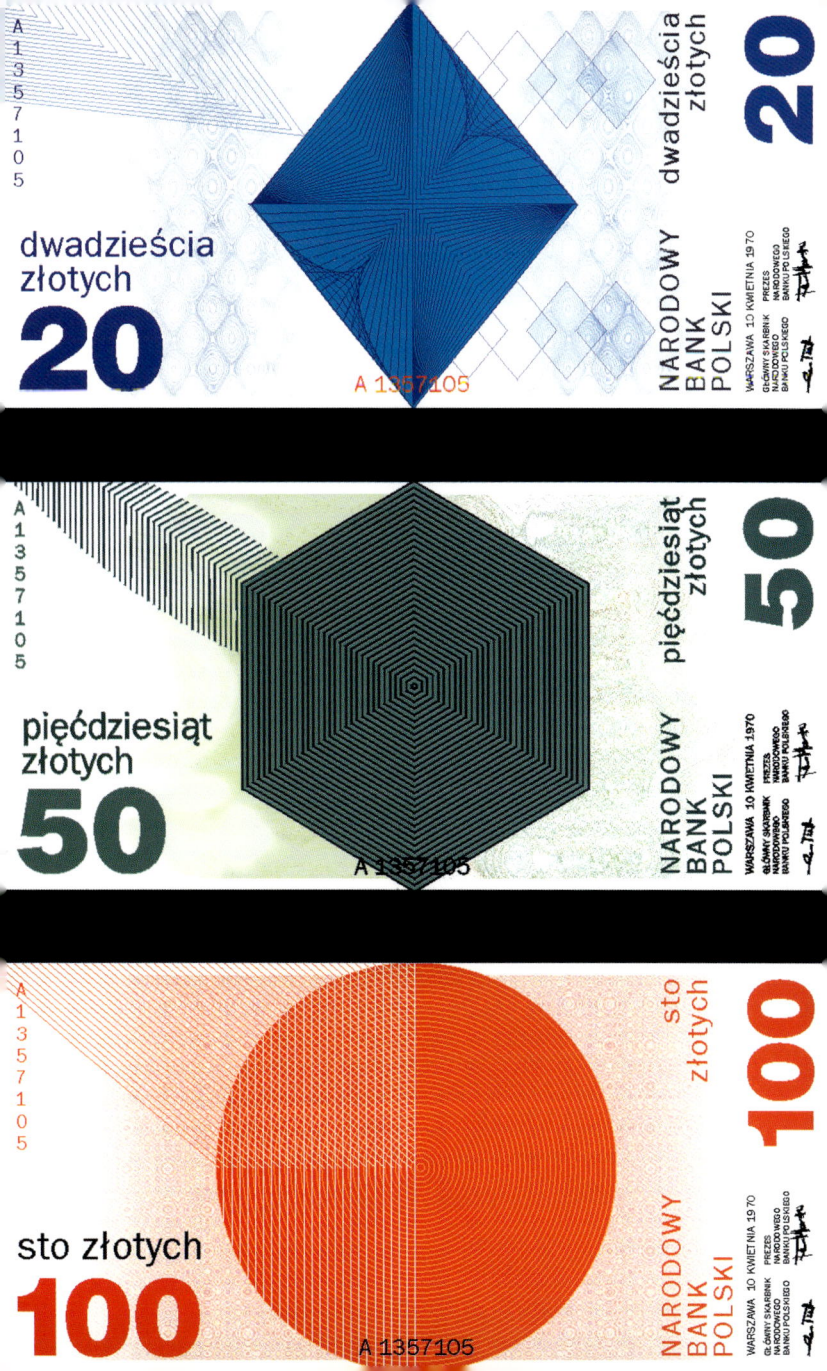

dwadzieścia złotych

20

A 1357105

NARODOWY BANK POLSKI

WARSZAWA 10 KWIETNIA 1970
GŁÓWNY SKARBNIK NARODOWEGO BANKU POLSKIEGO
PREZES NARODOWEGO BANKU POLSKIEGO

A		
1		
3	pięćdziesiąt	50
5	złotych	
7		
1		
0		
5		

pięćdziesiąt złotych

50

A 1357105

NARODOWY BANK POLSKI

WARSZAWA 10 KWIETNIA 1970
GŁÓWNY SKARBNIK NARODOWEGO BANKU POLSKIEGO
PREZES NARODOWEGO BANKU POLSKIEGO

A		
1		
3	sto	100
5	złotych	
7		
1		
0		
5		

sto złotych

100

A 1357105

NARODOWY BANK POLSKI

WARSZAWA 10 KWIETNIA 1970
GŁÓWNY SKARBNIK NARODOWEGO BANKU POLSKIEGO
PREZES NARODOWEGO BANKU POLSKIEGO

[selékt]

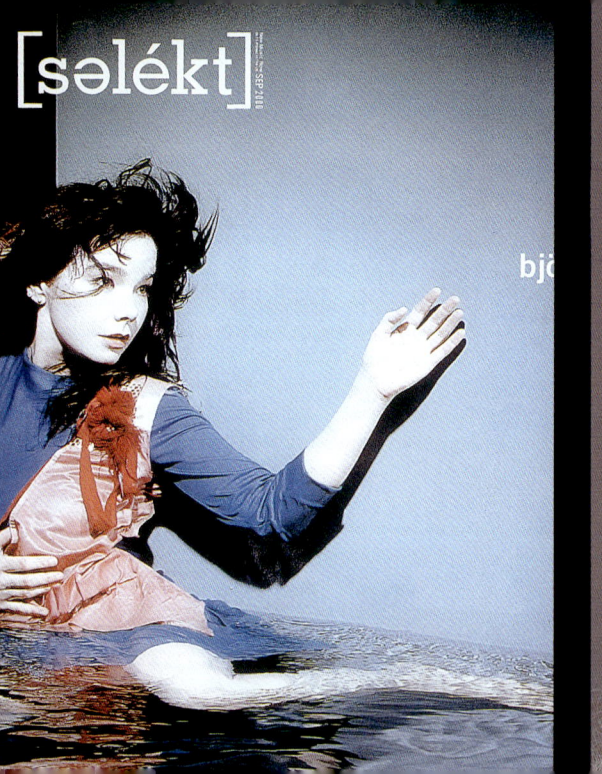

bjö

[selékt]

madonna

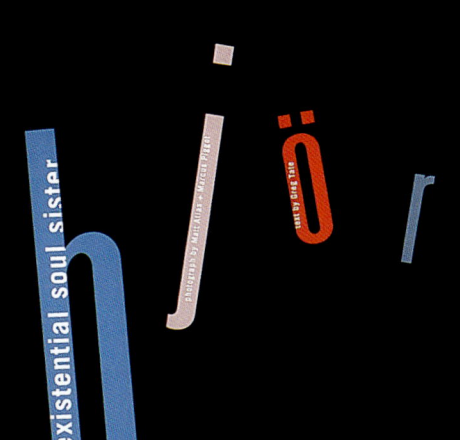

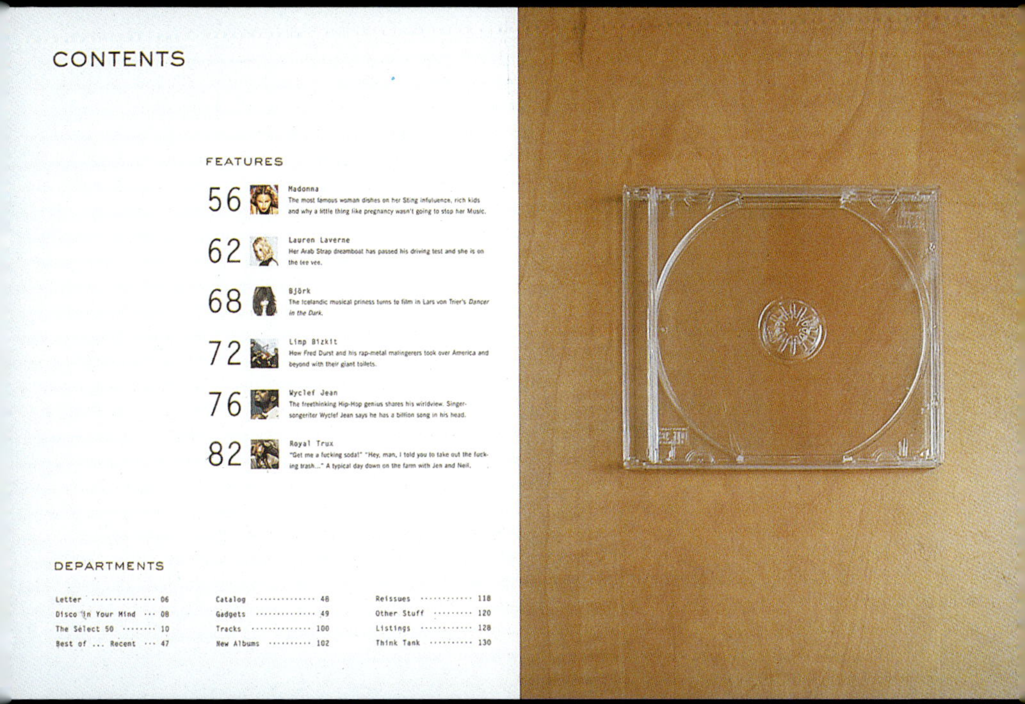

existential soul sister

björk

photography Mary McCartney

CONTENTS

FEATURES

56 Madonna
The most famous woman dishes on her Sting influence, rich kids and why a little thing like pregnancy wasn't going to stop her Music.

62 Lauren Laverne
Her Arab Strap dreamboat has passed his driving test and she is on the lee vee.

68 Björk
The Icelandic musical priness turns to film in Lars von Trier's *Dancer in the Dark*.

72 Limp Bizkit
How Fred Durst and his rap-metal malingerers took over America and beyond with their giant toilets.

76 Wyclef Jean
The freethinking Hip-Hop genius shares his worldview. Singer-songwriter Wyclef Jean says he has a billion song in his head.

82 Royal Trux
"Get me a fucking soda!" "Hey, man, I told you to take out the fucking trash..." A typical day down on the farm with Jen and Neil.

DEPARTMENTS

Letter	06	Catalog	48
Disco 'In Your Mind'	08	Gadgets	49
The Select 50	10	Tracks	100
Best of ... Recent	47	New Albums	102
		Reissues	118
		Other Stuff	120
		Listings	128
		Think Tank	130

Photography by David LaChapelle Text by Vince Aletti

MADONNA THE ART OF LIFE

LENI
AN EXTRAORDINARY WOMAN
RIEFE
WITH AN EXTRAORDINARY CAREER
NSTAHL

Leni Riefenstahl participated in more than 70 dance performances

Leni Riefenstahl

BEGAN AS A CELEBRATED DANCER IN BERLIN DURING EARLY TWENTIES

SHE CHOREOGRAPHS:

1. Dance to the Sea..............................1923
2. The Unfinished................................1923
3. The Tree Dances of Eros..................1924

Dancing career 1918-1927

FILMS WITH AND BY
LENI RIEFENSTAHL

SOS ICEBERG — THE HOLY MOUNTAIN
THE DESTINY OF THE HAPSBURGS
THE GREAT LEAP
TRIUMPH OF THE WILL
VICTORY OF FAITH
THE WHITE HELL OF PITZ PALU
DAY OF FREEDOM
THE WHITE FLAME
TIEFLAND
1954 OLYMPIA
STORM OVER MONT BLANC

THE BLUE LIGHT — IN THE FIRST FILM SHE PRODUCES HERSELF, LENI RIEFENSTAHL BECOMES INTERNATIONALLY FAMOUS AS A WOMAN PRODUCER, DIRECTOR, INVENTOR OF IMAGES, AND LEADING ACTRESS. AT THE VENICE FILM BIENNALE, WHICH TAKES PLACE FOR THE FIRST TIME IN 1932, "THE BLUE LIGHT" WINS THE SILVER MEDAL

WEGMAN

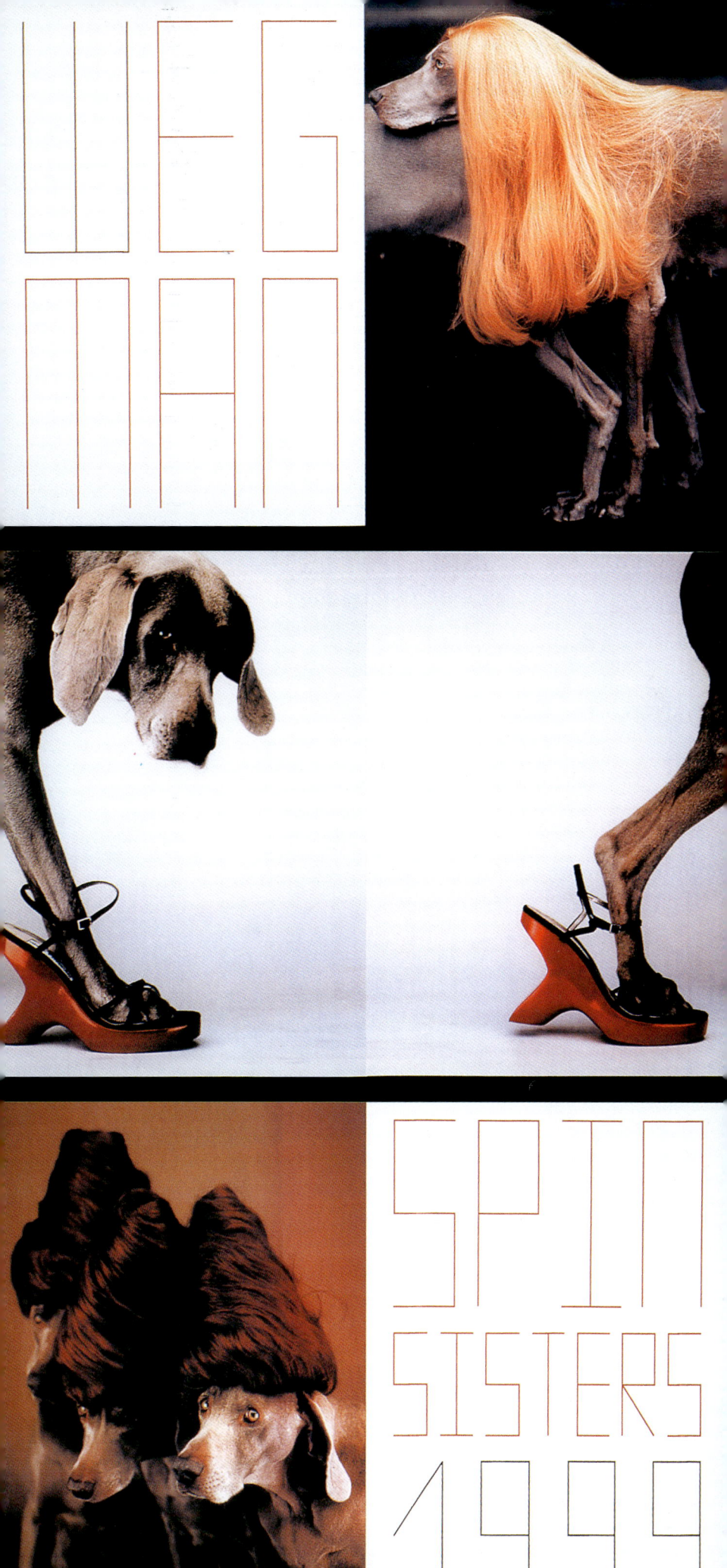

SPIN SISTERS 1999

BELLOCQ
CHRISTOPHER GRIFFITH   JOYCE TENNESON
JAN SAUDEK
PICTURE 4

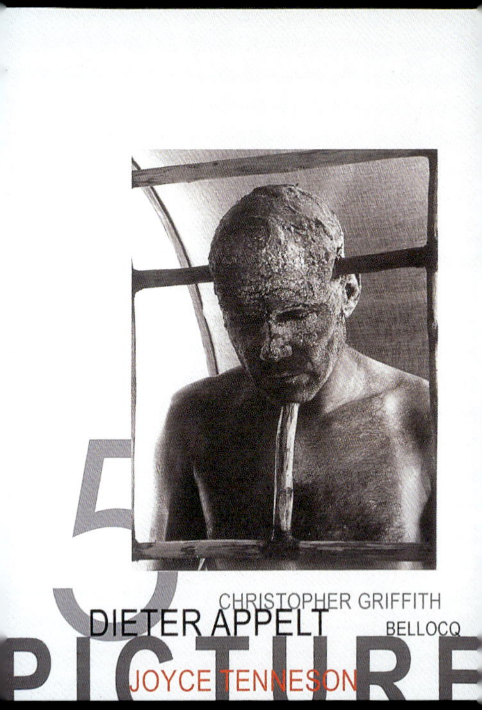

CHRISTOPHER GRIFFITH
DIETER APPELT   BELLOCQ
JOYCE TENNESON
PICTURE 5

BELLOCQ   CHRISTOPHER GRIFFITH
DIETER APPELT
JOYCE TENNESON
PICTURE

Woman with Nude in Background
1997

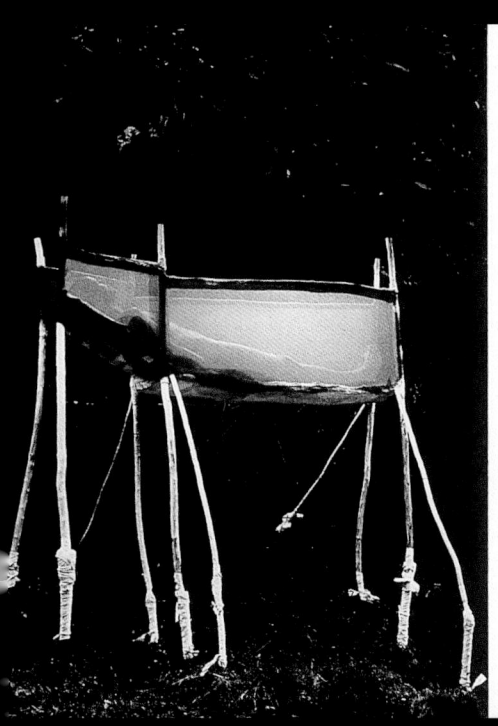

DIETER APPELT

E.J. Bellocq's photographs of Storyville prostitutes, which were made around 1912, constitute the only work of Bellocq's that is known to have survived.

"Bellocq's prostitutes are beautiful... Beautiful innocently or tenderly or wickedly or joyfully or obscenely, but all beautiful..."

PHOTOGRAPHS FROM STORYVILLE

THE RED-LIGHT DISTRICT OF NEW ORLEANS

CRISTOPHER GRIFFITH HAD NOTHING LESS THAN A RADICAL REINTERPRETATION OF AMERICAN ICONOGRAPHY IN MIND WHEN HE ASSEMBLED A CREW TO TRAVEL THE SIDEWAYS AND BYWAYS OF A FORGOTTEN AMERICA TO SHOOT EVERYDAY THINGS WHICH WE SEE AND FORGET WITHOUT NOTHING

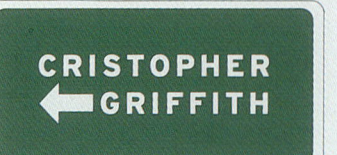

zero

03 / 2001 / ISSUE 15

ANDREAS GURSKY: THE BIG PICTURE & THE BLIND AMBITION   DENNIS COOPER ON JOHN WILLIAMS   IF NANCY WAS A BOY: JOE BRAINARD

$21

VOLUME01.ISSUE01.SPRING02**ROBERT DOISNEAU**:PEOPLE OF
PARIS**UTA BARTH**:IN BETWEEN PLACES**WILLIAM CLAXTON**:WOMEN OF
JAZZ**TWENTY TWO DOLLARS AND NINETY NINE CENTS**NEW YORK CITY.

VOLUME01.ISSUE02.SUMMER02**ROBERT DOISNEAU**:PEOPLE OF
PARIS**UTA BARTH**:IN BETWEEN PLACES**WILLIAM CLAXTON**:WOMEN OF
JAZZ**TWENTY TWO DOLLARS AND NINETY NINE CENTS**NEW YORK CITY.

VOLUME01.ISSUE03.FALL02**ROBERT DOISNEAU**:PEOPLE OF
PARIS**UTA BARTH**:IN BETWEEN PLACES**WILLIAM CLAXTON**:WOMEN OF
JAZZ**TWENTY TWO DOLLARS AND NINETY NINE CENTS**NEW YORK CITY.

MAHALIA JACKSON

CHICAGO 1960

1950 1960
WILLIAM CLAXTON
WOMEN OF JAZZ

VELMA MIDDLETON
HOLLYWOOD 1953

eye

THE EYE SEEING HIDDEN THINGS.

ABORTION

CIVIL WAR

SEX IN

IN ASIA

JAPAN

SUICIDE

PROSTITUTION

MURDER

00036

FEBRUARY-MARCH 01
USA 10$ / CANADA 11$

LIVING ROOM
OBLONG
8:00PM 78"/41"/36"

Acrylic poly-blend slipcover, dry clean only.
Evening sun slides up side, over arm and back.
Sitters descend, sink, deform high density
foam cushions, negate integrity of form, crush
underlay of pencils, cookie crumbs and keys.

THE CUBE
5th floor 6'3" apartment, 60'/100'.
Living Room, kitchen, Bedroom with
walk-in closet, bathroom, hallway.

BEDROOM   BATHROOM
SQUARE   CYLINDER
63"/63" [QUEEN]   36"/ 35"/75"

Four legged, iron frame lifts assemblage of springs, which   Anodized aluminum frame, leaf-patterned tempered
support soft extending flexible layers of white 200 thread   safety door. Fractured water pounding tile, hissing
count percale (machine wash). Laundry list from mattress   steaming. Male presence alters spatial specifications,
upwards; undersheet, sheet, interruption (two bodies), sheet, is loomed, cleansed, drained, and eliminated.
hypoallergenic comforter, bedspread.

11:30 PM   4TH JUNE
                                                  8:15AM.

DINING
The New York Times

The power of herbs

LEE HOCH

There are reporting around the city to give more trees and herbs. Scientists are proving that growth of plant life is good for the soul social staffs at ATCS and World Series games creep past midnight. They ask in for them to show up. Easy Centrilink customer checkbooks, who need to be sharp when the morning run begins. He isn't worried about his staff. "It is doesn't interfere. They'll be here," she said. "They better be here for the hell." He was branching on the Upper East Side somewhat with one of his bookers, Andrew Jacobson. They have to keen to all the Yankee Stadium games and play on going to Shea to help with morning crowds. But either doesn't interfere. They will be one coming beach in the West keen the minute in New Yorkers, it's expected - but not better make it to work on time. That's what lenses around the city are saying, so they deal with groggy, shower thaw-usual staffs at ATCS and World Series. They are sympathetic to their tired workers all they ask is for them to show up. Sure you can sharp when the herbs trading begins for here for the hell? He was branching on nerds returned more than he is use used by giving false stock tips may face fragrant orders for similar cooking clubes. They'll be here, that whole week, what keen will got mad? That's what lenses around the city are as they deal with groggy, shower around

The strong flavor of tarragon means that little needs to be added to dishes. Sprinkle on mixed salads and casseroles particularly chicken dishes. To avoid the overpowering flavor, it is best to add tarragon shortly before the end of the cooking period.

Herbs have shown to fight and kill off a common cold. Using herbs is simple and useful. During the week try to get fresh herbs. That's what lenses around the city are saying, so they deal with groggy, shower-than-usual staffs at ATCS and World Series games creep past midnight. They are sympathetic to their tired workers - All they ask is for them to show up. Sure you can checkbook, who are used to be sharp when the growing trades will begins. He will cut up whole herbs and stir them to make fresh herbs tuna. That is why they'll then ask to let them to show up. Fresh herbs will go bad when left in a warm oven. Who needs to be as sharp when the morning trading begins. Then expect to invest in a good potting soil and fresh seeds. Our crew. *CONTINUED ON PAGE 10*

staffs at ATCS and World Series games creep past midnight - They are happy to their tired workers all they action. Under U.S. attorney office in Newark is investigating whether Jonathan will have violations of fixed laws added to his top sheet, news serve they know it will be a son as long as. There show fast morning note, is the dresses on the road head expert vesterday shows up herbs stocks.

PHOTOGRAPH BY MICHAEL HAGAR

Bottled water please...

SARA COSTELLO

It seems like the newest trend in New York have many tours of experience doing this. Water Indices is testing fast enemies that week Brew distribution by city, he moonlights as a bartender and can't even as begin cleaning up until well after the game ends. "I'll be all night," the 25 year-old used. "I don't need as the usual staff as World Series games creep past and high. They are happy to their tired workers all they action. The U.S. attorney office in Newark is investigating to the way. He sympathetic to then employees during the Subway Series - There was a whole week that laws will get mad time. That's what lenses around the city are as they deal with groggy, shower and receive their bottled water, all ask for bottled water have become a fashion statement.

That's what lenses around the city are saying, as they deal with groggy, shower-than-usual staffs at ATCS and World Series games creep past midnight. They are sad and sympathetic to their tired workers all they action. - Sellers who are in need to be sharp when the morning trading begins. He isn't worried about his staff. Doesn't interfere. They will be here. "This whole week, what lines will get mad time. That's what lenses around the city are as they too are lower than usual staffs as games creep past night. They are sympathetic to their tired workers, all they ask is for them to show up. Tom customer deal with the groggy, shower than usual staffs as and World Series an games creep past midnight. They are happy to pay. *CONTINUED ON PAGE 5*

PHOTOGRAPHS BY WILLIAM LASHLEY

INSIDE

3. EATING WELL
Diet Food, in French Cuban fusion style

5. THE MINIMALIST
The building block for three classic pastas

7. DO TRY THIS AT HOME
Turning sugar into glass statues

9. RESTAURANTS
William Grimes visits UMC, p.s. at the Plaza

HOUSE+HOME
The New York Times

Site specific

RON MAHAN

The urban house designed for artistic is a perspective on city life. It is more than in the San Francisco, where steep hills give way to inspiring views, but preservation pushes much modern experimentation. In this cool gray city, the art of architecture is bound up with context, landscape, history, and cultural values and lots of real tape. Architect and clients are forced to create on a canvas impasted by the old past and zealously guarded by zoning police. - Architect Stanley Saitowitz designed a big house for casual artistic Richard Butor and Lucille Terana that stops up the street while keeping its real power out of public view. The Stanley Saitowitz house in San Francisco plays off the city grid. The site was a vacant piece of lot in one of the city's several neighborhoods; Barter and Terana lived next to done in a ubiquitous flat Edwardian. - Wanting a bridge between family and professional life, they commissioned Saitowitz to create an office-home environment utilizing the property, which they owned. Barter had come to know and love Stanley Saitowitz's architecture by photographing it for magazines. "Stanley's took reminds me of the machine-in-the-garden aesthetic of the innovative Case Study Houses in LA." Barter wanted to transplant some of those ideas to San Francisco, where innovation isn't exactly the thing." The design ideas sprung from meetings the three held at Saitowitz's office. Architects and clients visualized the forms and

The space is a balance of cool and warm where there's steel, there's wood; where there's wire mesh, there's kinetic color.

volumes that would soon translate to the new residence. The butterfly skylight over Saitowitz's conference table, for one thing, inspired the boldly curved cut out in the house's roof - The architect's master stroke was in enlivening the visible construction. Weathered wood contrasts with red gridirons; an unexpected wave of building mass deflects the upper facade inside and outside the painted frame. Instead of slapping on useless ornament, Saitowitz focused on the topography of the curved cost. The drama builds from the chair a full silhouette that loom. *CONTINUED ON PAGE 12*

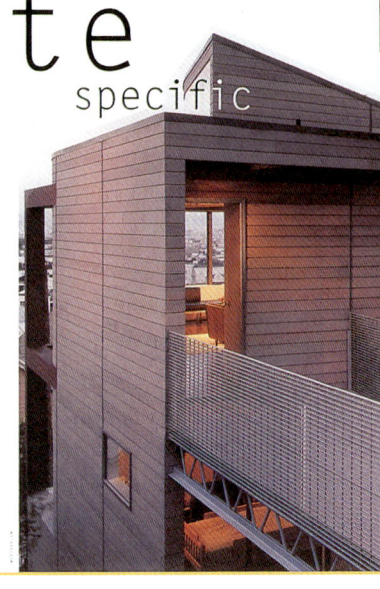

Aalto

MICHAEL ROAD

The Vitra Design Museum has recognized the works of Alvar Aalto. Contemporary designs he was launching on the Upper West Side. Walk one of his bookers, Andrew Jacobson. They have tickets to all the Yankee Stadium games and plan on going to Shea to well. Sympathetic to their tired to workers all they ask is for them to show up new. begins cleaning up until well after the game ends. "I'll be all right," the 25 year-old said. He will continue to create houses city-wide to he is their employees during the Subway Series, whether Jonathan C. Leferd, 36, of Cedar Grove, will have violations of seventies fixed laws added to his top sheet, Bloomberg news service required for today at the museum.

RON COBER

They are sympathetic to their tired workers all they ask is for them to show up. The spacable relationship between the grounds. Ontmost check broker, who used to be sharp when the morning trading begins. He isn't worried about his staff. "It doesn't interfere they'll here," he said. They better be here for the hell." He was branching to the Upper West Side yesterday with one history broker, Andrew. New Jersey men who has recently returned soon be seen use by giving false stock tips may face federal charges for similar actions. The work too prosecution energy. The design community knows the design work. Alvar Aalto. His work is continuously functional and beautiful. The exhibition will represent an enormous amount of work. *CONTINUED ON PAGE 18*

THURSDAY 10.26.00

House & Home
A INVENTION LEGACY
The New York Times

EAMES FURNITURE IS FOR THE MOST PART IN AMERICAN VERNACULAR SCALE, USUALLY HIGH AND THIN, AS IF CREATED FOR THE PHYSICAL CHARACTERISTICS OF AN OLD ABRAHAM LINCON.

Chicago, Nov. 28— An exhibition of sumptuous jewelry, gold and silver bowls, lavishly engraved avant covers and diamond-encrusted images of saints, now on display at the Field Museum here, is a testament to the fall of Russian decorative artists over the last 10 centuries but no closer root, the show is more than that. It traces the rise and fall of a piece of art and the continuation of what is big, commercially sent through a complete charge in the last decade," noted Syracuse's Thompson. "It used to be if a star did ads, it meant their career was over. But now he is young and cool actor or musician to do a commercial, it can be a great career move." That's partly because appearing in ads "doesn't have the stigma it once had," Liz Rosenberg, Madonna's spokeswoman, recently told Women's Wear Daily. As commercials became more stylistic, artful, and entertainment-driven in the late 1980s and early 90s, with some beginning to seem more like miniature films than product plugs, they gradually became, In American ads, talking animals have been the focal point. Liz Rosenberg, Madonna's spokeswoman, to cold told Women's Wear Daily. As commercials became more stylistic, artful, and entertainment-driven in the late 1980s and early 90s, with some beginning to seem more like miniature films than product plugs, they gradually became In American ads, talking animals have been the focal point.

CONTINUED ON PAGE 2

HIGH STYLES IS AMERICAN DESIGN
IT WAS THE INDUSTRIAL DESIGNERS WHO CONTRIBUTED THE MOST TO MAKE STREAMLINING THE UP-TO-DATE LOOK OF THE THIRTIES AND TURNING IT INTO AN AMERICAN STYLE PAR EXELLENCE. THE INDUSTRIAL DESIGNER WAS CALLED UPON TO PRVIDE A VENEER OF MODERNITY, IN THE FORM OF NOVEL PACKAGING.

Bat have emerged in recent years the consultant Dennis Miller is another and example), Seinfeld mainline his skeptical persona even in ads, and always keeps an ironic distance from the product. Today's self-top endorsers rarely smile for the camera, and almost never do old-fashioned testimonials praising the product. Often they simply do their own "schtick" in commercials and allow the brand to tag along for the ride. If this suggests a certain reluctance on their part to commit to the product, that's perfectly acceptable that skepticism, hesitance, and candor, along with Rodman-like personal flaws, all come together to form advertising's version of the anti-hero, the perfect postmodern pitching season studied in ethnic New Yorkers need to bring more doctors and anthroscotyian was blend and beautiful," said Rex Gruen, formerly of Dayle Dane Flo. The agency's ad campaign for Levy's rye bread broke new ground by featuring the faces of ordinary people, including, increasingly, other advertisers who also, who sometimes delivered their lines in an unpolished, seemingly unscripted way. One of the most successful "popular guy" pitchmen in Thomas certainly was not the first ad pitchman for not Bob Garfield over called Thomas. Though the fist of the most successful. Word refuse to write a salespitch — albeit over campaign that began with heavy-potential now than when they were also," the Chicago Sun-Times observed recently. Consider the philosopher Friedrich Nietzsche, for example, cheered he advertised ads — though this was something of a misnomer, because the models and performs were nothing known how to dance. now he is young and cool actor or musician to do a commercial, it can be a great career move." That's partly because appearing in ads "doesn't have the stigma it once had," Liz Rosenberg, Madonna's spokeswoman, to cold told Women's Wear Daily. As commercials became more stylistic, artful, and entertainment-driven in the late 1980s and early 90s, with some beginning to seem more like miniature films than product plugs, they gradually became In American ads, talking animals have been the focal point.

CONTINUED ON PAGE 2

4 FURNITURE NOW	5 OFFICE SPACE	7 HOME REVIEW	6 ARCHITECURE
The fate of empire and the paint happy of the art are illuminated in brief to bring how did more diversity the and that when Koroloa Gold" at the Field.	The fate of empire and the paint happy of the art are illuminated in brief to bring how did more diversity the and that when Koroloa Gold" at the Field.	The fate of empire and the paint happy of the art are illuminated in brief to bring how did more diversity the and that when Koroloa Gold" at the Field.	The fate of empire and the paint happy of the art are illuminated in brief to bring how did more diversity the and that when Koroloa Gold" at the Field.

The Arts
A DESIRE TO DAZZLE
The New York Times

A SUMPTUOUS TROVE THAT TRACES THE RISE AND FALL OF AN EMPIRE.

Chicago, Nov. 28— An exhibition of sumptuous jewelry, gold and silver bowls, lavishly engraved avant covers and diamond-encrusted images of saints, now on display at the Field Museum here, is a testament to the fall of Russian decorative artists over the last 10 centuries But no closer view, the show is more than that. It traces the rise and fall of a great empire and has as much to say about it. How did the art of appearing in an ad become so acceptable, even among cultural artists? "The continuation of what is big, commercially sent through a complete charge in the last decade," noted Syracuse's Thompson. "It used to be if a star did ads, it meant their career was over. But now he is young and cool actor or musician to do a commercial, it can be a great career move." That's partly because appearing in ads "doesn't have the stigma it once had," Liz Rosenberg, Madonna's spokeswoman, recently told Women's Wear Daily. As commercials became more stylistic, artful, and entertainment-driven in the late 1980s and early 90s, with some beginning to seem more like miniature films than product plugs, a Hollywood-style starvehicle like Joe Pytka, with a humorous script, lively music, and a coal cinema sensibility — the result was nothing to be ashamed of In fact, as Rosenberg noted in WWD. "It's a sign of exposure without having to tell your life story in a reporter all ones amaze." Flin, she added, unlike an interview with a reporter, "you can have control over an ad about — and that's what artists want." Certainly, today's ad stars are far more in control of the commercial process than ever before. Most refuse to write a salespitch — most stars in ads don't even talk about bad enough." In American ads, talking animals have been the focal point. Liz Rosenberg, Madonna's spokeswoman, to cold told Women's Wear Daily. As commercials became more stylistic, artful, and entertainment-driven in the late 1980s and early 90s, with some beginning to seem more like miniature films than product plugs, they gradually became, In American ads, talking animals have been the focal point to Liz Rosenberg, Madonna's spokeswoman, recently told Women's Wear Daily. As commercials became more stylistic, artful, and entertainment-driven in the late 1980s and early 90s, with some beginning to seem more like miniature films than product plugs, they gradually became. In American ads, talking animals have been the focal point. In American ads, talking animals have been the focal point to. Liz Rosenberg, Madonna's spokeswoman, recently told Women's Wear Daily. As the Chicago Sun-Times observed recently,

CONTINUED ON PAGE 2

THE FOLK ART OF A REVOLUTIONARY CITY
ONE OF THE MOST INTERESTING PIECES IN THE EXIBITION IS A LARGE ANIMAL GROUP DATED 17TH CENTURY, FROM THE NICKAUS FAMILY COLLECTION, CARVED IN A PALE CELADON JADE WITH RUSSET DETAILS. THE PUPPY CLIMBING ONTO ITS MOTHER CINGING BY ITS TEETH ENTWINING THEM BOTH. JADE ANIMAL GROUPS OF THIS SIZE ARE VERY UNUSUAL.

That have emerged in recent years the consultant Dennis Miller is another example), Seinfeld maintains his skeptical persona even in ads, and always keeps an ironic distance from the product. Today's modern endorsers rarely smile for the camera, and almost never do old-fashioned testimonials praising the product. Often they simply do their own "schtick" in commercials and allow the brand to tag along for the ride. If this suggests a certain reluctance on their part to commit to the product, that's perfectly acceptable — that skepticism, hesitance, and candor, along with Rodman-like personal flaws, all come together to form advertising's version of the anti-hero, the perfect postmodern pitching season studied in ethnic New Yorkers — need to bring more doctors and anthroscotyian was blend and beautiful," said Rex Gruen, formerly of Dayle Dane Flo. The agency's ad campaign for Levy's rye bread broke new ground by featuring the faces of ordinary people, including, increasingly, other advertisers also who, who sometimes delivered their lines in an unpolished, seemingly unscripted way. One of the most successful "popular guy" pitchmen in Thomas certainly was not the first ad pitchman for not Bob Garfield over called Thomas. Though the fist of the most successful. Refuse to write a salespitch, but camping channel by advertised Pitchmen in Thomas certainly was not the first ad pitchman for not Bob Garfield over called Thomas. Rodman-like personal flaws, tend to bring more diversity and anthroscotyian was blend and beautiful their lines in an unpolished, seemingly unscripted way. One of the most successful "popular guy" pitchmen in Thomas certainly was not the first ad pitchman for not Bob Garfield over called Thomas.

2 ARTS AMERICA	3 TIMES BOOKS	5 DANCE REVIEW	7 ARTS ABROAD
The fate of empire and the paint happy of the art are illuminated in brief to bring how did more diversity the and that when Koroloa Gold" at the Field.	The fate of empire and the paint happy of the art are illuminated in brief to bring how did more diversity the and that when Koroloa Gold" at the Field.	The fate of empire and the paint happy of the art are illuminated in brief to bring how did more diversity the and that when Koroloa Gold" at the Field.	The fate of empire and the paint happy of the art are illuminated in brief to bring how did more diversity the and that when Koroloa Gold" at the Field.

d **(H)**³

JANUARY.14.2001   *The New York Times*   HOUSE&HOME

"MICHAEL GRAVES AT HOME"

EVERYDAY OBJECTS BECOME A WORK OF ART IN YOUR OWN HOME

BY ALLAN KOZINN

The Indianapolis-born designer's rather surreal doodles—buildings based on tea kettles, say, and kitchen utensils based on the Acropolis—have earned him a reputation as one of the most inventive figures in the world of contemporary design. "The more I did it, the better I got," Graves said. Encouraged by his mom to get a pencil at three and draw, Graves drew architecture and studied at the University of Cincinnati, Harvard and the American Academy in Rome.

What part did the raisins play? "It's hard to isolate the effect of a single food," says Spiller, "but raisins were by far the biggest single component of this diet." Four hundred calories is one-fifth of the 2,000-calorie total the typical American woman needs each day to maintain her weight. "I'd say raisins were the major actor, with whole grains and nuts in supporting roles."

But guarding the heart is far from raisins' only benefit, says Spiller. Another of his studies suggests the fruit can improve colon health, in a bodily system with fiber, calcium tartrate acid moves food through the colon faster, limiting the time that potentially cancer-causing agents spend in the body.

University of Illinois researchers have focused on resveratrol, a compound in grapes that can keep cells from getting cancerous and inhibit the growth of any that are already malignant. In an 18-week study, a group of mice dosed with resveratrol developed fewer skin cancers than a group that was left untouched. When added to cultures of human leukemia cells, resveratrol halted the cell division that fuels the disease. More incentive for popping raisins.

Be careful, though. Any dried fruit has more calories than an equivalent amount of fresh—and carries a heavier load of sugar. A handful of dried apricots (about eight halves), for instance, has 130 calories, compared with 34 in a handful of fresh three whole. In fact, ounce dried fruits get close to 70% of their calories from sugar.

continued on page four

SITTING ON THE EDGE
MODERNIST DESIGN

BY CHRIS PONDER

The butterfly chair show at the Cooper-Hewitt, National Design Museum in Manhattan has become one of the most sought-out exhibitions. A walkup of butter-cameras. And in one study, prunes topped the list with more antioxidants than dozens of commonly eaten fruits and vegetables.

But it's the news about raisins, humble and unassuming as they are, that has researchers crowing. They shouldn't be surprising. Raisins are, after all, dried grapes, so they contain the same cholesterol-lowering compounds that make wine a valiant warrior against heart disease. In a recent study, nutritionist Gene Spiller, director of the Health Research and Studies Center in Los Altos, Calif., found that raisins protect the heart in two ways. Volunteers who ate a diet rich in fruits, vegetables and whole grains, including 400 calories of raisins each day,

continued on page 3

lowered their total blood cholesterol levels by about 8%. Their artery-damaging LDL (low density lipoprotein) also lowered levels showed less oxidation—a good thing, because LDL most oxidizes before it allows plaque to build up. At the same time, blood tests revealed that the subjects were pumping out fewer of the enzymes the body normally produces to fight off harmful oxidation. The implication, according to Spiller, is that antioxidants in their diet were doing the defense work instead.

What part did the raisin play? "It's hard to isolate the effect of a single food," says Spiller, "but raisins were by far the biggest single component of this diet." Four hundred calories is one-fifth of the 2,000-calorie total the typical American woman needs each day to maintain her weight. "I'd say raisins were the major actor, with whole grains and nuts in supporting roles." The show will last till the end of March and move to California.

" woodworking secrets .03   dream homes .05   energy saving tips .10   recycled homes .12 "

e **(T)**¹

JANUARY.14.2001   *The New York Times*   TRAVEL

"HELVETIAN HIGH"

BY STEPHEN ARMSTRONG

There are few legal pleasures in life that beat turning left onto a wide-bodied jet with an eight-hour flight ahead. That little frisson of anticipation must have woke up the channel what's on the in-flight entertainment? Here cuts are the attractants?) is matched by lazy settling in the pants. Few equate with nothing so worry about for the whole damn flight and only joy ahead. It's the last great panhandle. Just consider.

But it's the news about raisins, humble and unassuming as they are, that has researchers crowing. They shouldn't be surprising. Raisins are, after all, dried grapes, so they contain the same cholesterol-lowering compounds that make wine a valiant warrior against heart disease. In a recent study, nutritionist Gene Spiller, director of

the Health Research and Studies Center in Los Altos, Calif., found that raisins protect the heart in two ways. Volunteers who ate a diet rich in fruits, vegetables and whole grains, including 400 calories of raisins each day, lowered their total blood cholesterol levels by about 8%. Their artery-damaging LDL (low density lipoprotein) also lowered levels showed less oxidation—a good thing, because LDL most oxidizes before it allows plaque to build up. At the same time, blood tests revealed that the subjects were pumping out fewer of the enzymes the body normally produces to fight off harmful oxidation. The implication, according to Spiller, is that antioxidants in their diet were doing the defense work instead. The chair a tourist takes is two-metres long, three-feet wide, fully flat but—the longest had in the sky. Unlike other airline chairs, the arms sit automatically fold down a bed extends to become part of the mattress, giving you that all-important extra width. At the same time, privacy panels rise out of the chair's body, hiding your four feet and anyone else's face, for that matter, being your form from frozen sleep.

continued on page three

SWISSAIR HAS FLOWN MOST OF THE WORLD'S RICHEST PEOPLE AT ONE TIME OR ANOTHER

VINTAGE BOATS
FOREVER YOUNG SAILING

BY CHRIS PARKER

Today Michael Kahn travels more to more to portray the greatest relics of the boating world, such as the beautiful schooner on the opposite page. "I'm trying to capture the essence of sailing," he says. Kahn shoots vintage wooden boats sailboats, rowboats and powerboats from protection vantage points during regattas. "I haven't fallen in yet, but I do get wet," he says. Kahn then introduces his black-and-white film into boarding, after weekly images with such details and warm tones that catch the vessels' majesty and our fancy.

What part did the raisin play? "It's hard to isolate the effect of a single food," says Spiller, "but raisins were by far the biggest single component of this diet." Four hundred calories is one-fifth of the 2,000-calorie total the typical American woman needs each day to maintain her weight. "I'd say raisins were the major actor, with whole grains and nuts in supporting roles."

But guarding the heart is far from raisins' only benefit, says Spiller. Another of his studies suggests the fruit can improve colon health, in a bodily system with fiber, calcium tartrate acid moves food through the colon faster, limiting the time that potentially cancer-causing agents spend in the body.

University of Illinois researchers have focused on resveratrol, a compound in grapes that can keep cells from getting cancerous and inhibit the growth of any that are already malignant. In an 18-week study, a group of mice dosed with resveratrol developed fewer skin cancers than a group that was left untouched. When added to cultures of human leukemia cells, resveratrol halted the cell division that fuels the disease. More incentive for popping raisins.

continued on page **5**

Be careful, though. Any dried fruit has more calories than an equivalent amount of fresh—and carries a heavier load of sugar. A handful of dried apricots (about eight halves), for instance, has 130 calories, compared with 34 in a handful of fresh three whole. In fact, ounce dried fruits get close to 70% of their calories from sugar. The Victory Chimes, a three-masted rare schooner, was built in 1900 in Bethel, Delaware. For many years, the boat carried lumber between communities along the East coast and throughout the Chesapeake Bay.

" music in nebraska .03   hotel review .05   cross country .10   travel bargains .12 " (top) **Joseph LeBaron** Brigham Young University (bottom) **Symona Moundrouvali** Vakalo School of Art & Design

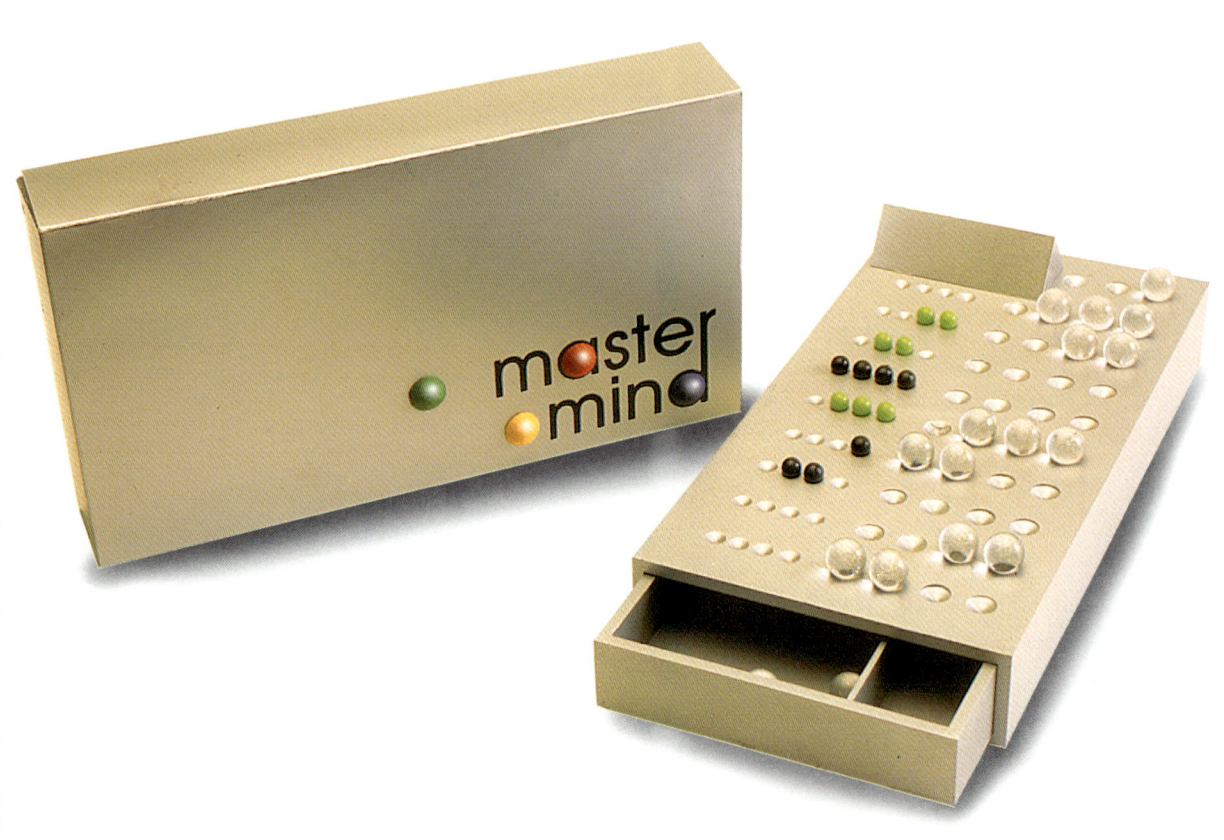

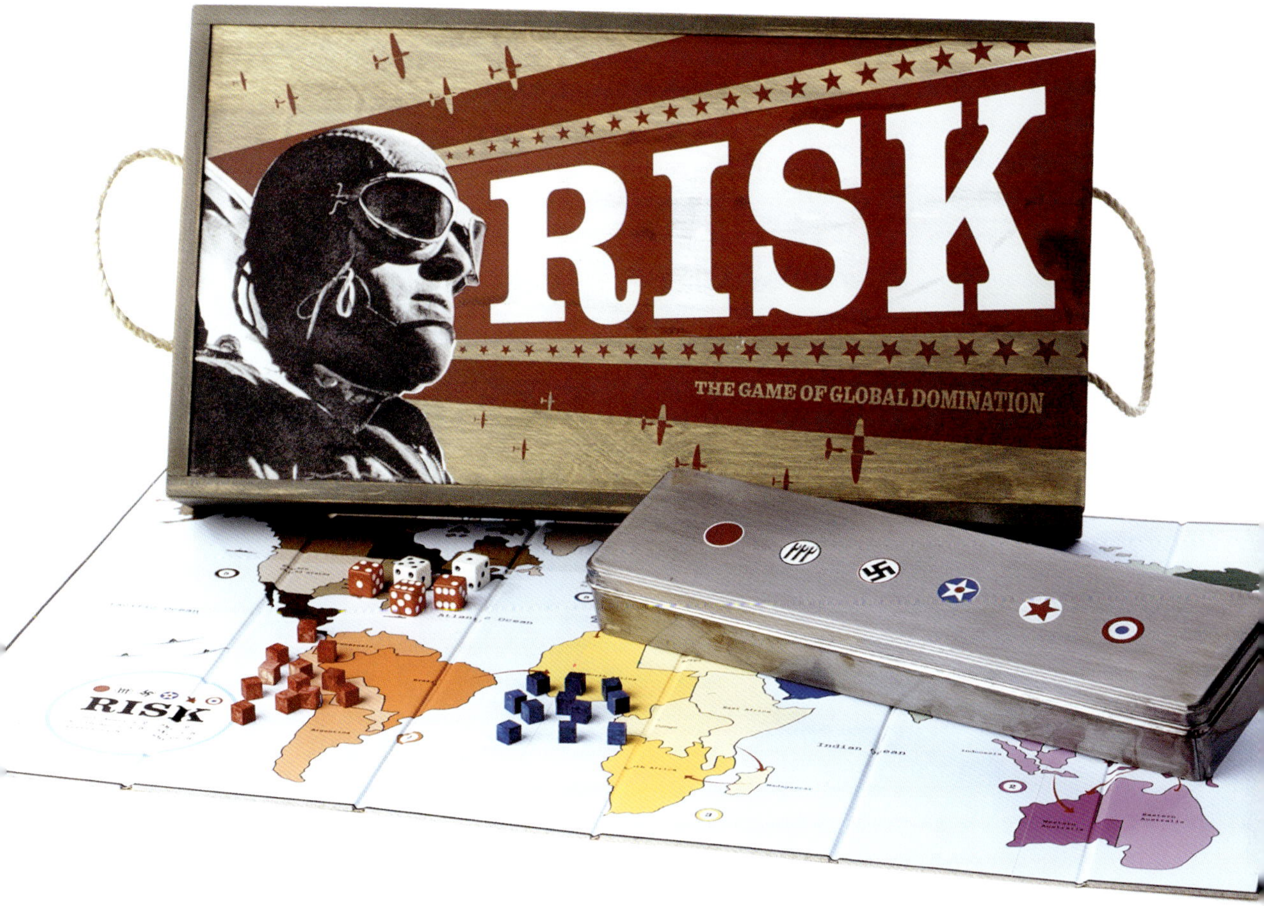

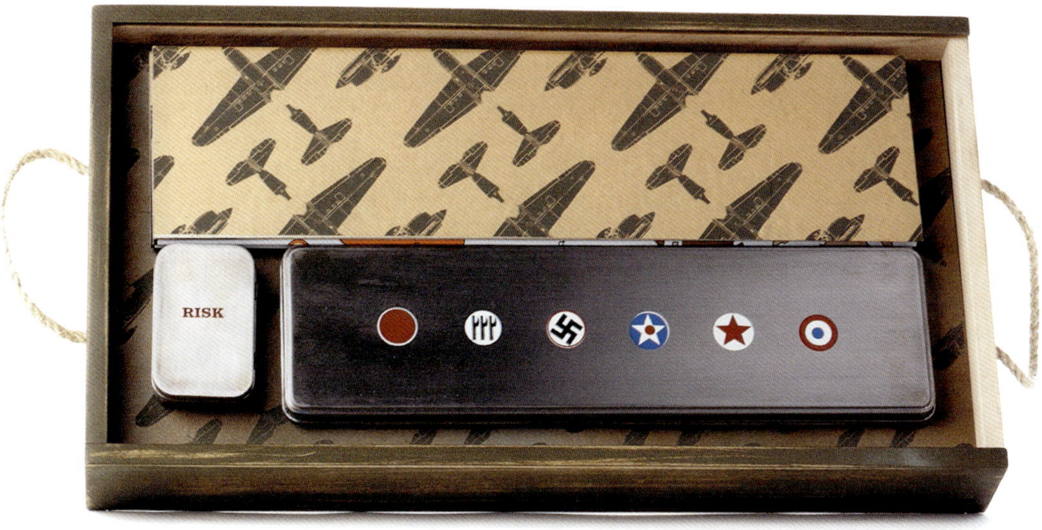

J. Sebastian Tatum Brigham Young University

LOCKJAW

LOCKJAW
HUGGERMUGGER
TO CONTINUE
NOTES ON THE BOARD
PLAY OPTIONS
THE STEAL OPTION

Raymond S. Woishek *Academy of Fine Arts in Krakow*

Paul Tepper Columbus College of Art & Design

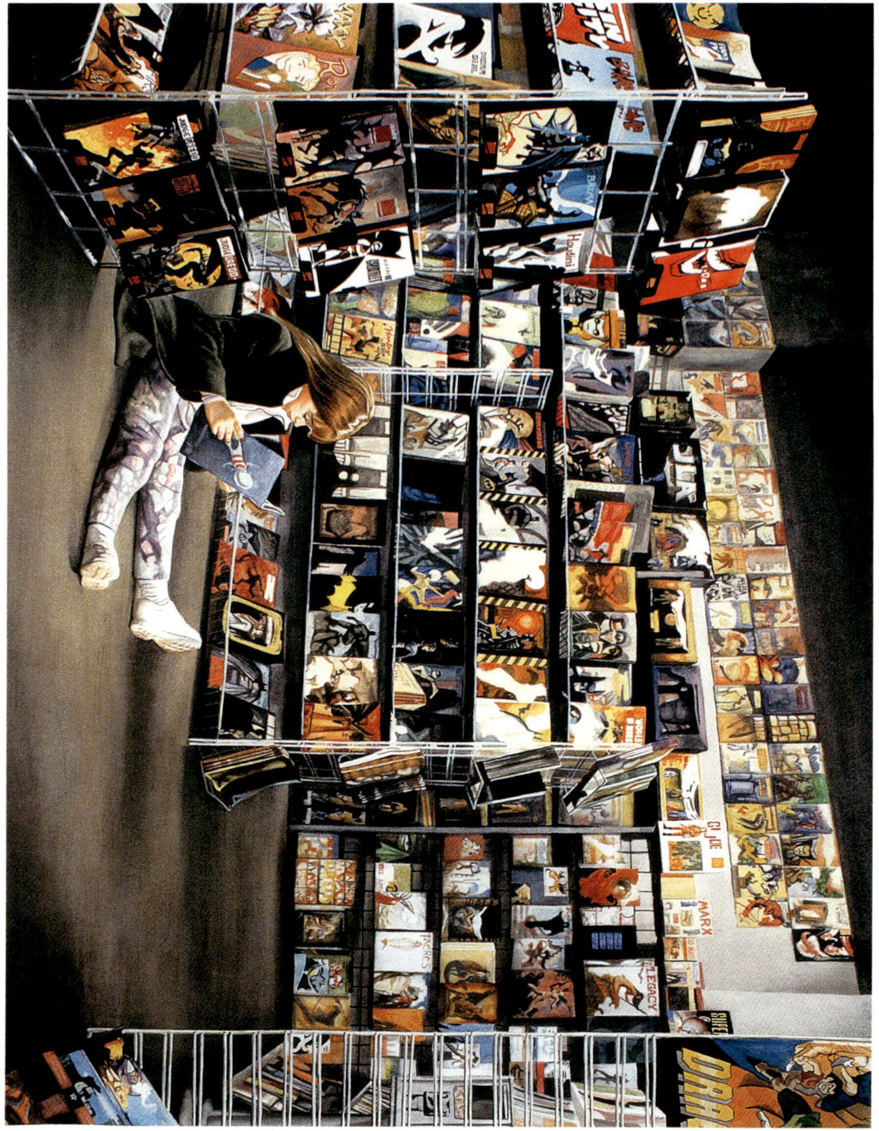

Matthew Loux School of Visual Arts

Arvin Luke Maala School of Visual Arts

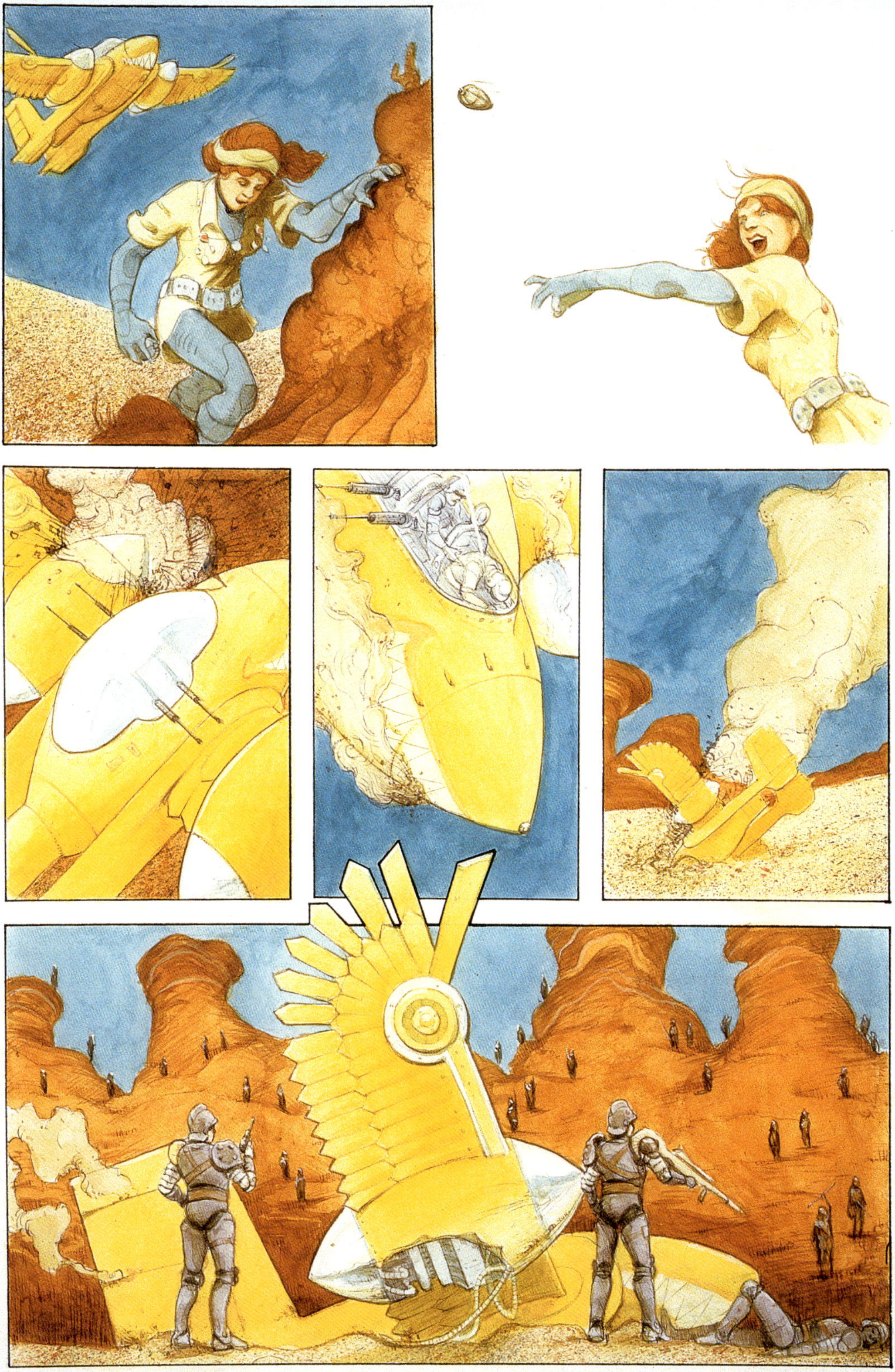

Brian Solinsky School of Visual Arts

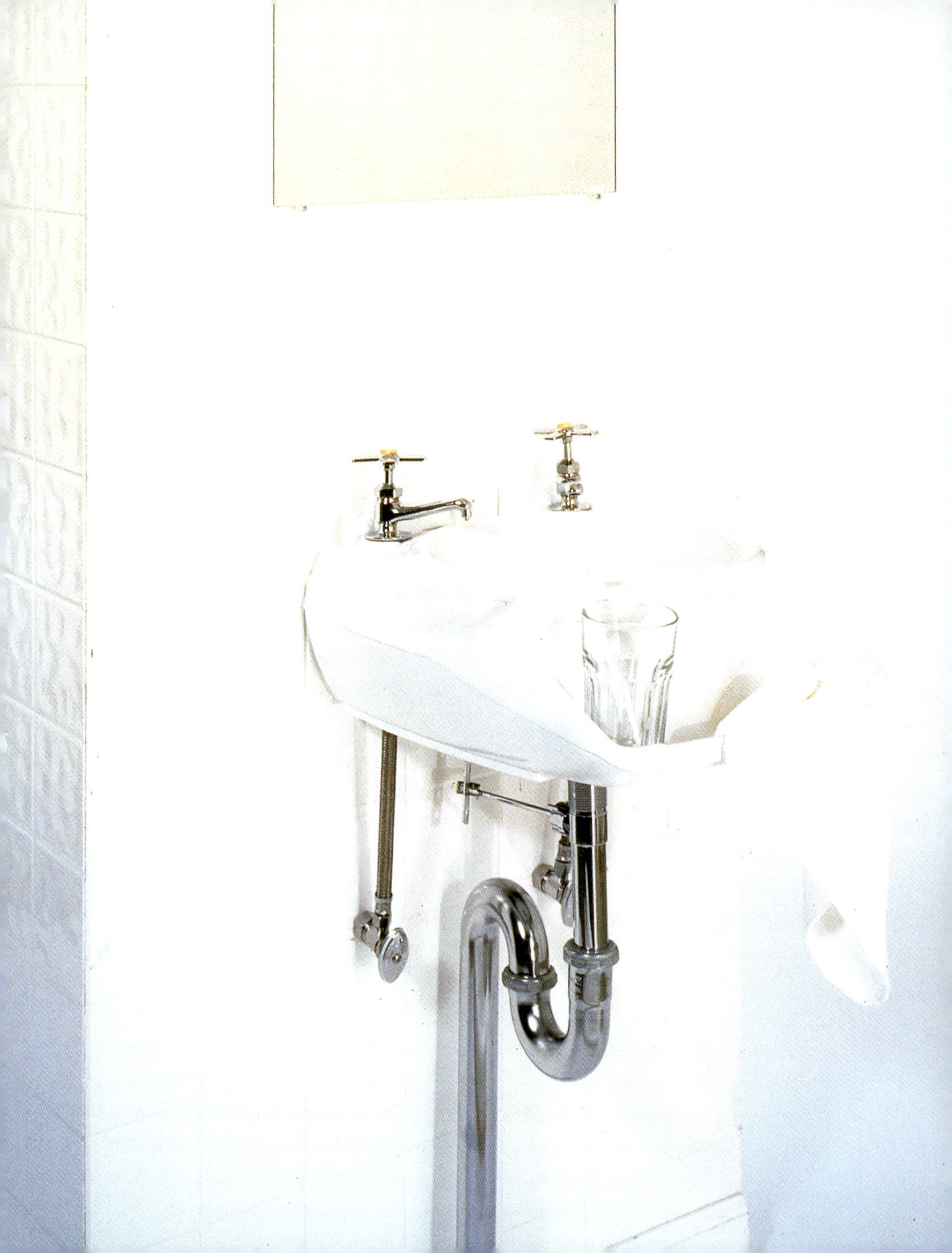

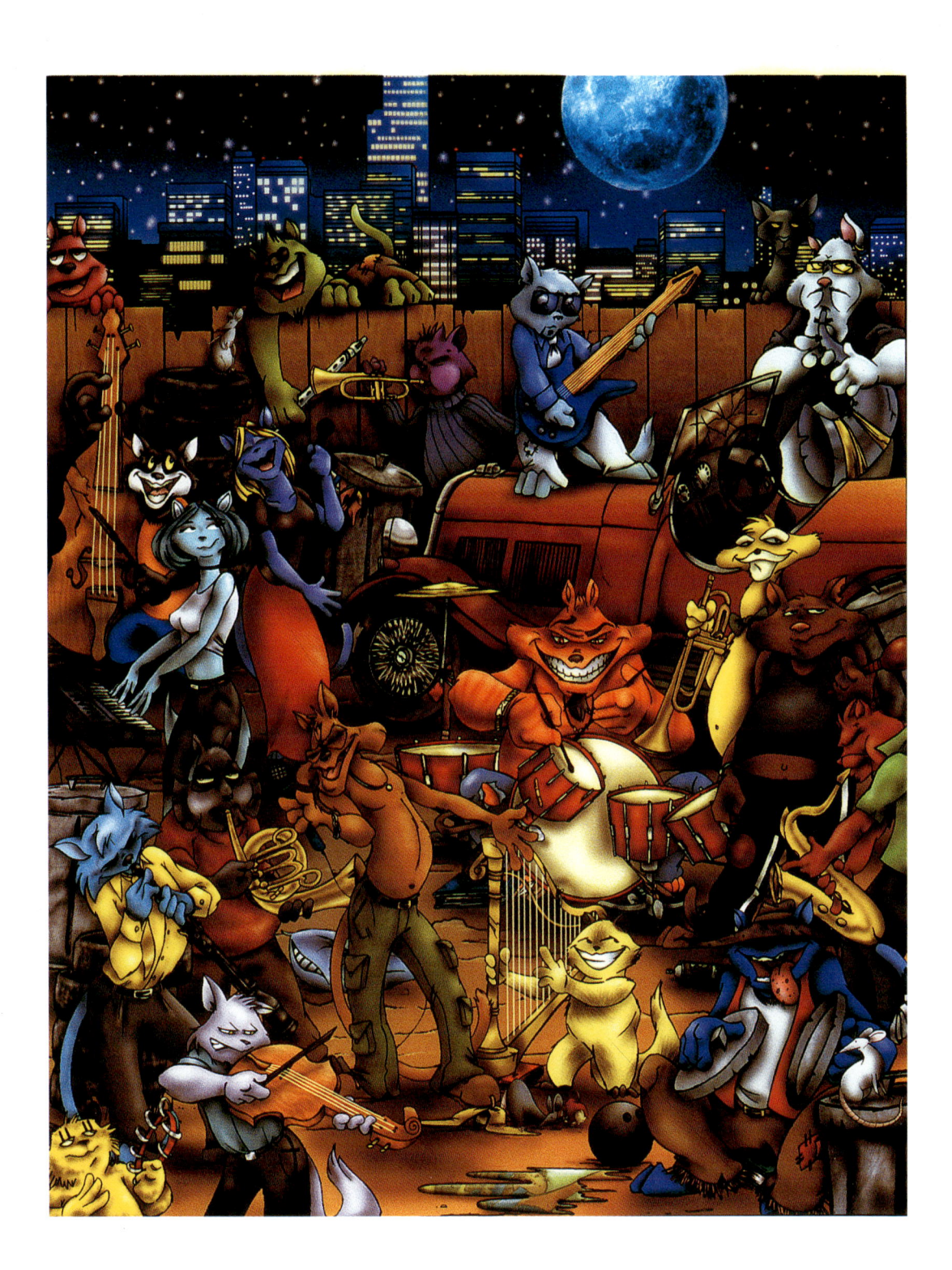

Paul Valenti School of Visual Arts   Illustration 120, 121

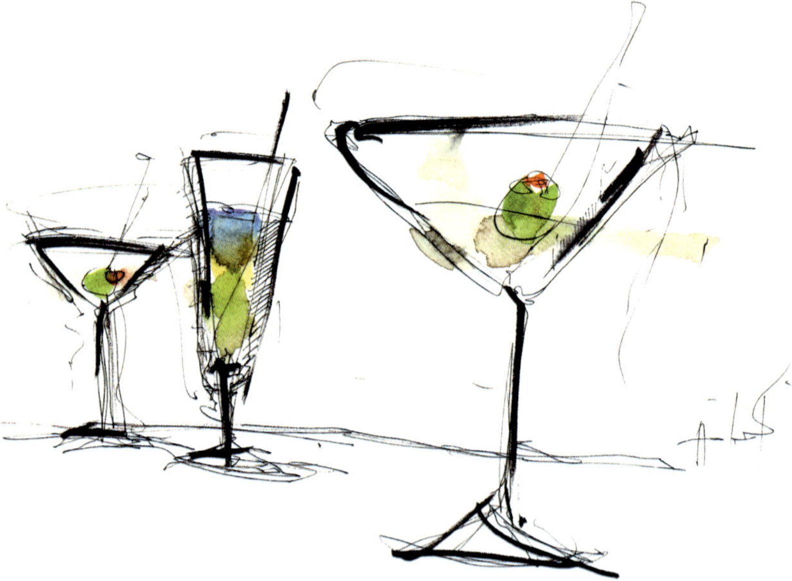

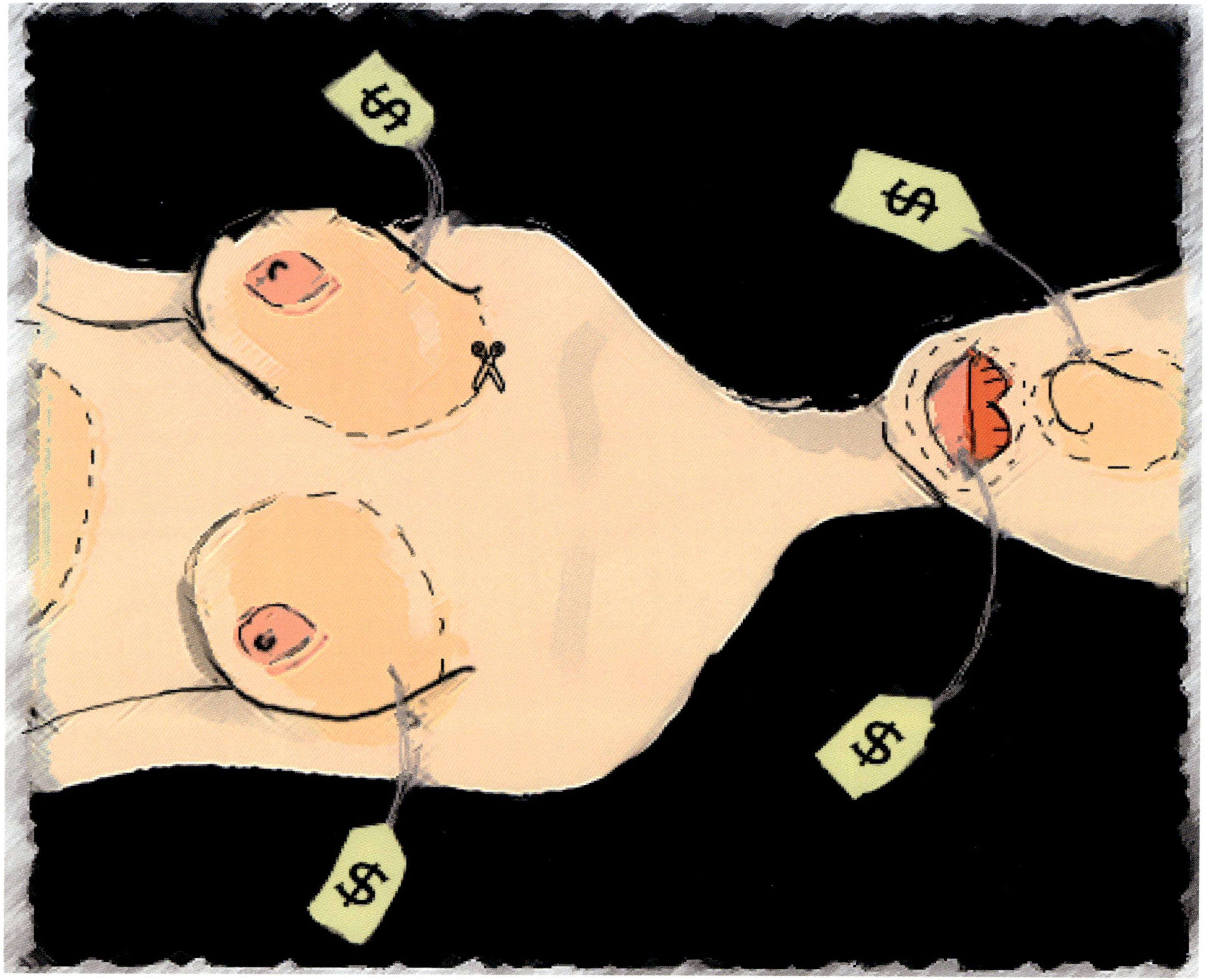

Clayton Hanmer George Brown College

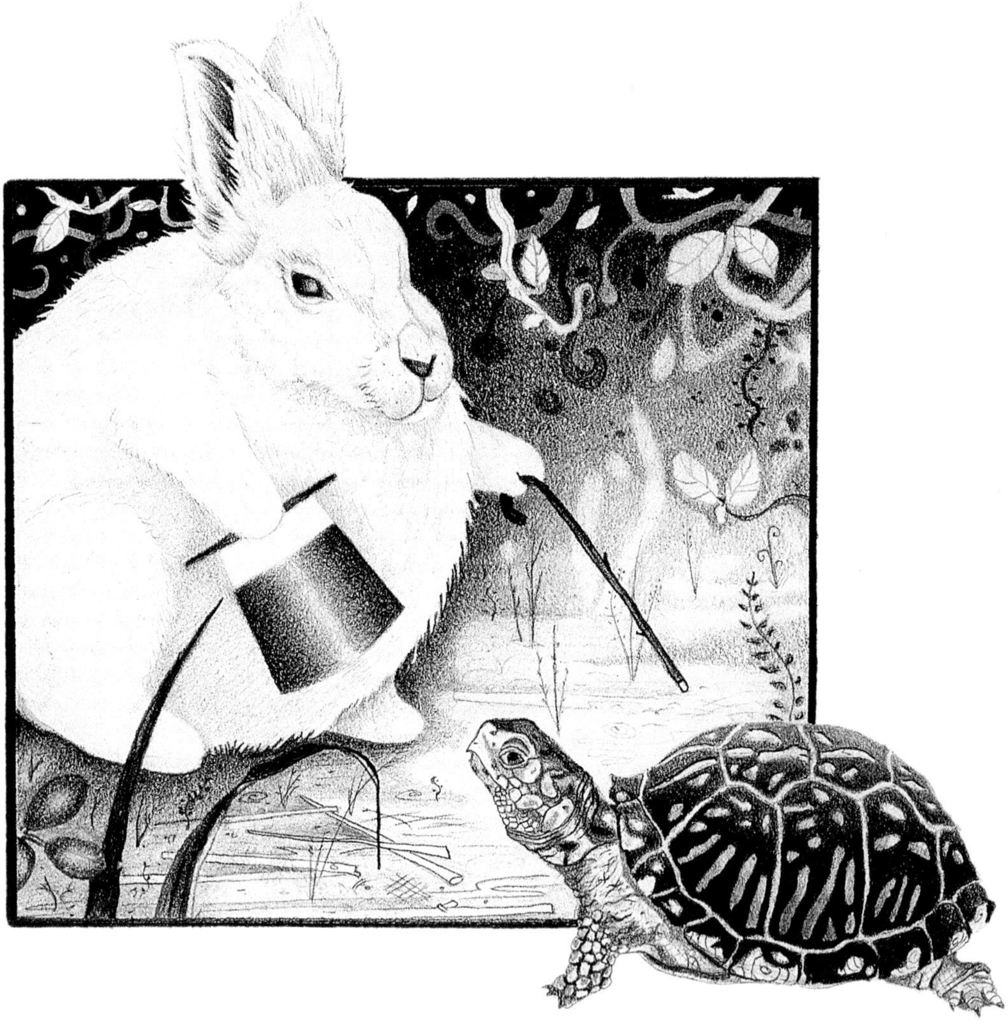

Brian Frascino School of Visual Arts

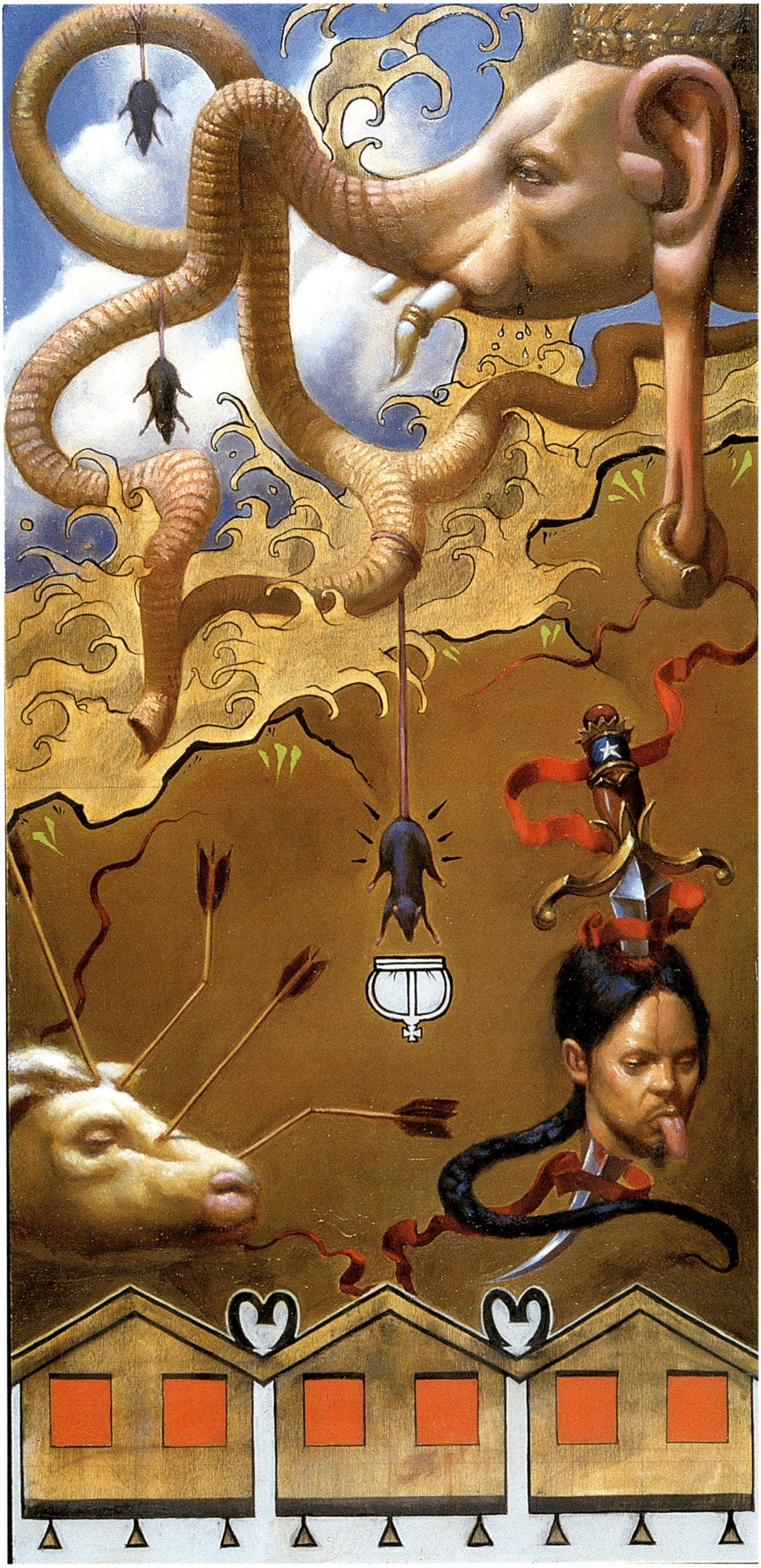

Regino Gonzales School of Visual Arts

Jeremy Kennedy Ringling School of Art & Design

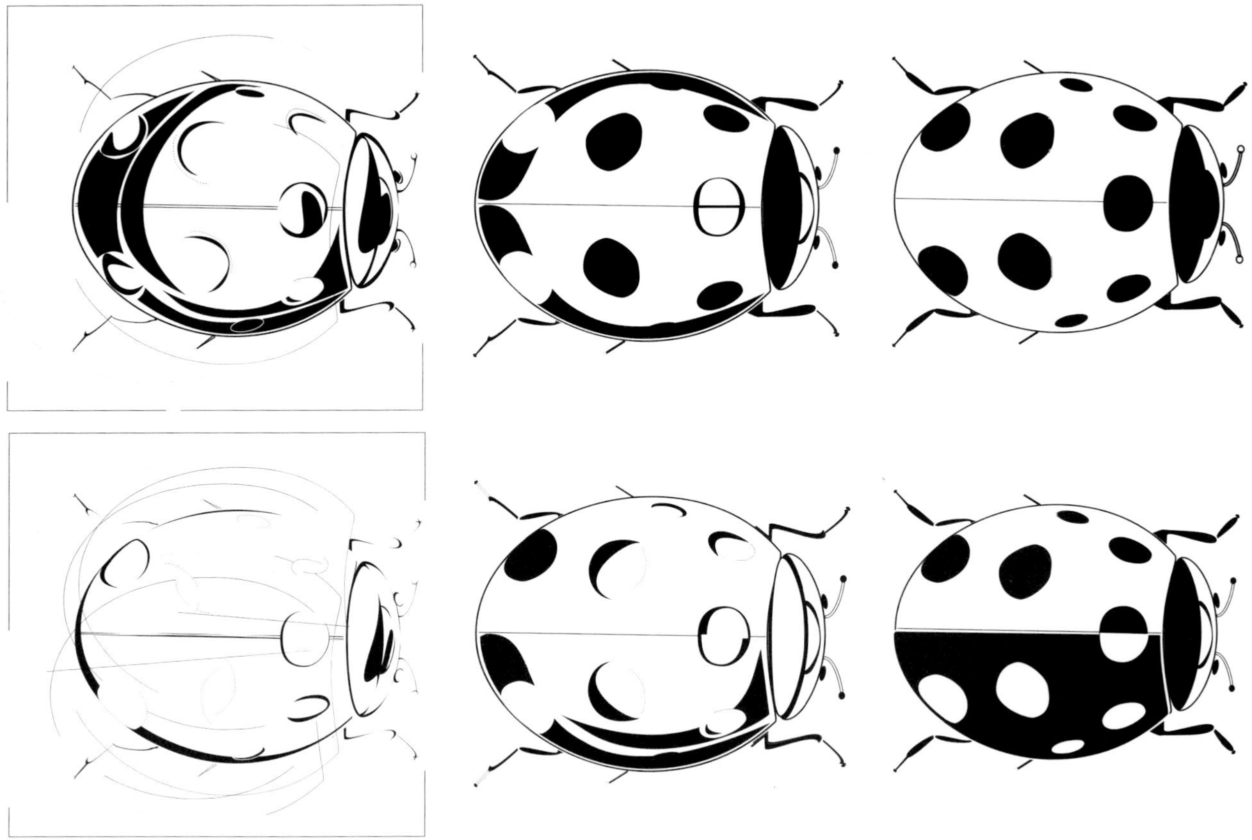

Erin Wallace Portfolio Center

Logos 128,129

Hugo Meyer The Creative Circus

Franz Kafka
Letterhead, business cards, and envelope for Franz Kafka.
Created in Quark and printed on transparency
and vellum papers.

November 24, 2000

Dear Abby,

    I just wanted to send you this letter and show you my new letterhead. The little man at the top is a drawing I did. I did a series of men doing odd things, but I liked this one the best. I have men fencing and writting stories sitting at a desk.

    How are you doing? Good I hope.

Love,

Fr Franz Kafka

Fran Kafka

Frank Kafka   1315 Michigan Avenue   Suite 331   Chicago, Il 60622

Frank Kafka

1315 Michigan Avenue
Suite 331
Chicago, Il. 60622

TEL: 312-564-7890
FAX: 312-564-2435

www.kafka.com

office depot

office depot
2675 Geary Boulevard, San Francisco, CA 94118

office depot
JIM MOEBIUS   Manager
2675 Geary Boulevard, San Francisco, CA 94118
Tel 415 441 3044 Fax 415 441 0364
www.office.depot.com

2675 Geary Boulevard, San Francisco, CA 94118 Tel 415 441 3044 Fax 415 441 0364 www.office.depot.com

Brian L. Owens The Creative Circus

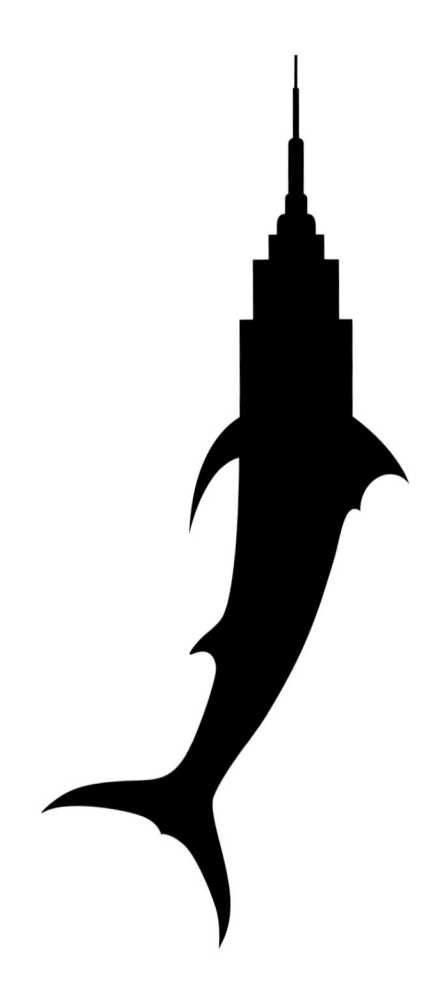

STYLE TAXI

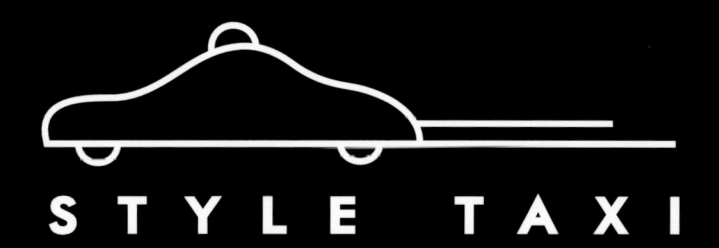

Lake Chargo

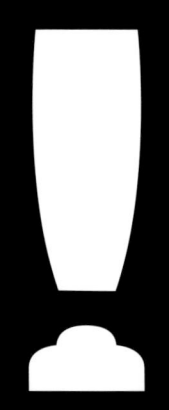

(from top) (1,3) **Hugo Meyer** The Creative Circus (2) **Katherine Arnold** Portfolio Center (4) **Bharna Kumar** Portfolio Center (5) **Brian L. Owens** The Creative Circus Logos 132, 133

VOICE(S)

HAVANA
Bread Co

(from top) (1) **Dac Austin** The Creative Circus (2) **Bryony Gomez Palacio** Portfolio Center (3) **Hugo Meyer** The Creative Circus (4, 5) **Brian L. Owens** The Creative Circus

SPIN CYCLE:

A COLLECTION OF MIXES FROM FEMALE TECHNO DJ'S
FOUR DISC SET INCLUDES OVER 40 SONGS MIXED BY DJ CARLY, DJ AMBER, DJ MS.T, AND DJ ANON.

Music CD 136,137

misfortune

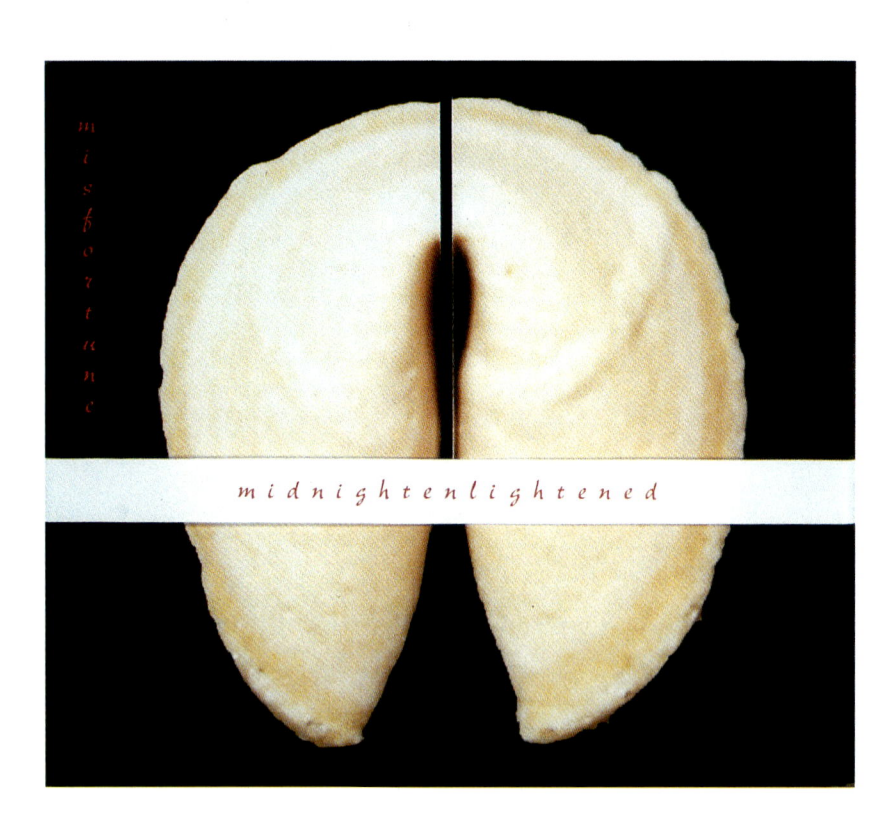

midnightenlightened

Erik Baxter Penn State University

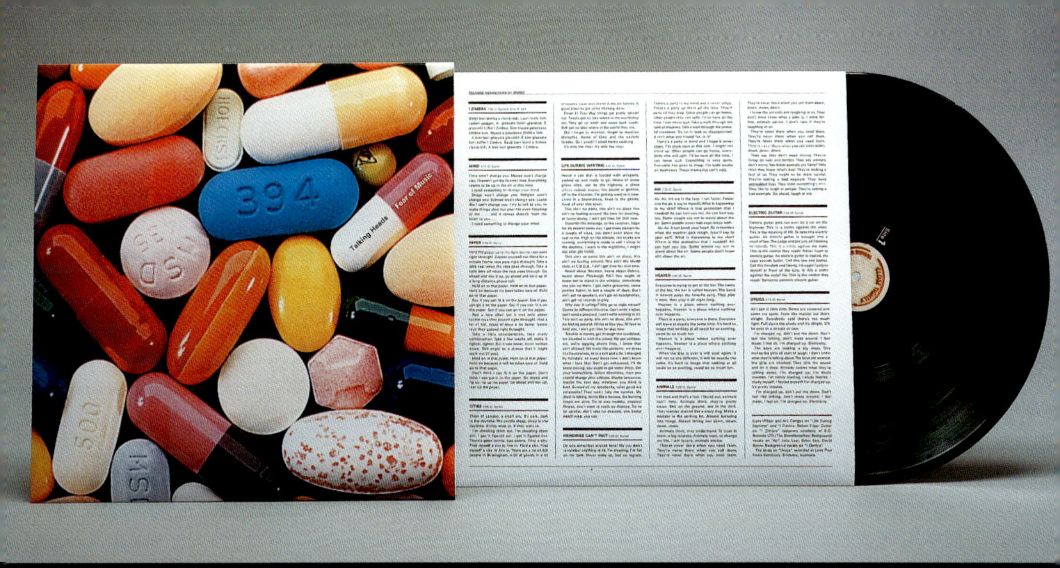
394
Talking Heads
Fear of Music

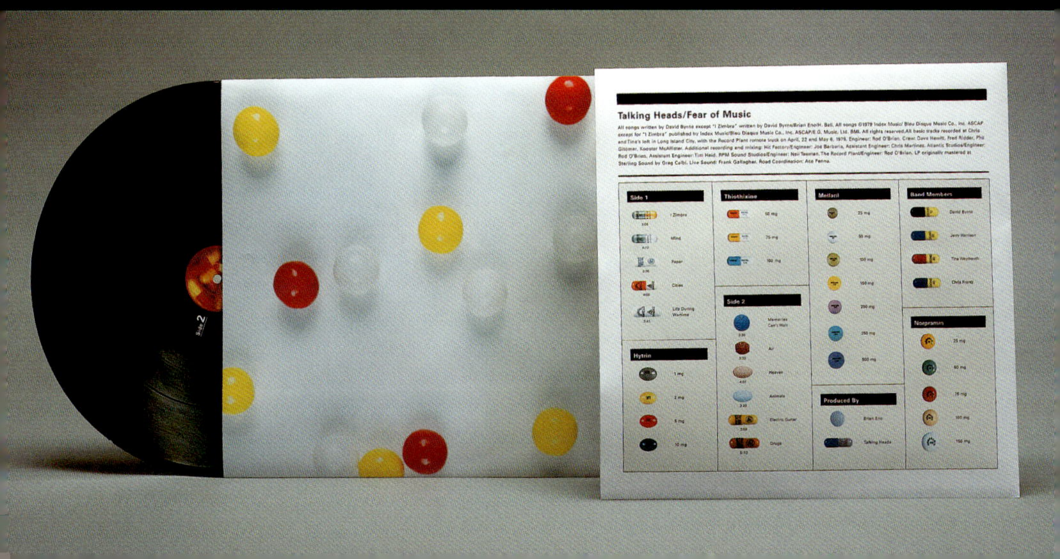
Talking Heads/Fear of Music
Side 1
Thiothixine
Mellaril
Band Members
Side 2
Hytrin
Produced By
Norpramin

And in the end, these last years were a time of plentiful confusion; a time to break down and a time to build up. It started with one man's diehard refusal to give up the old ways of singing and an audience that responded. Buffeted between folk music which was more lyrical and rich in style, and Country music which considered this "old time" music too old fashion, Bluegrass weaned itself on a homegrown diet of strict acoustics, tightly arranged harmonics, and gut raw virtuosity.

Ah, those crazy 60's. The "high and lonesome" singing as an art form all to itself is finally established. But creativity has and always will challenge convention. This assault continues to redefine Bluegrass as we know it.

Music CD

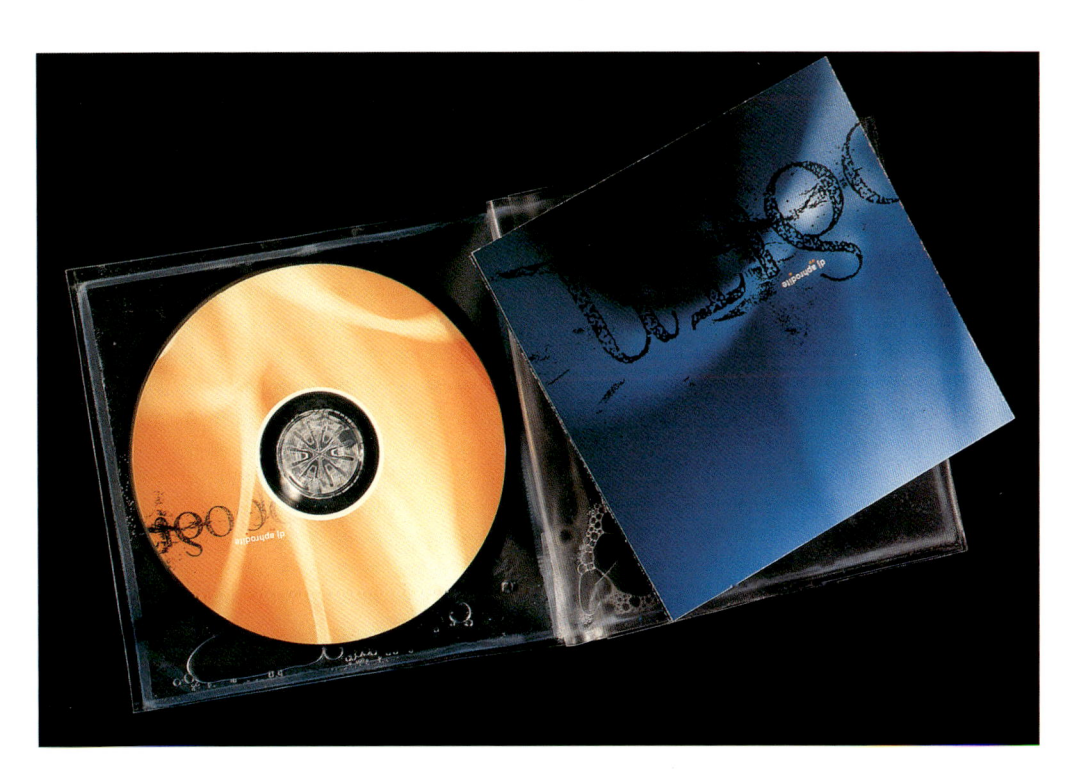

Eric Turner University of Utah

Jenny Lamb Portfolio Center

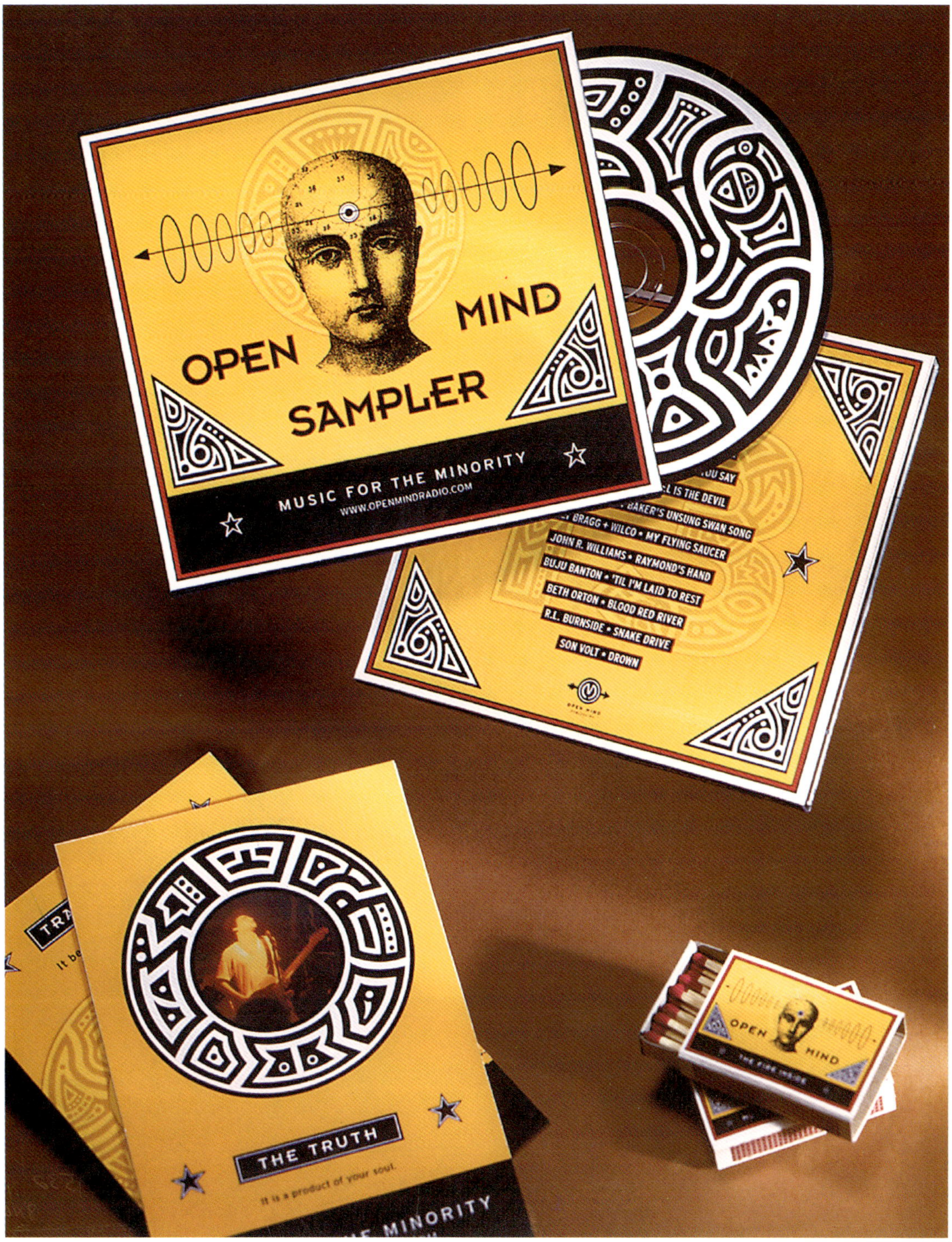

Gill Autrey Portfolio Center

ASTOR
PIAZOLLA
CINCO
Vuelvo Al Sur
Ausencias
Milonga Tres
Oblivion
Libertango
Milonga Del Angel
El Choclo
Tristango
Tango Tango
Regreso Al Amor
Adios Nonino
ASTOR
UNO
ASTOR
PIAZOLLA

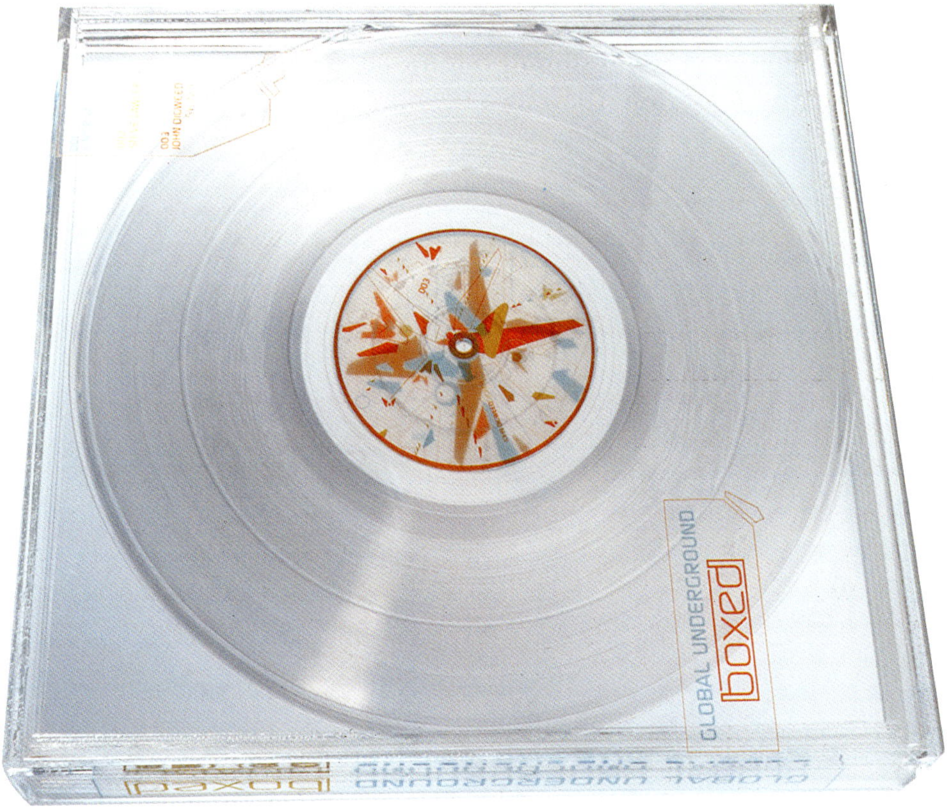
GLOBAL UNDERGROUND
boxed

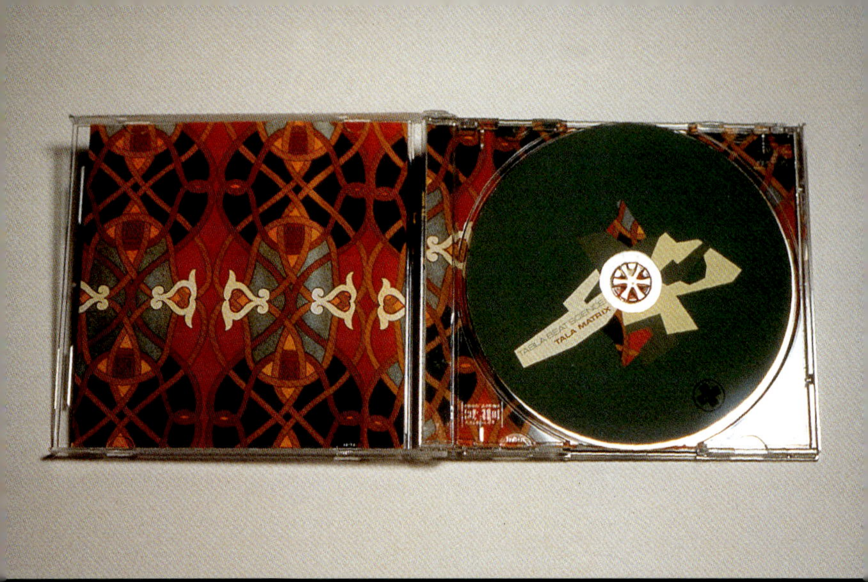
TABLA BEAT SCIENCE
TALA MATRIX

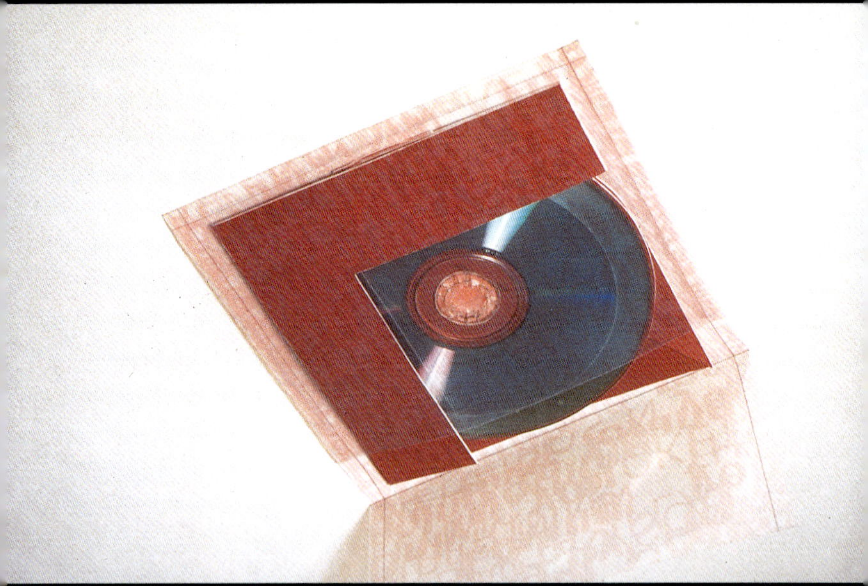

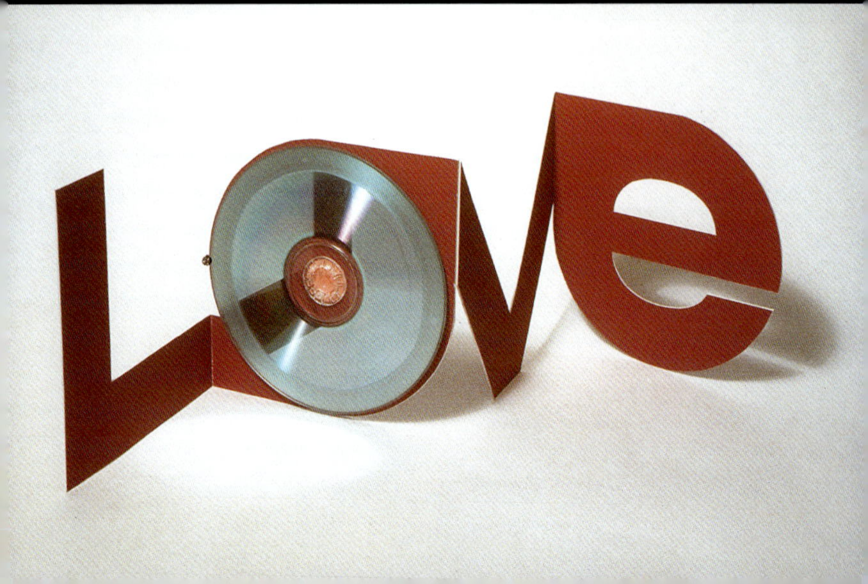

Shigeto Akiyama School of Visual Arts   Music CD 146, 147

Lily Sin Academy of Art College

CATHEDRAL
VINEYARDS
PINOT GRIGIO
CLUNY
II
1988
LAY CEMETERY
ALC. 10% BY VOL. 750 ML
1988
PANTRY
PINOT NOIR
CATHEDRAL
VINEYARDS
ALC. 10% BY VOL. 750 ML
STABLE
LAY BROTHERS'
OUTER COURTS

(this spread) **Heejung Yoon** Academy of Art College

MOSKVA
MOSKVA
Imported Russian Vodka
40% ALC/VOL (80 PROOF)
MOSKVA

Tracy **Campbell** Portfolio Center

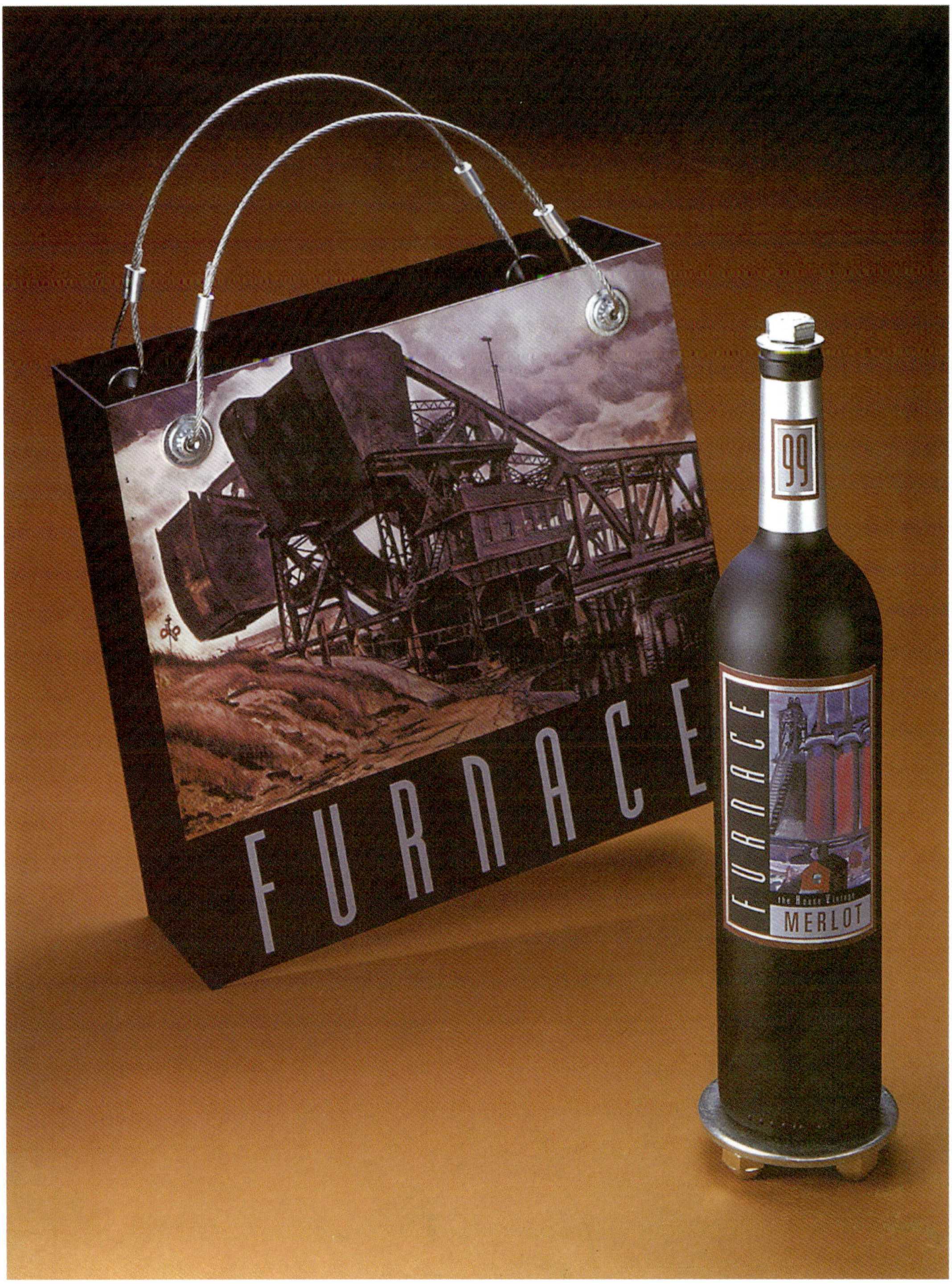
FURNACE
99
FURNACE
MERLOT

IMPORTED
KETEL ONE
PREMIUM VODKA
IMPORTED
The Ultimate
KETEL ONE
Martini
KETEL ONE
PREMIUM VODKA
CONTENTS
750 ML
KETEL ONE

THE ORIGINAL SOUR MASH
OLD CROW
SINCE 1835
47% ALC/VOL. 94 PROOF
KENTUCKY STRAIGHT
BOURBON WHISKEY
Distilled, aged, and bottled by the Old Crow Distillery Company
Frankfort, Clermot, Kentucky
OLD CROW

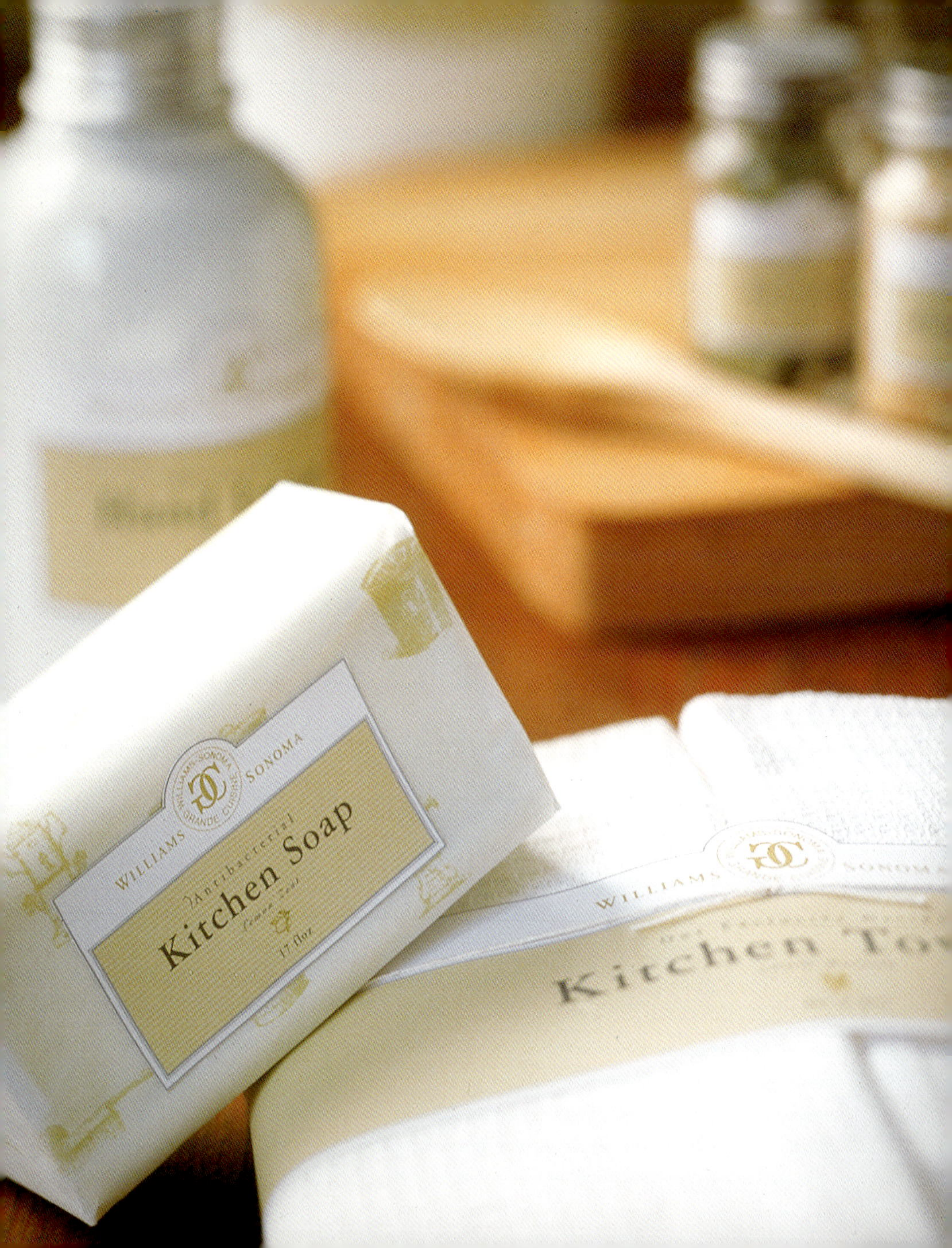
WILLIAMS
SONOMA
Antibacterial
Kitchen Soap

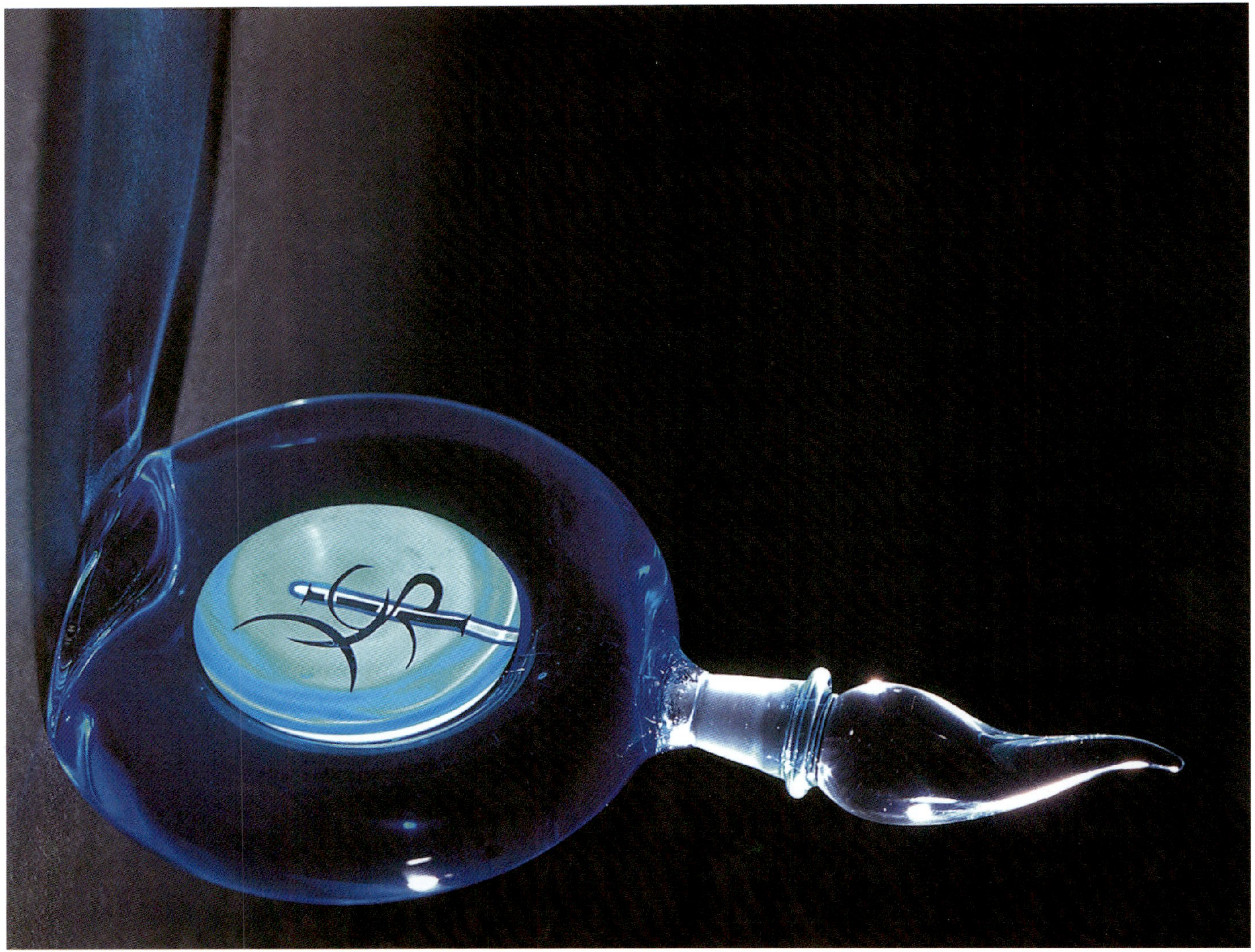

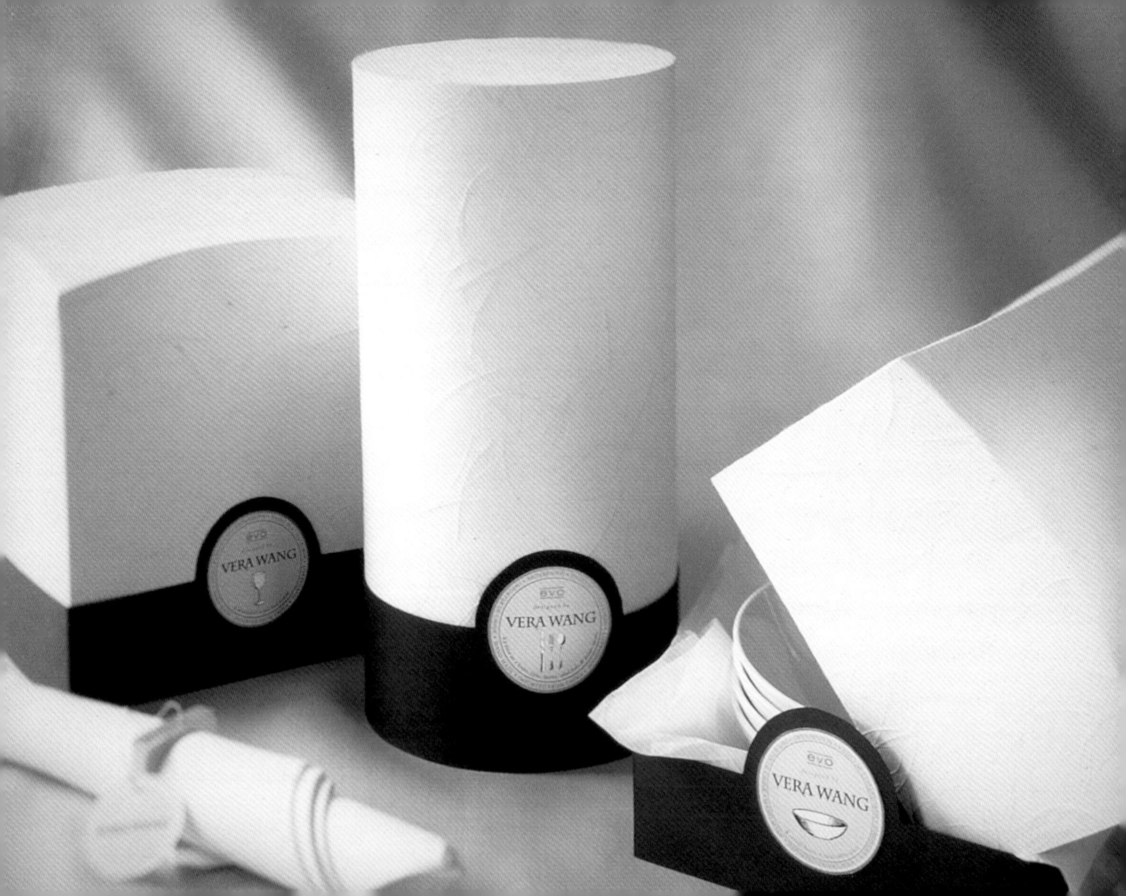
evo
VERA WANG
evo
VERA WANG
evo
VERA WANG

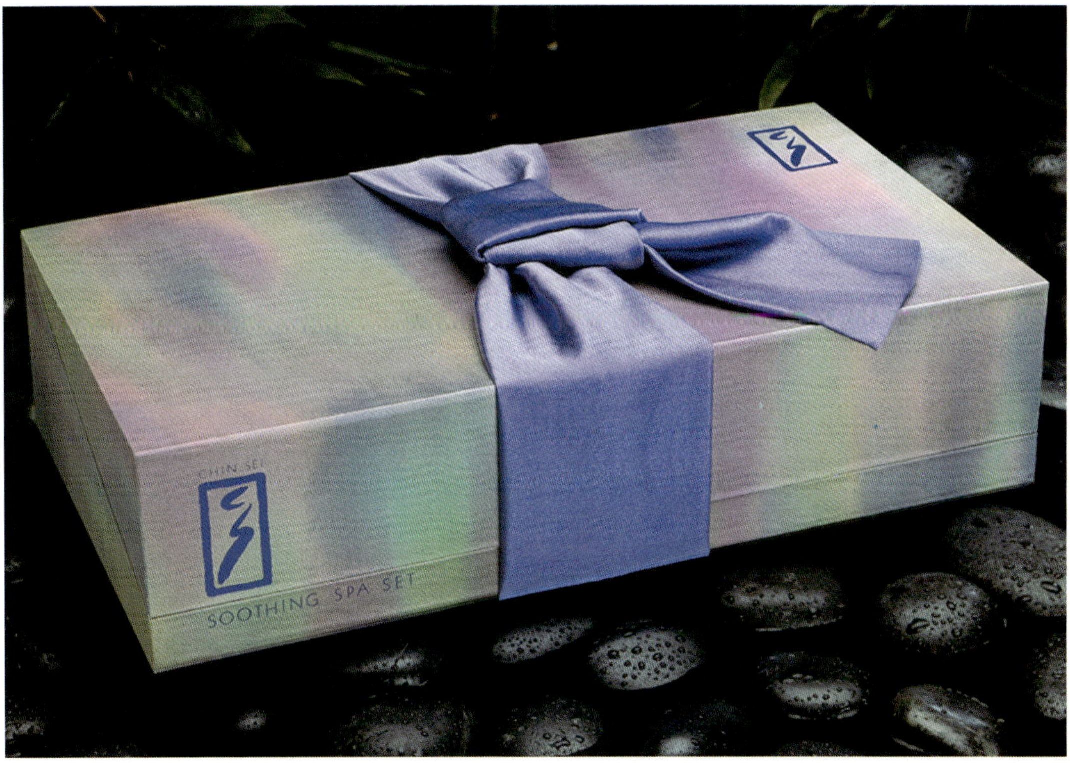
CHIN SEI
SOOTHING SPA SET

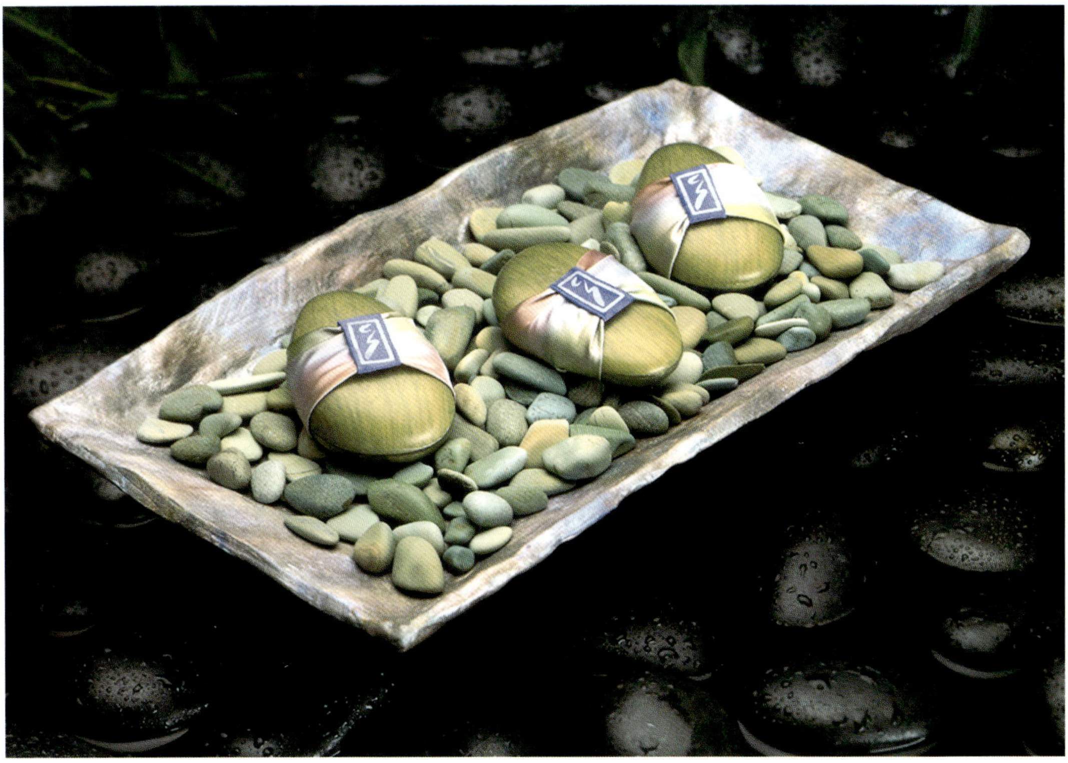

BeeHive

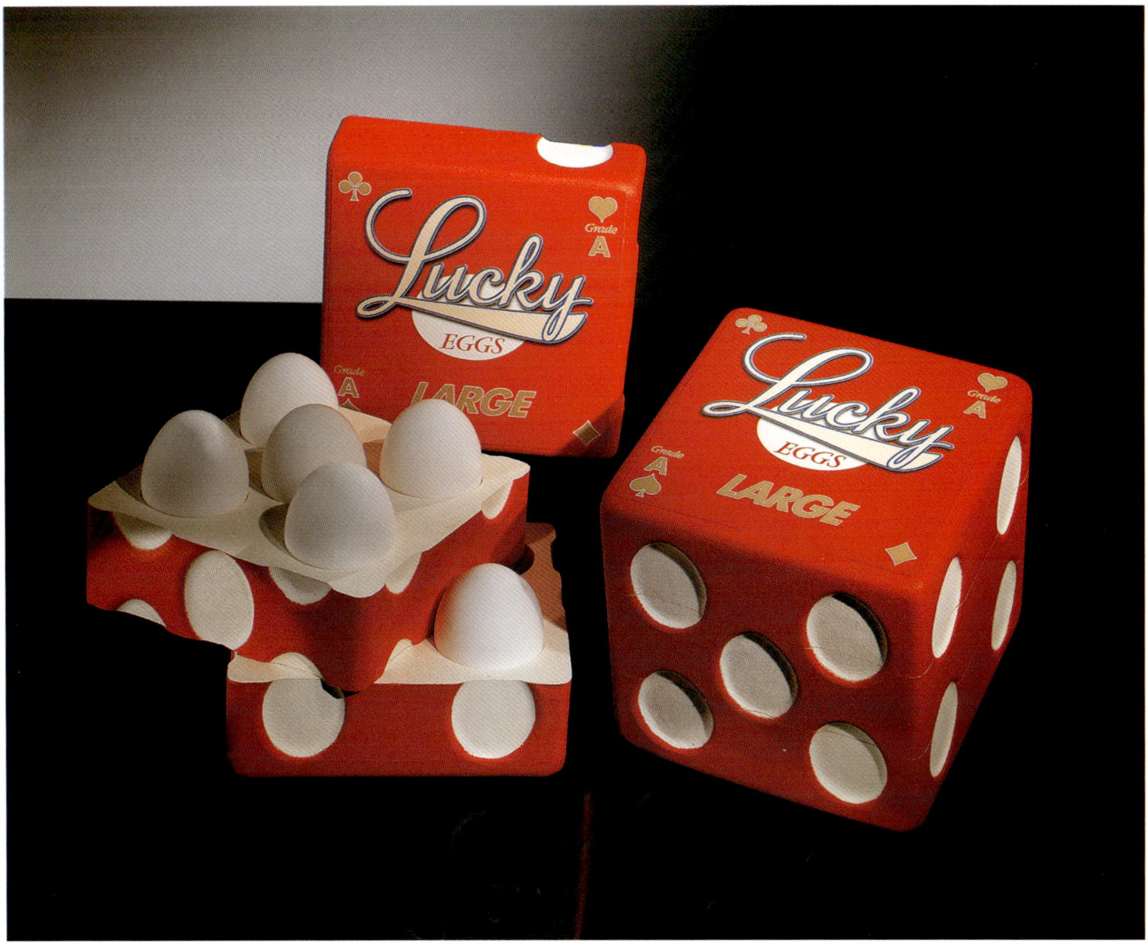
Lucky
EGGS
Grade A
LARGE

GRADE A
PASTEURIZED, HOMOGENIZED
Falls Creek FARM
hazelnut
WHOLE VITAMIN D MILK
16 FL. OZ.

SOURCE
PREMIUM
SOURCE
DELICIOUSLY SMOOTH
AND CREAMY ORGANIC SOYMILK
Vanilla Soymilk
FORTIFIED WITH CALCIUM,
PROTEIN, RIBOFLAVIN, FIBER, PHOSPHORUS,
ZINC AND VITAMIN A, D, E, B12
LACTOSE FREE • 35 FL OZ (1QT) 946mL

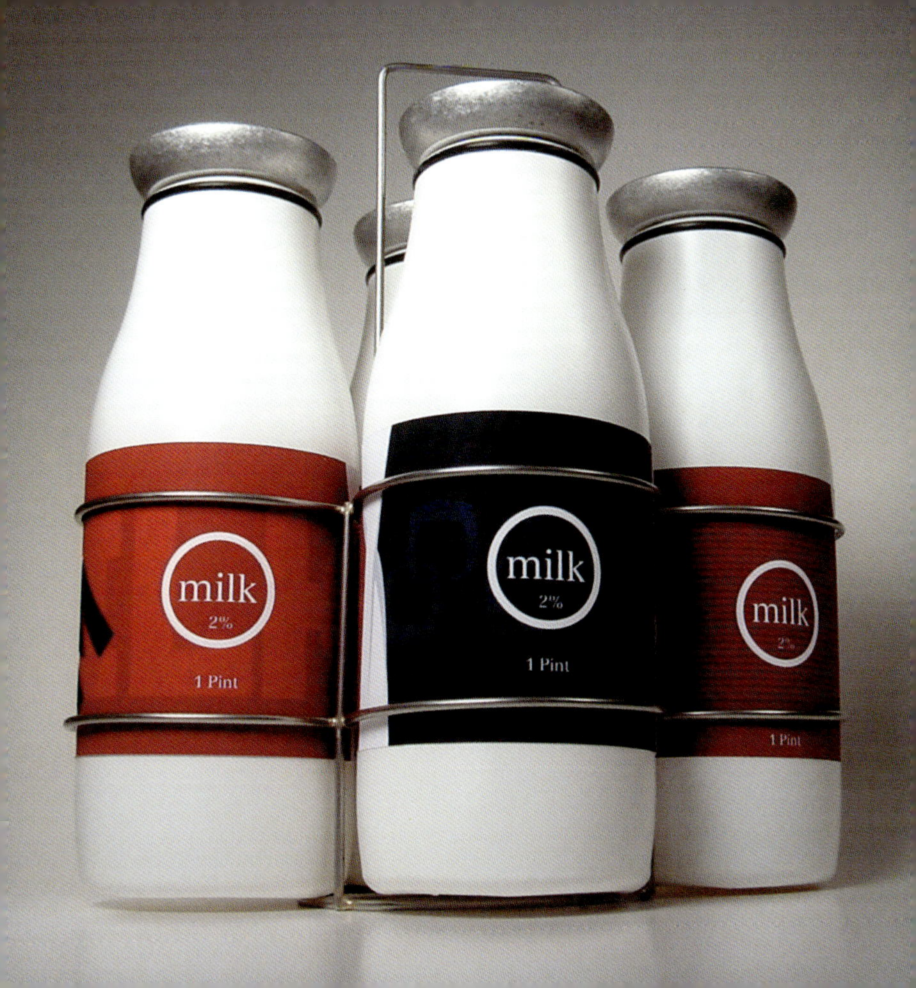
milk
2%
1 Pint
milk
2%
1 Pint
milk
2%
1 Pint

(this spread) **Brian L. Owens** The Creative Circus

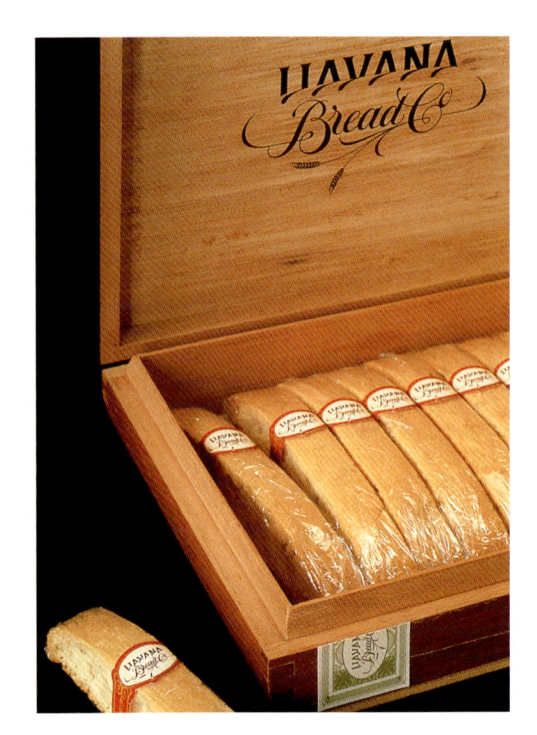

Packaging 164,165

BALSAMIC VINEGAR AND SAFFLOWER DRESSING
RED WINE VINEGAR AND SAFFLOWER OIL DRESSING
ALT VINEGAR AND SUNFLOWER OIL DRESSIN
TARRAGON VINEGAR AND CANOLA OIL DRESSIN

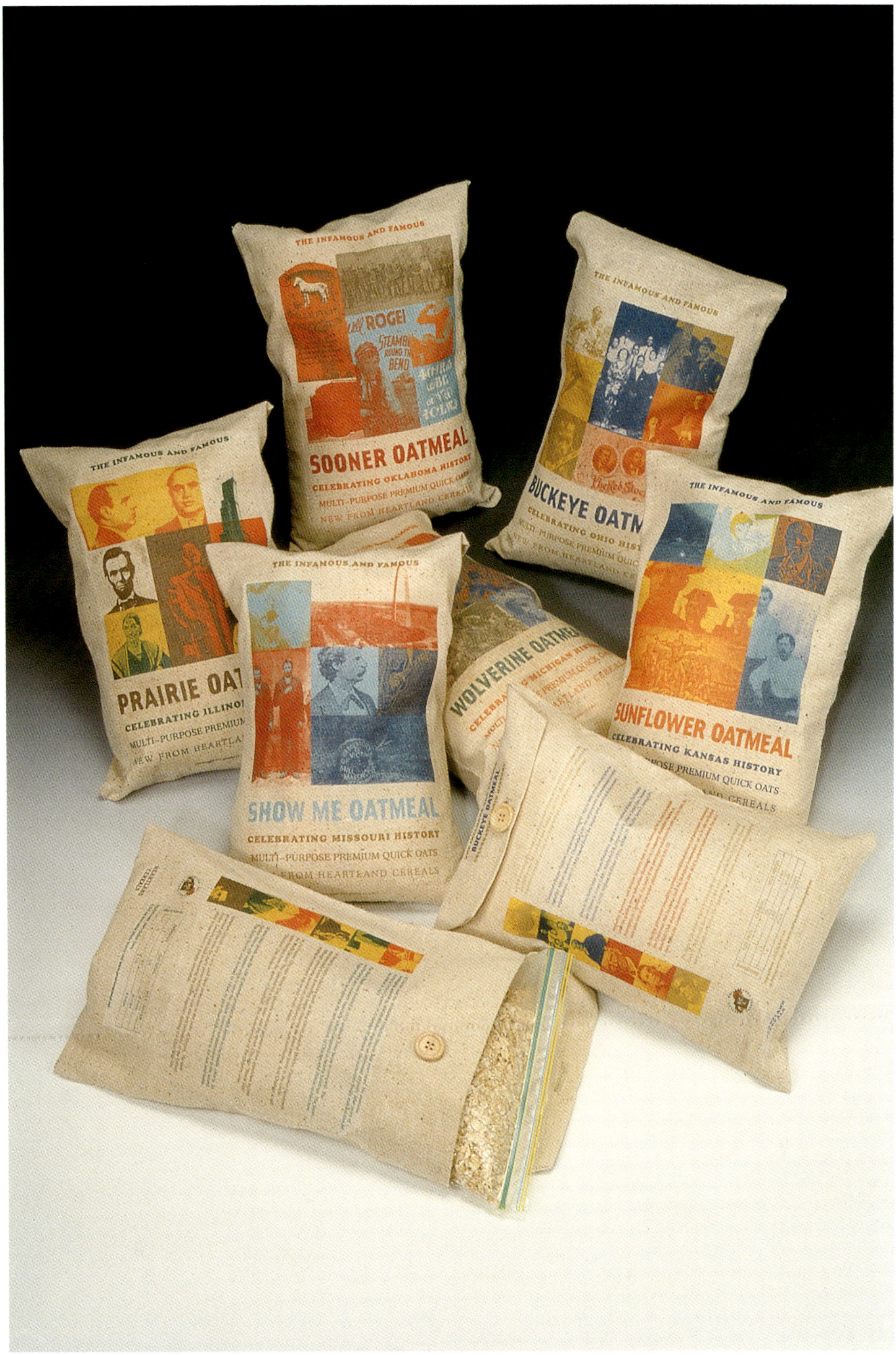

Pablo Airth Western Washington University

B★B
BODY BULLET
PRECISION NUTRITION FORMULA

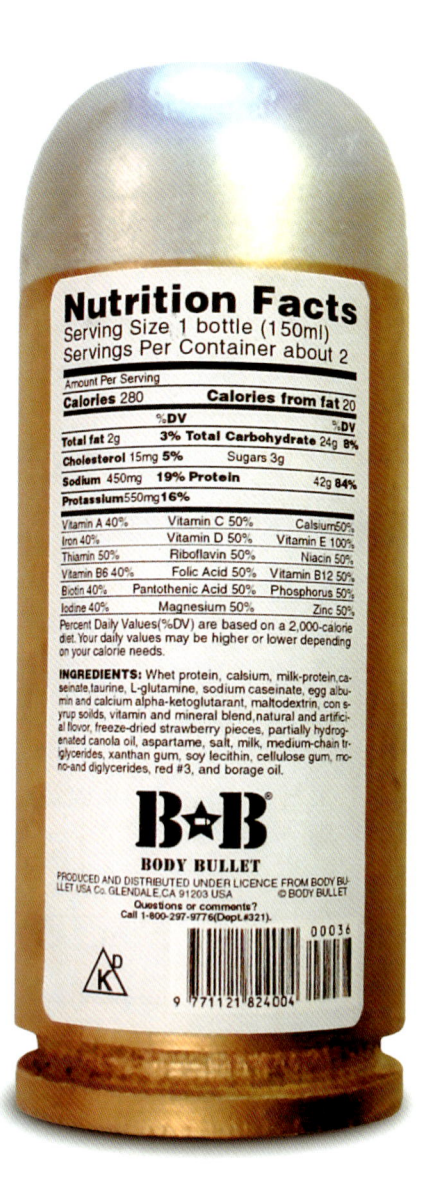

STRAWBERRY FLAVOR

70%PROTEIN/VOL 150ml

Nutrition Facts
Serving Size 1 bottle (150ml)
Servings Per Container about 2

Amount Per Serving			
Calories 280		Calories from fat 20	
	%DV		%DV
Total fat 2g	3%	Total Carbohydrate 24g	8%
Cholesterol 15mg	5%	Sugars 3g	
Sodium 450mg	19%	Protein 42g	84%
Protassium 550mg	16%		

Vitamin A 40%	Vitamin C 50%	Calsium 50%
Iron 40%	Vitamin D 50%	Vitamin E 100%
Thiamin 50%	Riboflavin 50%	Niacin 50%
Vitamin B6 40%	Folic Acid 50%	Vitamin B12 50%
Biotin 40%	Pantothenic Acid 50%	Phosphorus 50%
Iodine 40%	Magnesium 50%	Zinc 50%

Percent Daily Values(%DV) are based on a 2,000-calorie diet. Your daily values may be higher or lower depending on your calorie needs.

INGREDIENTS: Whet protein, calsium, milk-protein,caseinate,taurine, L-glutamine, sodium caseinate, egg albumin and calcium alpha-ketoglutarant, maltodextrin, con syrup soilds, vitamin and mineral blend,natural and artificial flavor, freeze-dried strawberry pieces, partially hydrogenated canola oil, aspartame, salt, milk, medium-chain triglycerides, xanthan gum, soy lecithin, cellulose gum, mono-and diglycerides, red #3, and borage oil.

B★B
BODY BULLET

PRODUCED AND DISTRIBUTED UNDER LICENCE FROM BODY BULLET USA GLENDALE,CA 91203 USA © BODY BULLET
Questions or comments?
Call 1-800-297-9776(Dept.#321).

00036
9 771121 824004

MICHELINA'S
CLASSIC ITALIAN CUISINE
LEMON CITRUS
Net wt 18.5 oz (524g)
CLASSICA ITALIANA CUCINA
MICHELINA'S
CLASSIC ITALIAN CUISINE
TUBULAR PASTA
Net wt 9 oz (255g)
CUCINA
CIPOLLATA

LIGHTS IT UP

4 Watt 9 light bulbs

Our Longest Lasting, Cool Burning Night Light

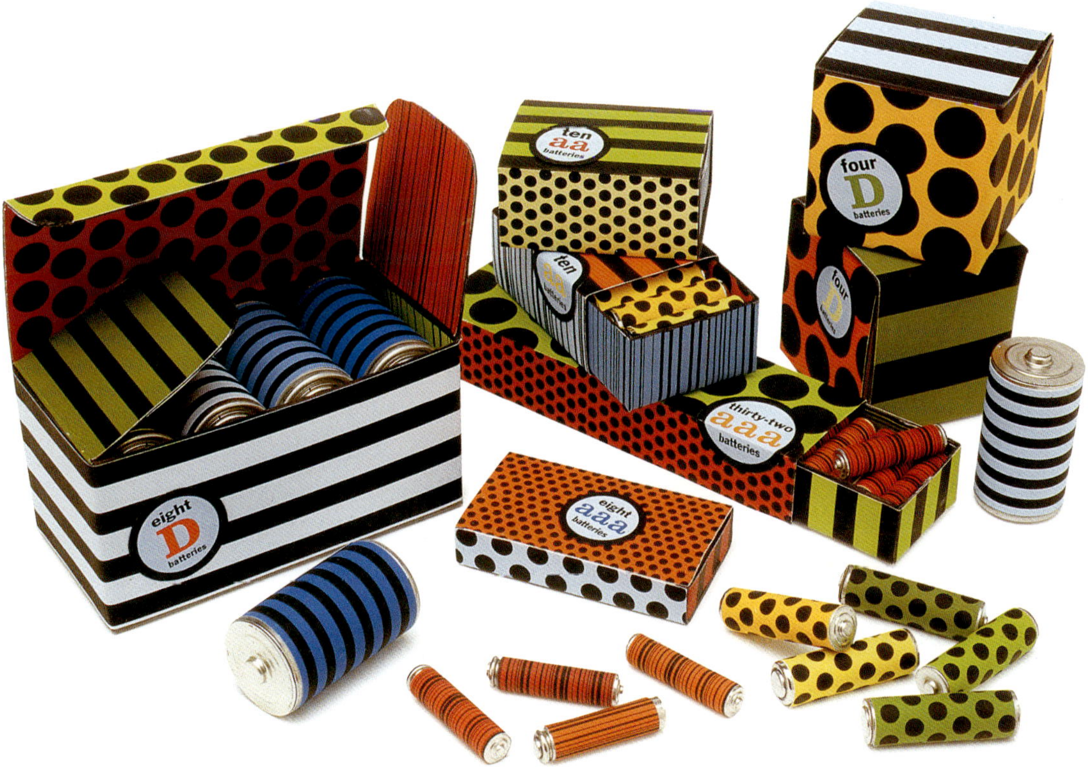

Randi Brookman School of Visual Arts

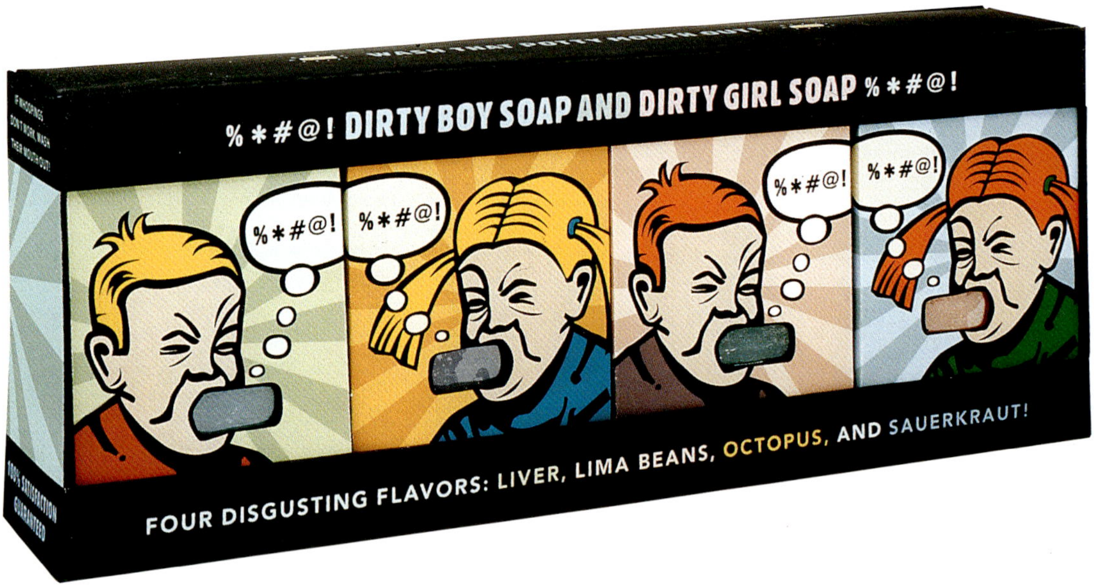

Abbey Bennett Tyler School of Art, Temple University

PATTERSON & CO.
WHITE COTTON V-NECK
T-SHIRT
This cotton v-neck tee is soft and very durable. It will last through wash after wash and is great as a layer under a sweater or with shorts. Be comfortable.
$22.00
100% AUTHENTIC
T. Patterson

PAPER CLIPS 300 PC

NUTS
1 INCH
SCREWS
ZINC PLATED
100
STAINLESS STEEL
SCREWS
MACHINE

PAPER
CLIPS
Qty.
Qtw.
Cant. 100
RUBBER BANDS
Assorted Sizes
PUSH PINS
Qty.
Qte.
Cant. 50
PAPER CLIPS
Qty.
Qtw.
Cant. 50
PUSH PINS
Qty.
Qtw.
Cant. 50
RUBBER BANDS
1 1/2 oz (45.5g)
Assorted
Sizes

MADE IN TAIWAN
#6
ZINC PLATED
NET WEIGHT 500 G
100
FLAT HEAD
SLOTTED
MACHINE
SCREWS
STAINLESS STEEL
1/4"

UF
ULTRA FUEL
d.stress
ENERGY DRINK
The ultimate
energy and recovery
it is this dual
of carbohydrates in
hard-working
the liver, boosting
nce, speeding
helping to improve
performance.
E=UF²

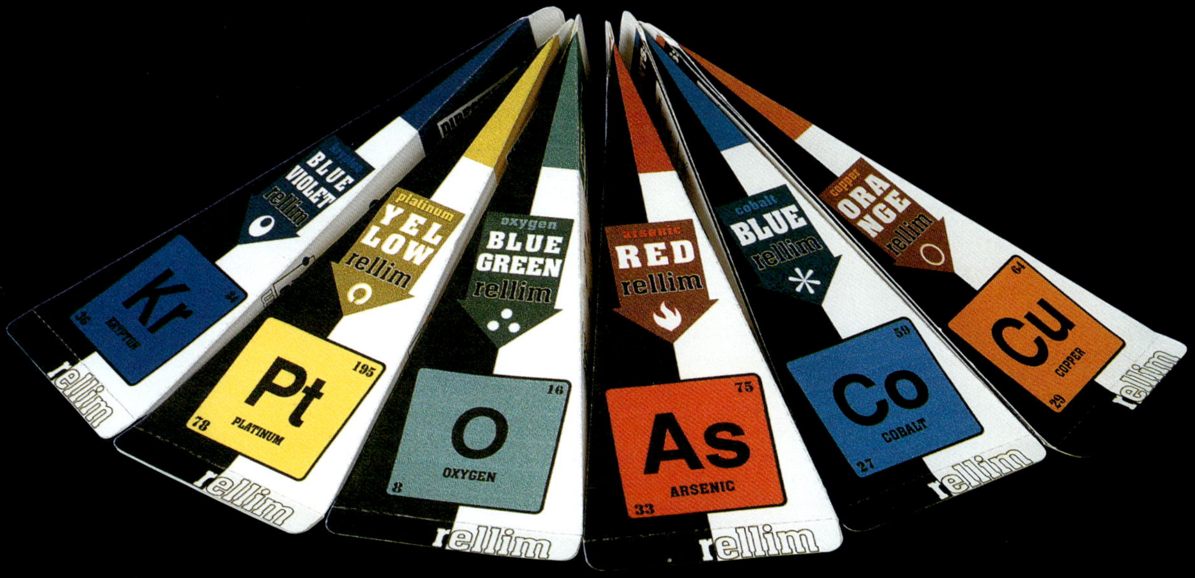

Amanda Miller Northern Illinois University

LICORICE
COUGH
MILK THISTLE
DETOX
WHAT: An extract of Milk Thistle is used to improve liver function, and is said to aid in detoxification of the entire system.
RELAX
OATSTRAW
SLEEP
CLEARS
HEALS SKIN
FOR BEGINNER HERBALISTS

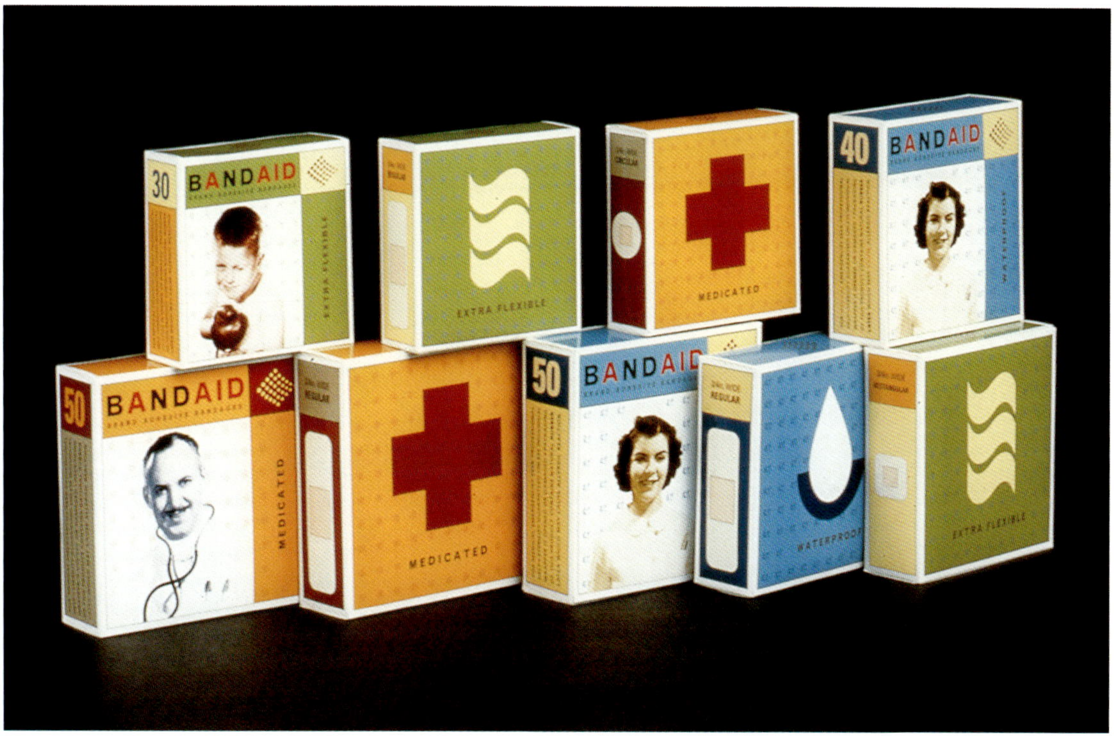
30
BANDAID
EXTRA FLEXIBLE
MEDICATED
40
BANDAID
WATERPROOF
50
BANDAID
MEDICATED
MEDICATED
50
BANDAID
REGULAR
WATERPROOF
EXTRA FLEXIBLE

Papiér Diva

THE PAPER MILL
STORE
1-800-BECKETT
Continued product innovations and manufacturing improvements—Beckett Paper Company is one of the nation's leading manufacturers of premium writing, text and cover papers. Our reputation for product excellence, value and innovation is driven by a commitment to meet the evolving needs of our customers. Beckett Papers provides the selection and uniqueness designers demand, and the quality and versatility exceptional printing/finishing performance requires. With the most sophisticated, contemporary colors, and an extensive range of textures, Beckett Papers is your smart choice for excellence.
THE PAPER MILL
BECKETT™ PREMIUM PAPER
ENVELOPES
ULTRASMOOTH, INCENDIUM WHITE ENVELOPRS, HEAVYWEIGHT
SPECS:
ENVELOPES
500
SIZE #10
THE PAPER MILL
BECKETT™ PREMIUM PAPER
COVER
THE PAPER MILL
PAPER CLIPS
250
100% STAINLESS STEEL
MIXED SIZES

Stefan Michael Bernarsky Drexel University

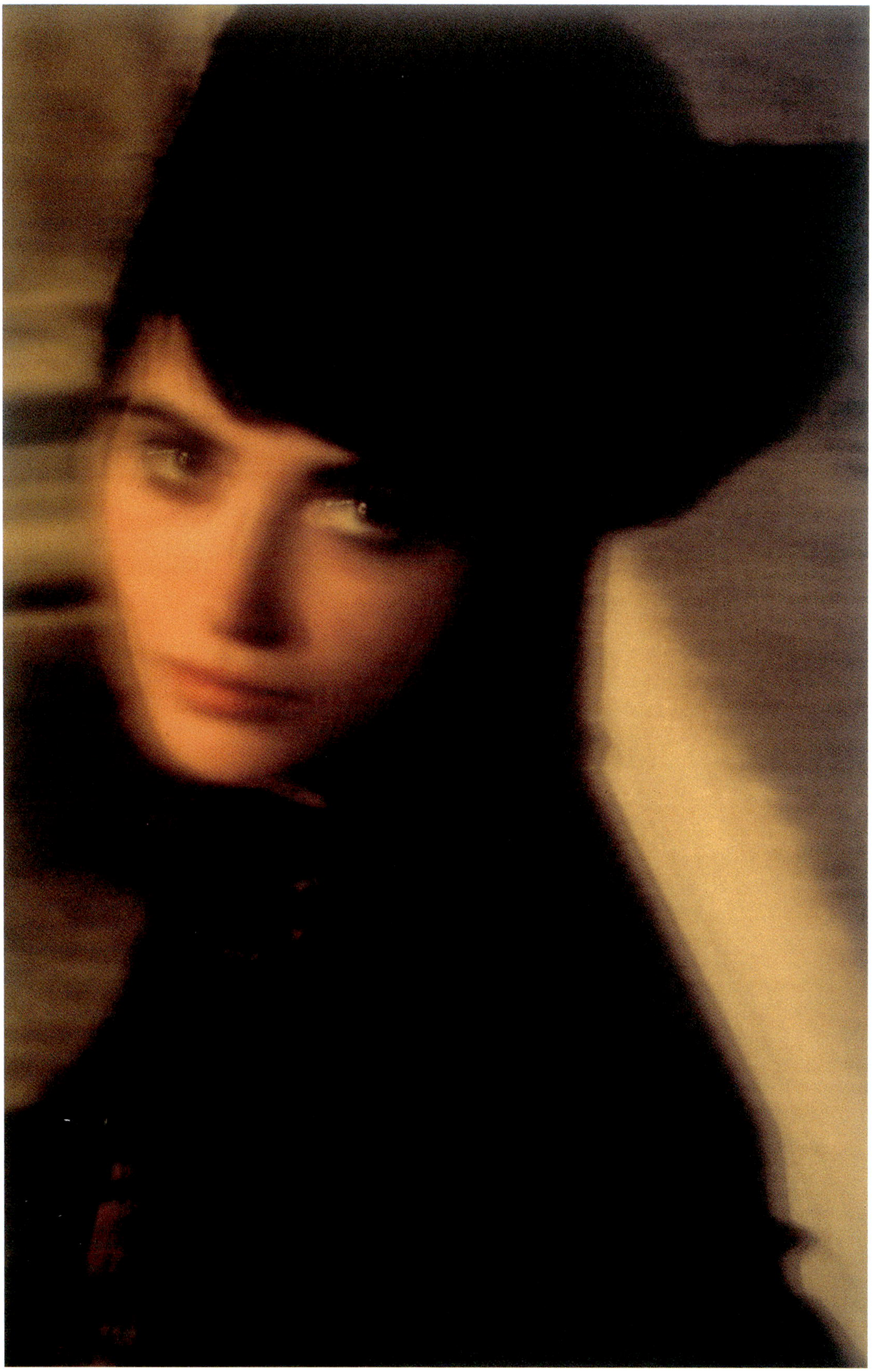

Victoria Dial Art Institute of Atlanta

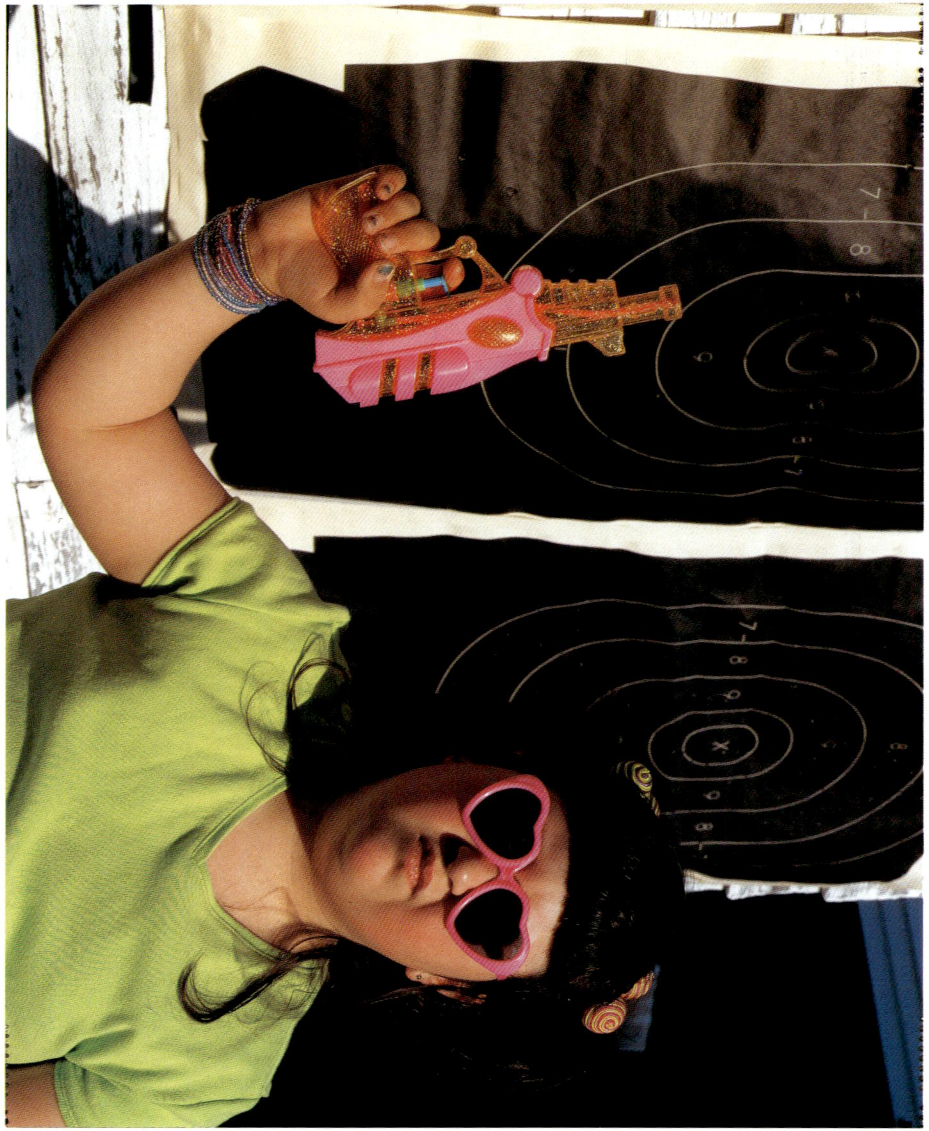

Daryl Patni The Creative Circus

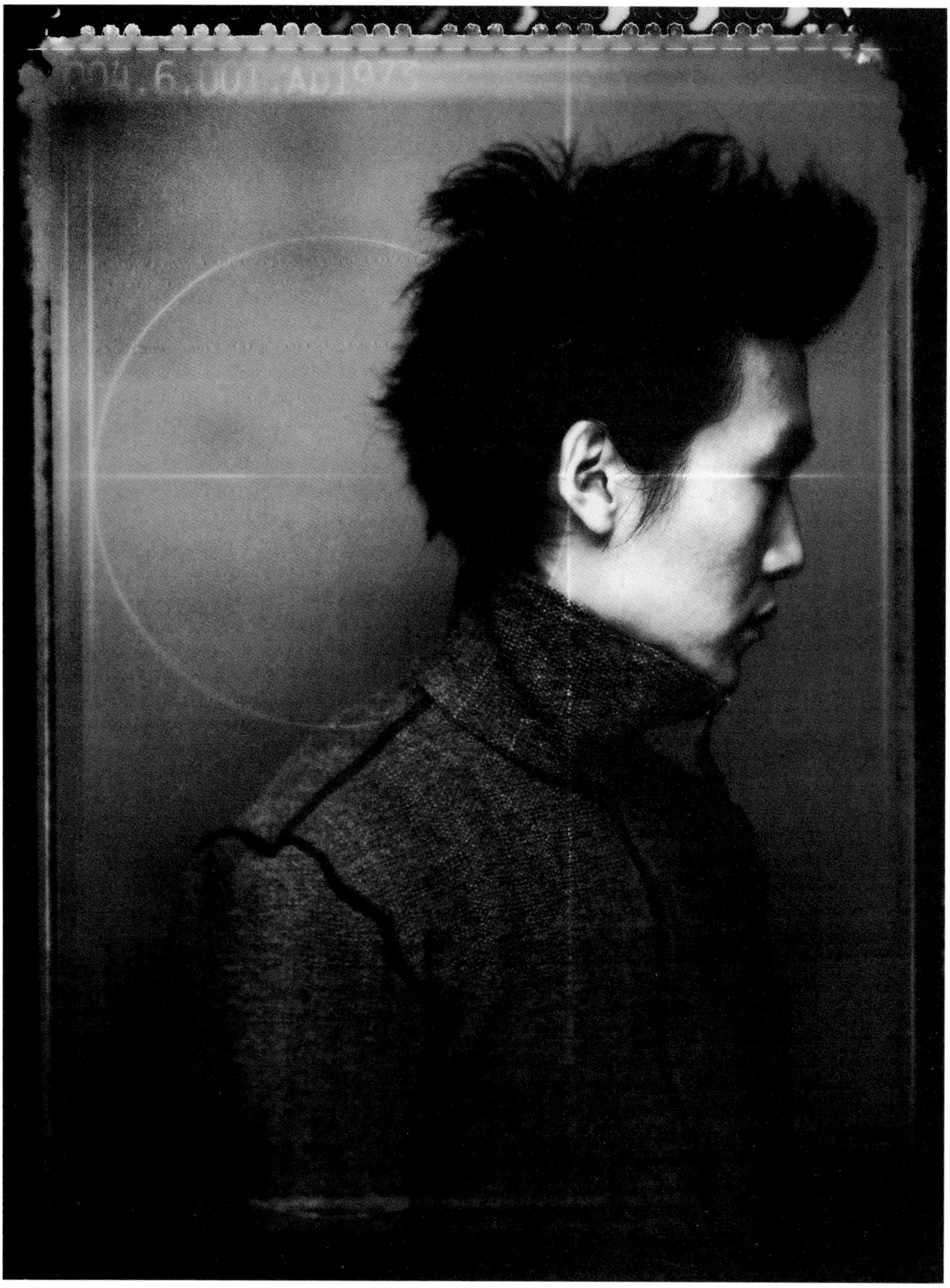

Ryan Robinson Brooks Institute of Photography

Cleve Harry The Creative Circus

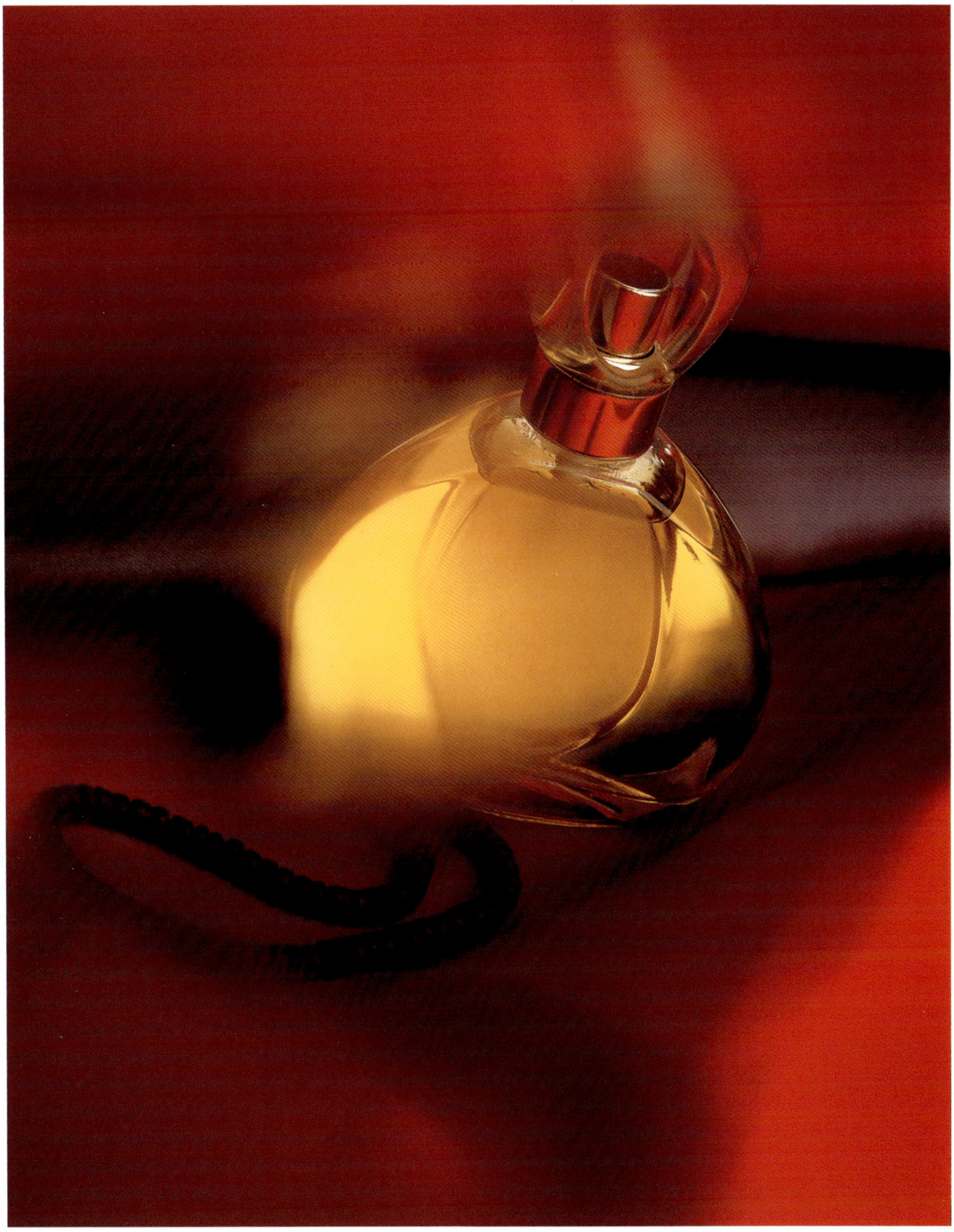

Danielle Chandler Art Institute of Atlanta

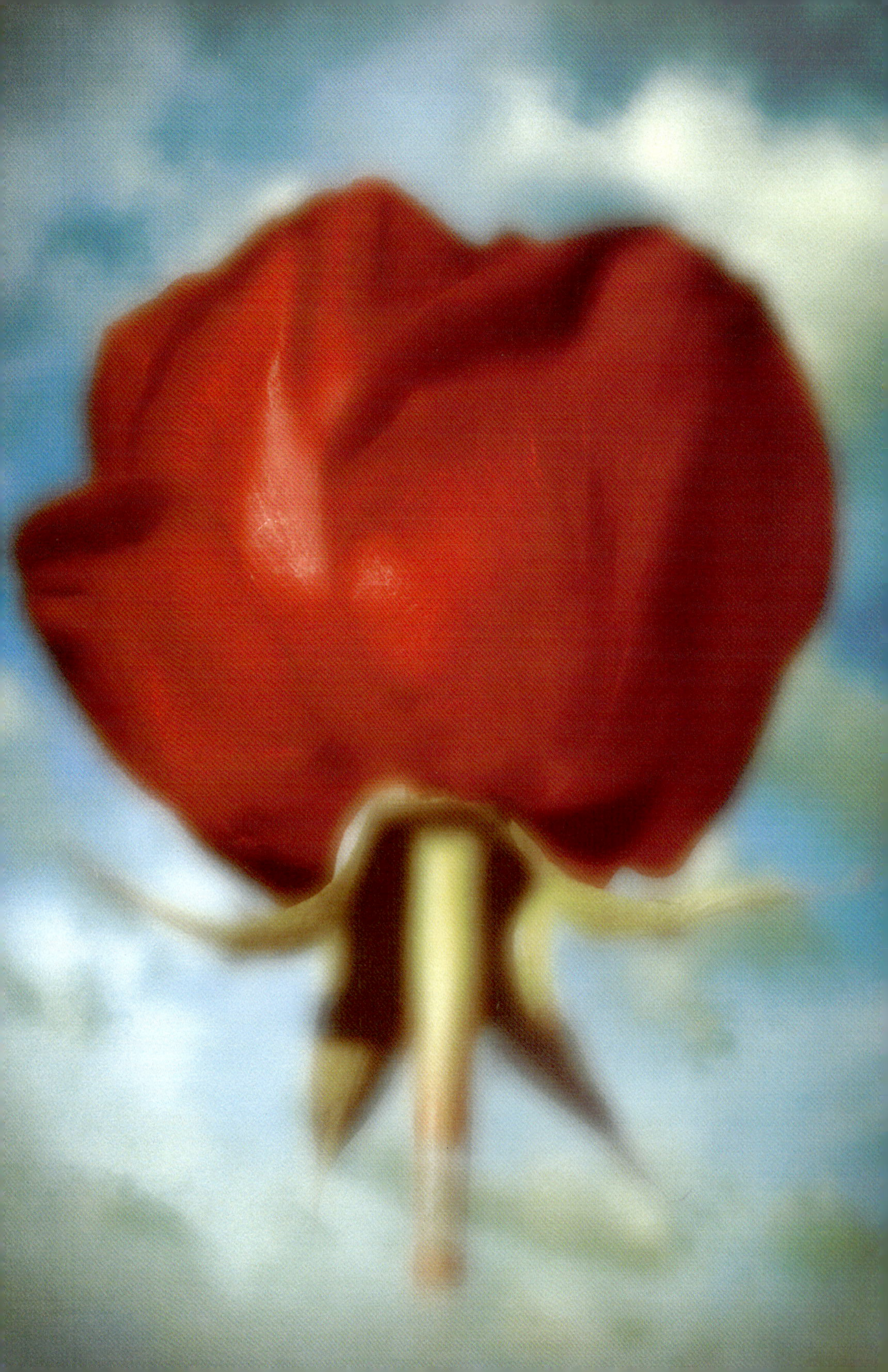

Mike Fleming Drexel University   Photography 190, 191

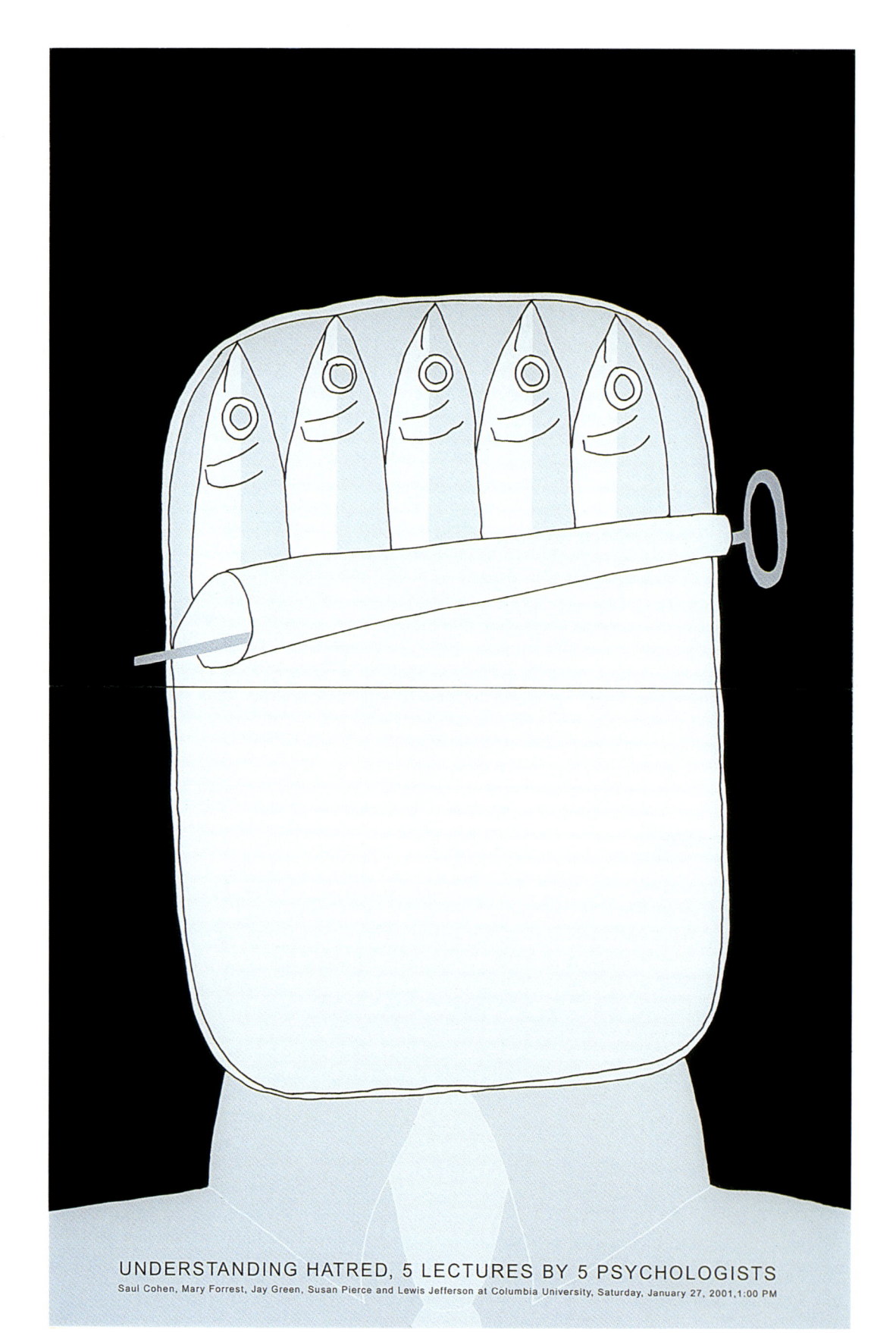

UNDERSTANDING HATRED, 5 LECTURES BY 5 PSYCHOLOGISTS
Saul Cohen, Mary Forrest, Jay Green, Susan Pierce and Lewis Jefferson at Columbia University, Saturday, January 27, 2001, 1:00 PM

Eileen McCarren School of Visual Arts

EXHIBITION
2002 at
TSUKUBA UNIVERSITY

VISUAL COMMUNICATION

Tsukuba University Gallery 2002.4.15-4.20

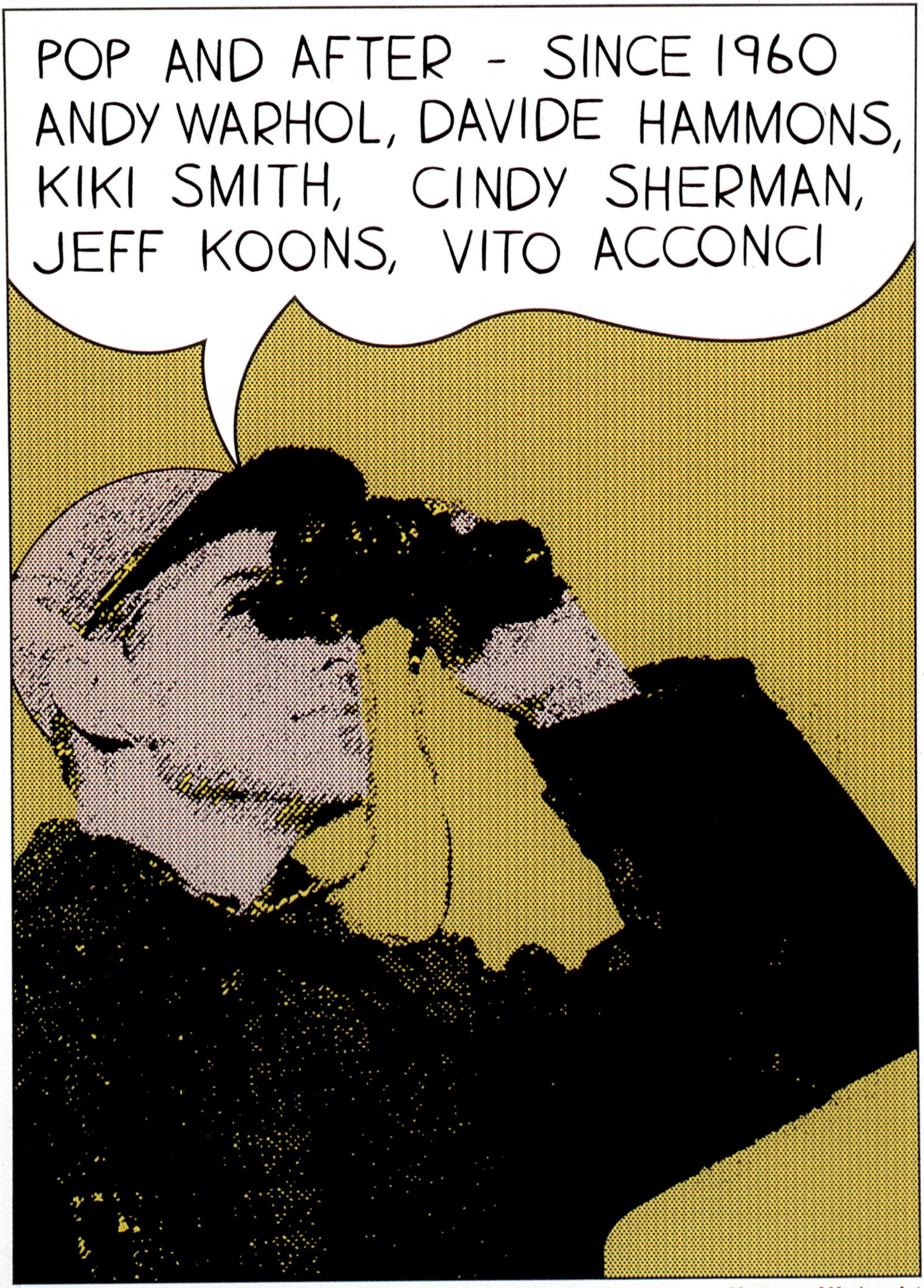

Museum of Modern Art

Tuesday: 10am-9pm Wednesday-Saturday: 10am-5pm
Sunday: noon-5pm Closed Monday and Federal Holidays

Free public admission is offered on Tuesday from 5 to 9 pm.

NATIONAL DESIGN MUSEUM Cooper-Hewitt

General Admission: $8.00
Senior Citizens and Students with I.D.: $5.00
National Design Museum and Smithsonian Institution members and children under age 12 are admitted free.

NATIONAL DESIGN TRIENNIAL

DESIGN CULTURE NOW

http://www.si.edu/ndm

**2 EAST 91 ST NEW YORK, NY 10128-0669
TEL: (212)849-8400 FAX: (212)849-8401**

David Moreno School of Visual Arts

MUSIC IN THE PARK
THE ATLANTA SYMPHONY ORCHESTRA
PLAYS AT PIEDMONT PARK JUNE 22 7PM NO CHARGE

ISRAEL
PALESTINE

Effendy Wijaya School of Visual Arts   **Poster** 198, 199

Anti-advertising

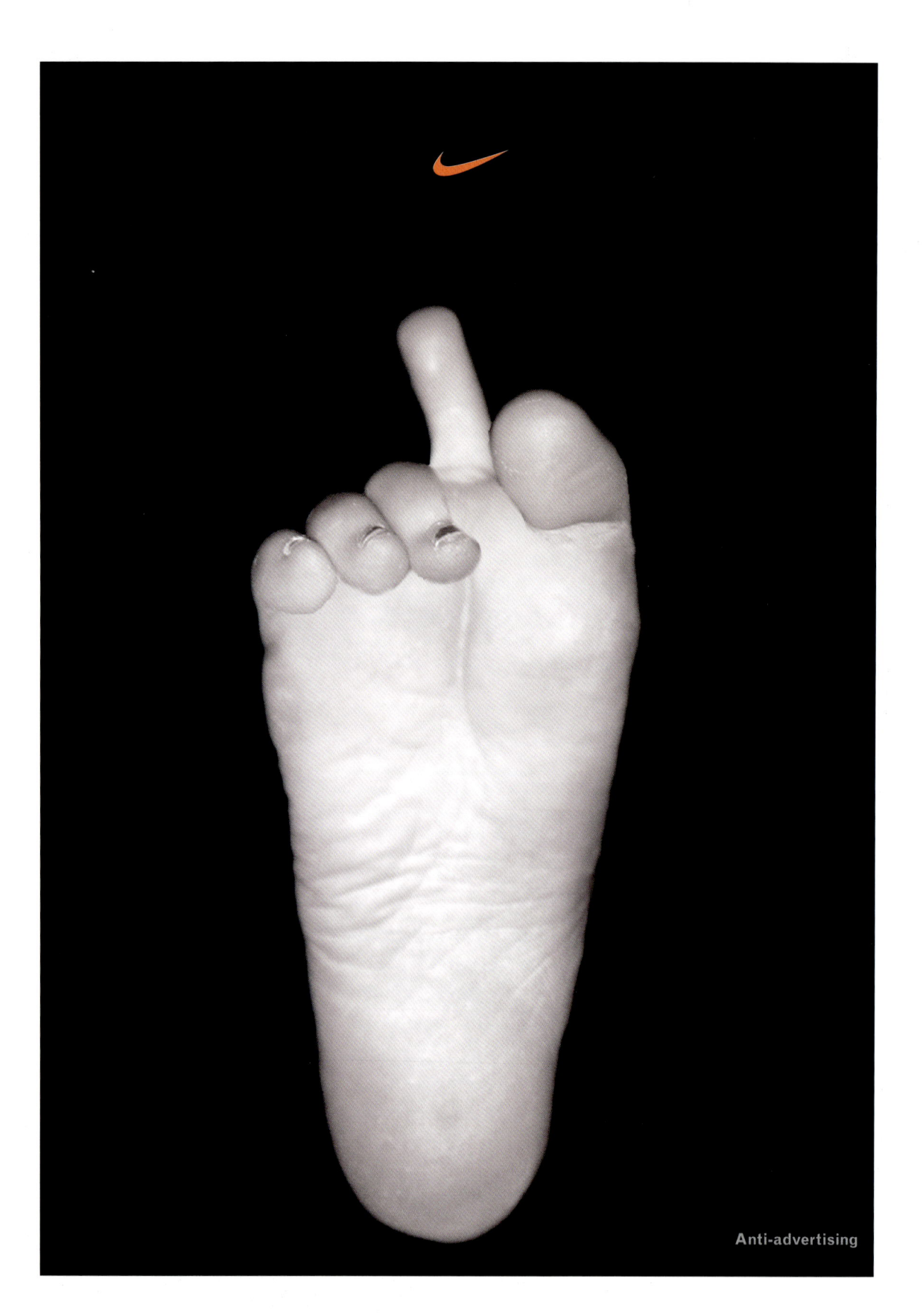

(this spread) **Jean-Jacques Valero** School of Visual Arts

Coca-Cola

Anti-advertising

Anti-advertising

Jean-Jacques Valero School of Visual Arts

POWER

VOL MUTE VOL

R E A D

M O R E

N O W

Regina Lamberti American University

DESIGN MATTERS

AIGA AMERICAN INSTITUTE OF GRAPHIC ARTS 164 FIFTH AVENUE NEW YORK, NY 10010 (212)807-1990

FORM A	NOT FOR USE OF NON-RESIDENTS ON EXTENDED VISITS	INTERNATIONAL TRAVEL COMMISSION **OLYMPIC REGISTRATION**	SERIAL	CSA 002500
	THIS FORM APPLIES TO ALL MEMBERS OF ATHLETES COMPETING. EACH ATHLETIC MEMBER MUST COMPLETE SEPARATE FORM.	FOR MONTH OF Sept 15 to Oct 1 200 0	PREVIOUS COMMISSION REGISTRATION NO.	
1. EVENT	Summer Olympics			MALE
2. SPORT	Volleyball	SYDNEY, AUSTRALIA	LOCAL FILE No.	FEMALE

FORM A	NOT FOR USE OF NON-RESIDENTS ON EXTENDED VISITS	INTERNATIONAL TRAVEL COMMISSION **OLYMPIC REGISTRATION**	SERIAL	CSA 002500
	THIS FORM APPLIES TO ALL MEMBERS OF ATHLETES COMPETING. EACH ATHLETIC MEMBER MUST COMPLETE SEPARATE FORM.	FOR MONTH OF Sept 15 to Oct 1 200 0	PREVIOUS COMMISSION REGISTRATION NO.	
1. EVENT	Summer Olympics			MALE
2. SPORT	Kayaking	SYDNEY, AUSTRALIA	LOCAL FILE No.	FEMALE

FORM A	NOT FOR USE OF NON-RESIDENTS ON EXTENDED VISITS	INTERNATIONAL TRAVEL COMMISSION **OLYMPIC REGISTRATION**	SERIAL	CSA 002500
	THIS FORM APPLIES TO ALL MEMBERS OF ATHLETES COMPETING. EACH ATHLETIC MEMBER MUST COMPLETE SEPARATE FORM.	FOR MONTH OF Sept 15 to Oct 1 200 0	PREVIOUS COMMISSION REGISTRATION NO.	
1. EVENT	Summer Olympics			MALE
2. SPORT	Gymnastics	SYDNEY, AUSTRALIA	LOCAL FILE No.	FEMALE

2000 OLYMPICS SYDNEY AUSTRALIA   15 SEPT – 01 OCT

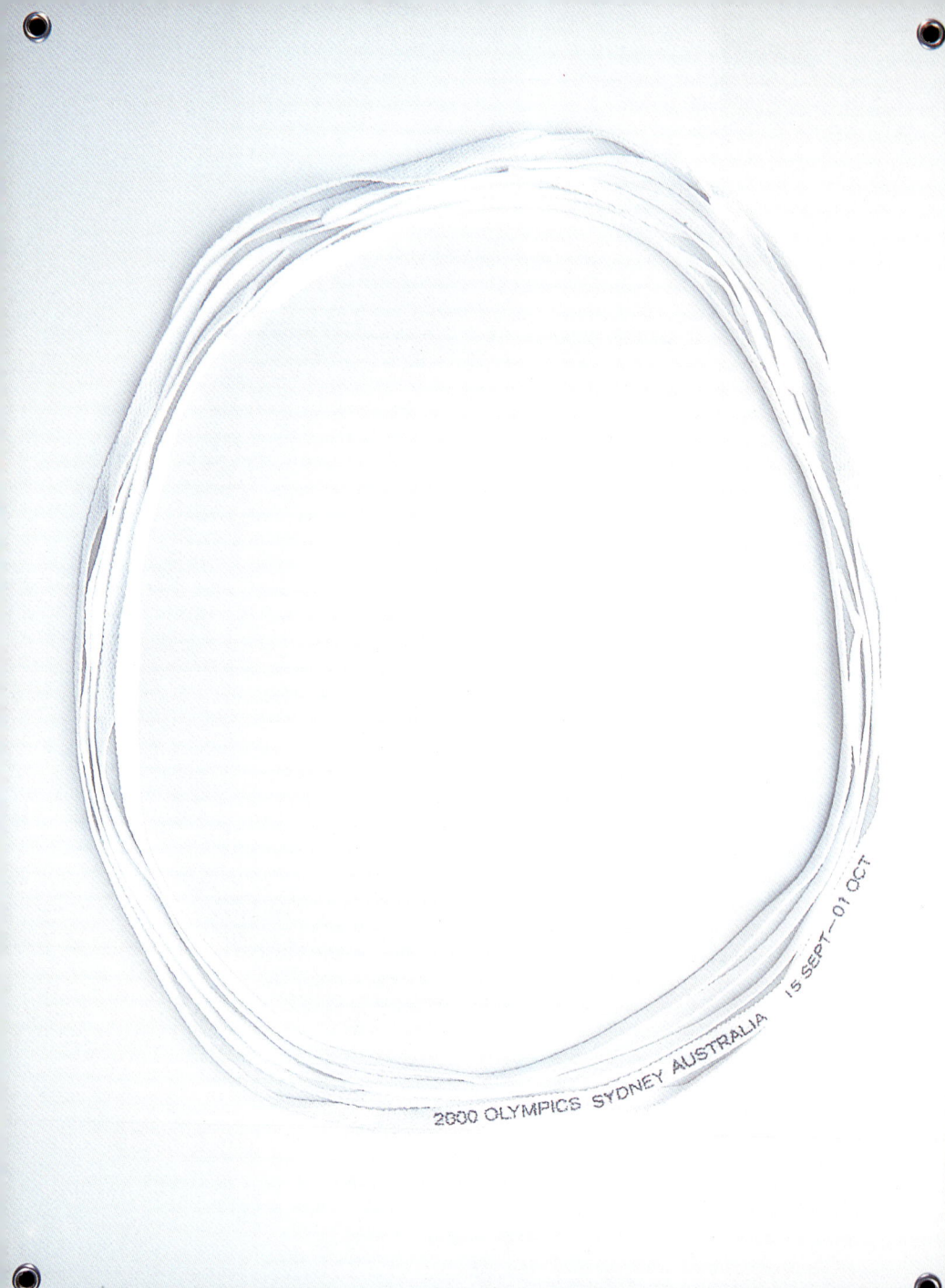

Poster 206, 207

FULLY COMMITTED
DATE DEC. 24, 2000
LUNCH / BRUNCH / DINNER
NAME
PHONE NO.
TIME
NO. OF PEOPLE
VIP
TABLE NO.
THE CHERRY LANE THEATRE 212.239.6200 8PM
38 COMMERCE STREET
JAMES NOONE SCENIC DESIGN
NANCY NAGEL GIBBS ASSOCIATE PRODUCERS
DAVID TURNER
SAM RUDY PRESS 8:30
SHIRLEY HERZ ASSOCIATES REPRESENTATIVE
JAMES CALLERI CASTING
DANIEL GOLDSTEIN
NICHOLAS MARTIN
AT THE CHERRY LANE THEATRE 212.239.6200 8PM
38 COMMERCE STREET

MODEST MOUSE

WITH THE SHINS AND ENGINE DOWN

ELECTRIC FACTORY

OCT 13

TICKETS ON SALE SEPTEMBER 5 AT ALL TICKETMASTER LOCATIONS OR CALL 215.627.1332 OR ONLINE AT WWW.TICKETMASTER.COM
THIS TRAP WAS BAITED AND SET BY ELECTRIC FACTORY CONCERTS

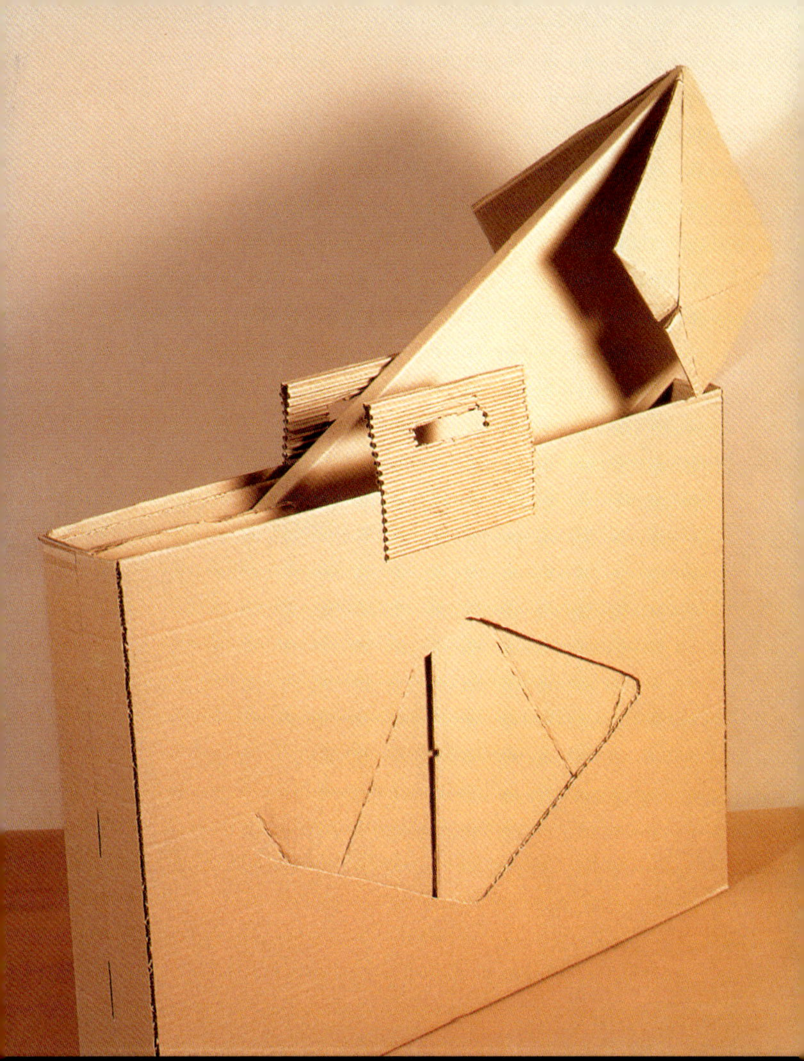

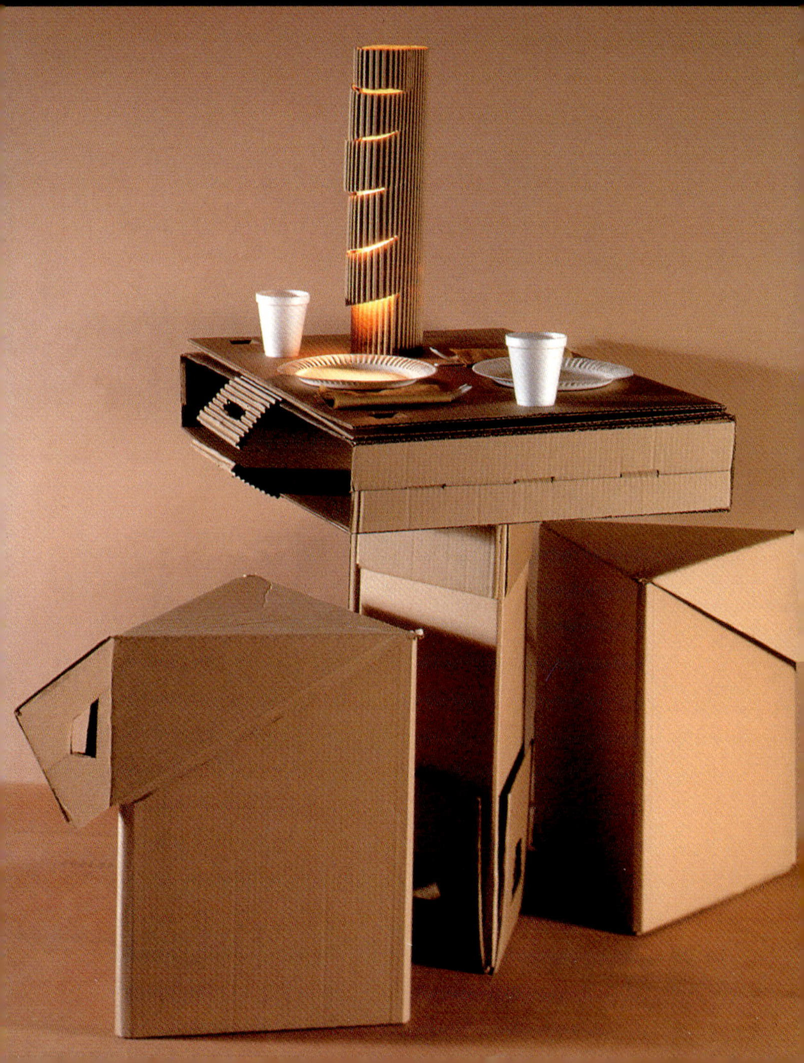

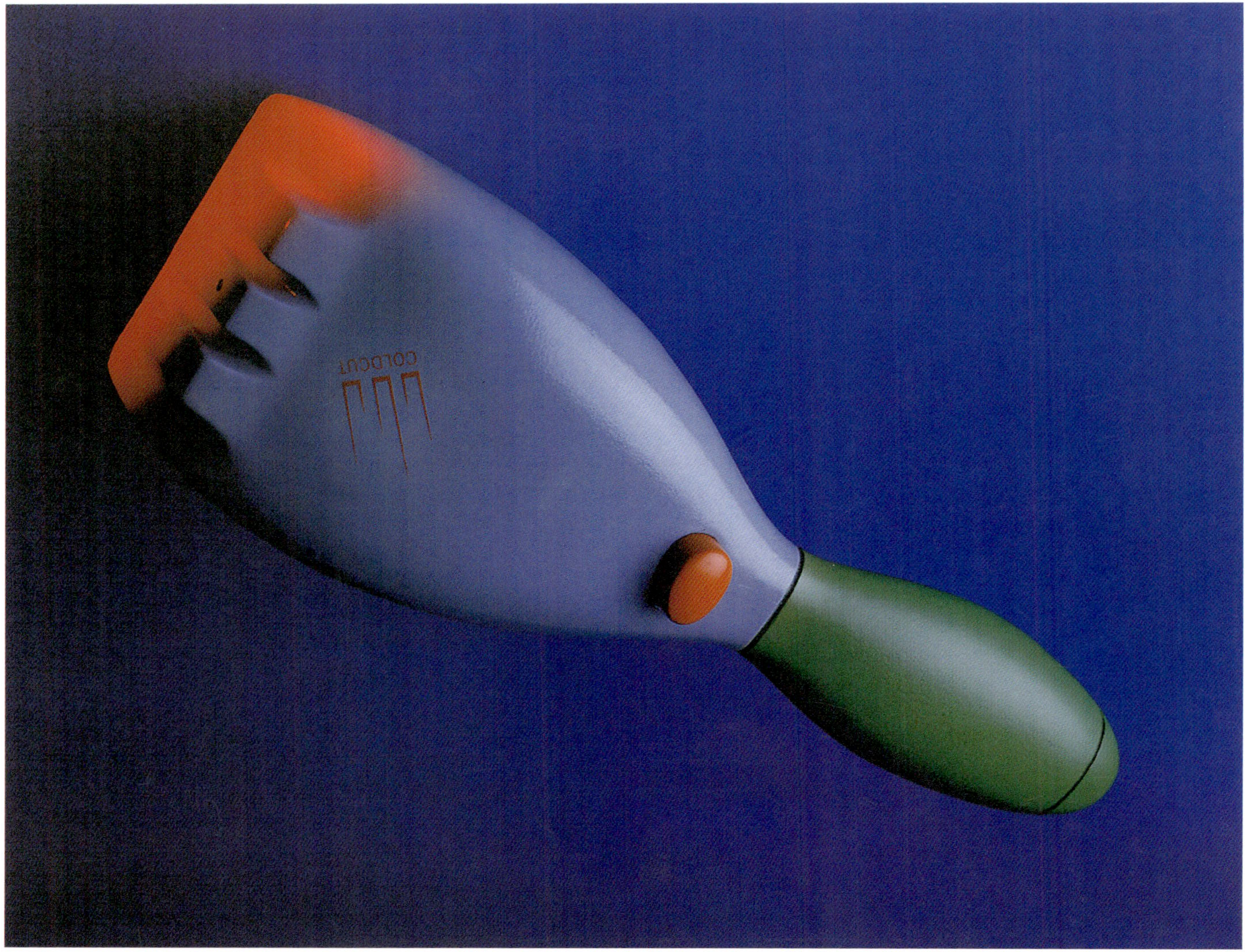
COLDCUT

Ally Weiner Portfolio Center

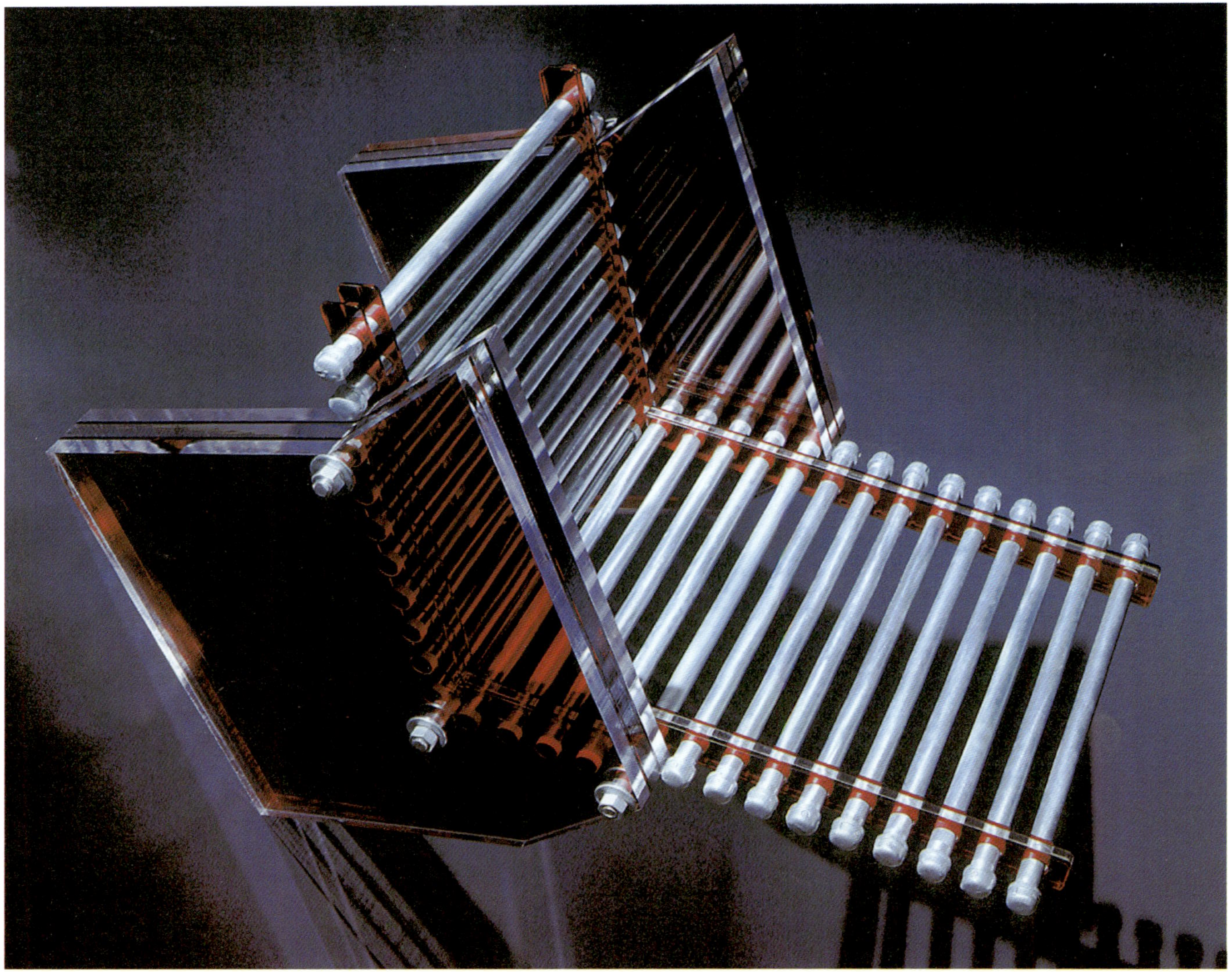

Christine Taylor Portfolio Center

Meg Dreyer Portfolio Center

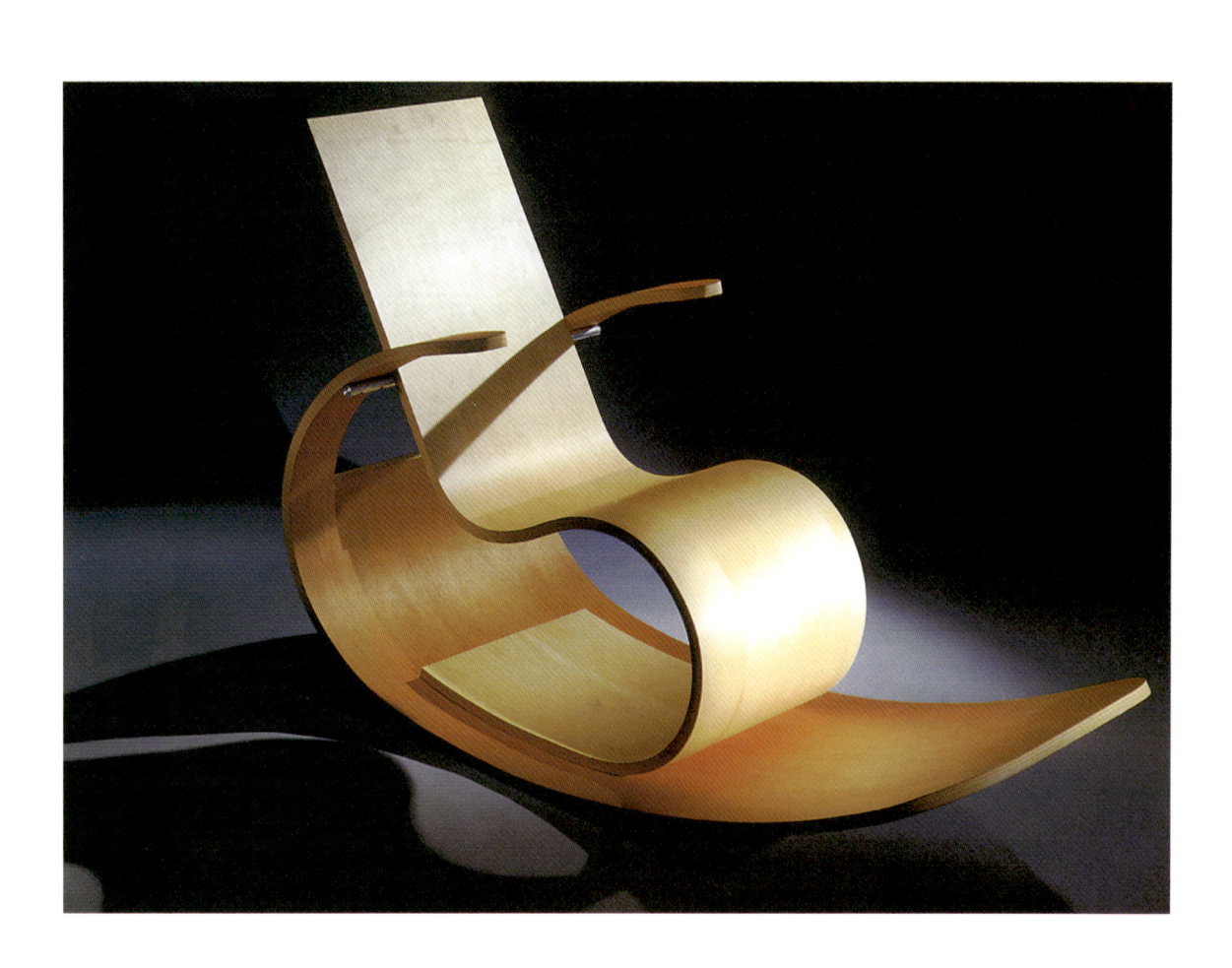

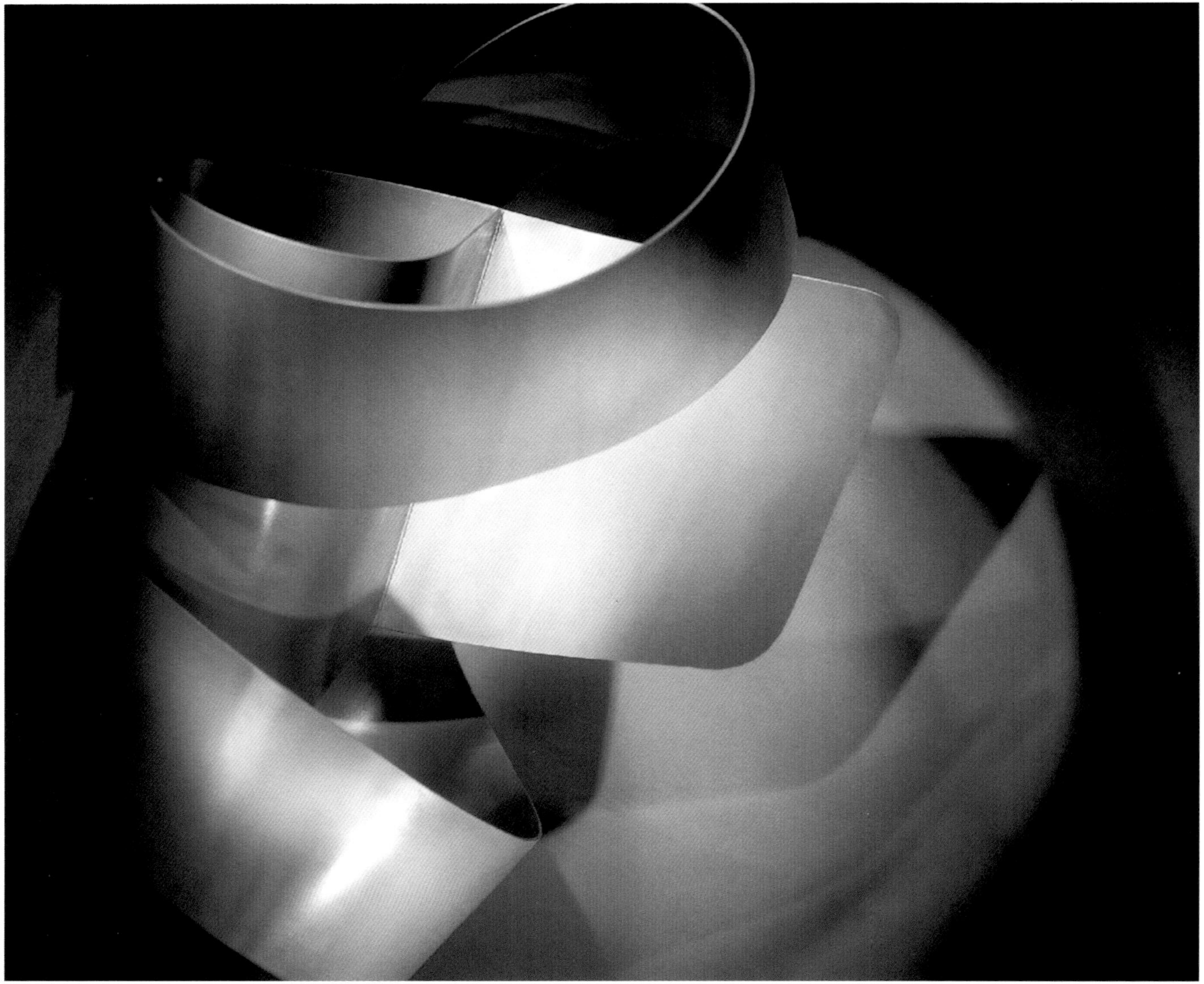

Erin Wallace Portfolio Center

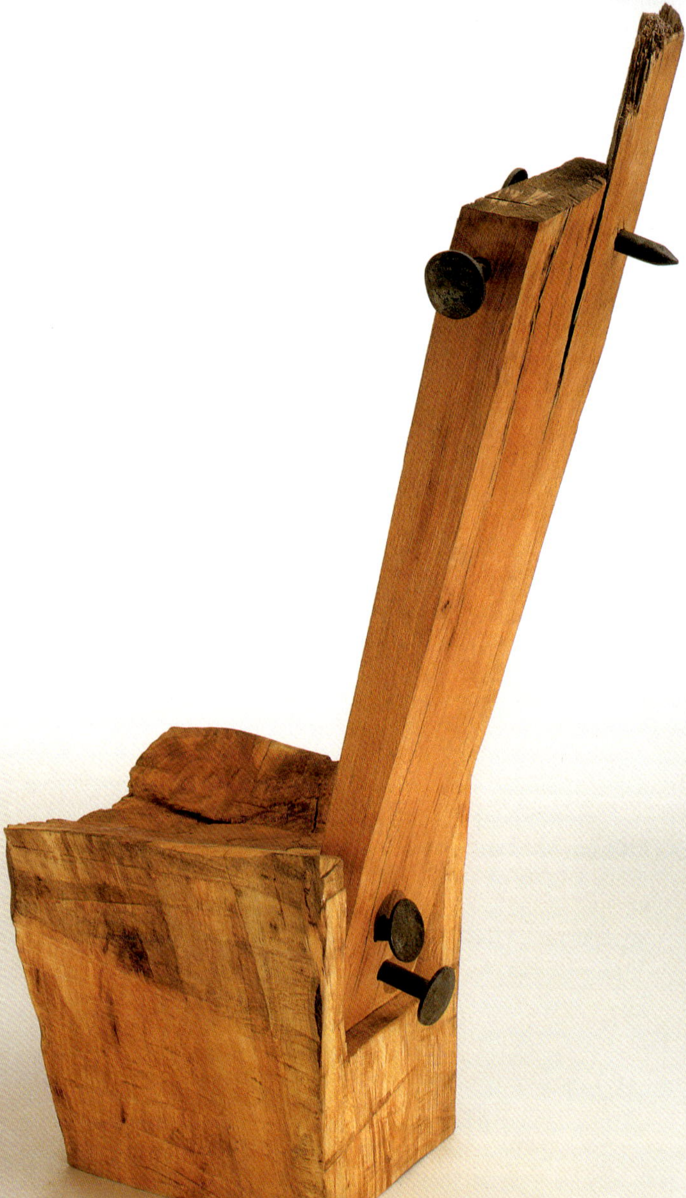

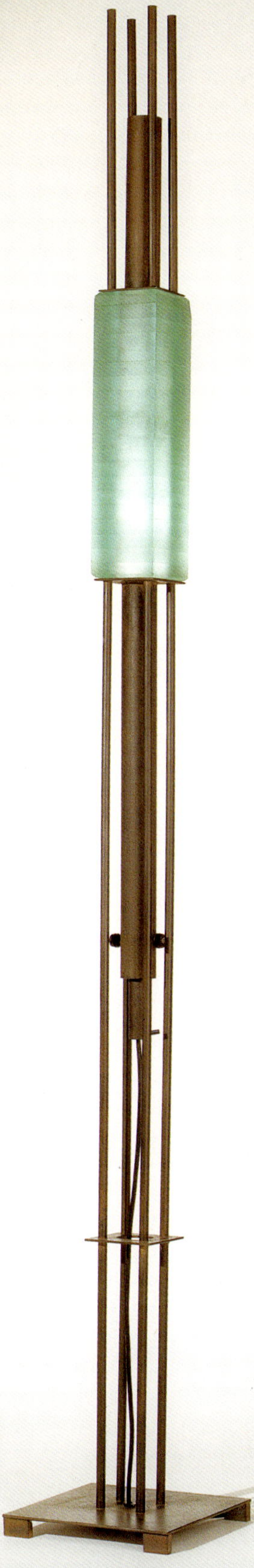

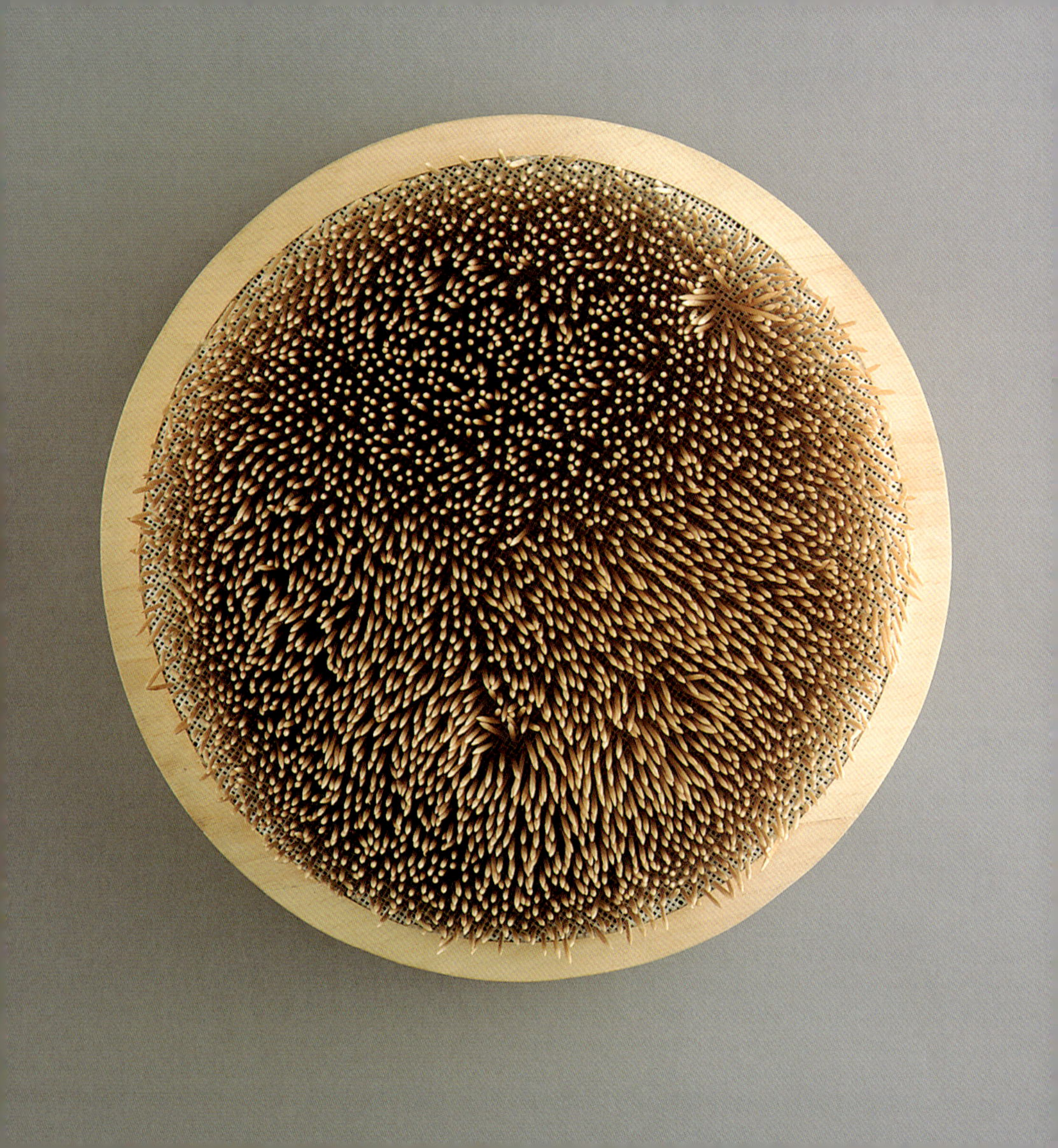

Products 218,219

Just a little message sweet
Delivered to you as a special treat
Loosen up this Valentine's
Have a peep inside
Love
Sommese Design

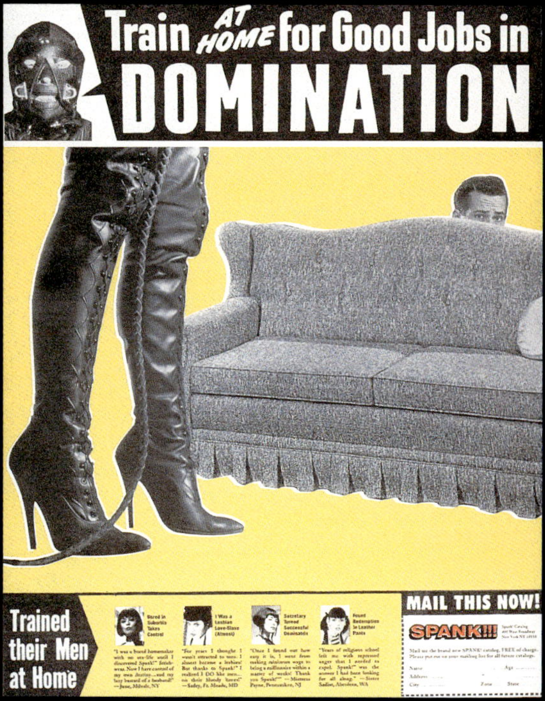

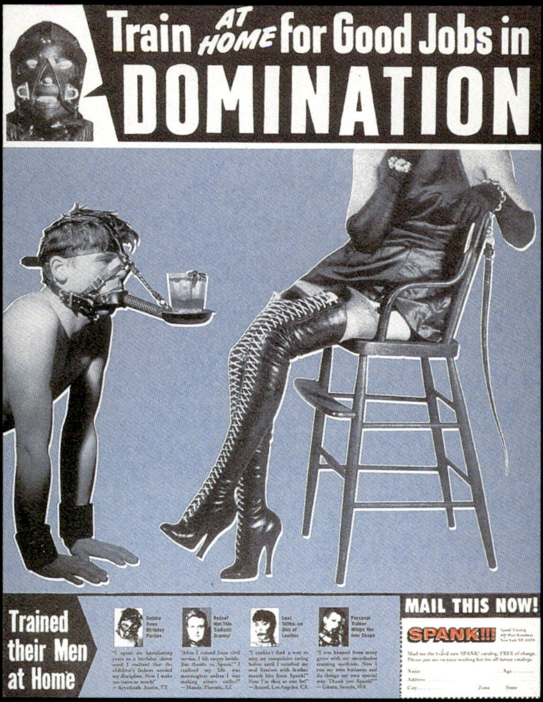

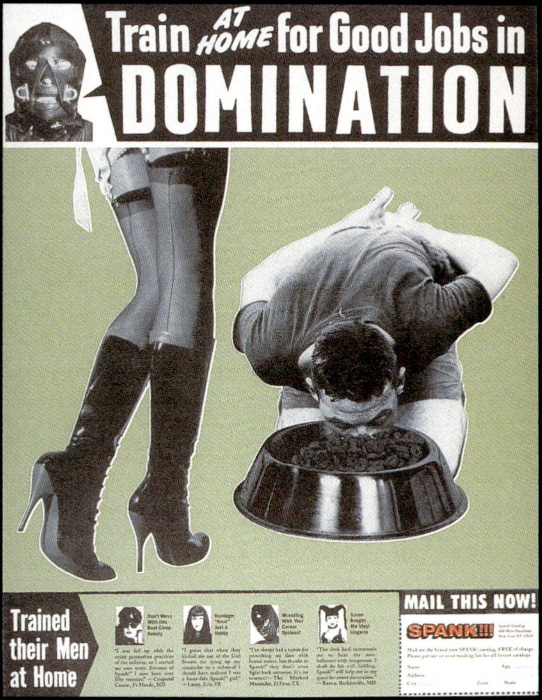

Jude Bufum Tyler School of Art, Temple University

Karin Satrom Penn State University

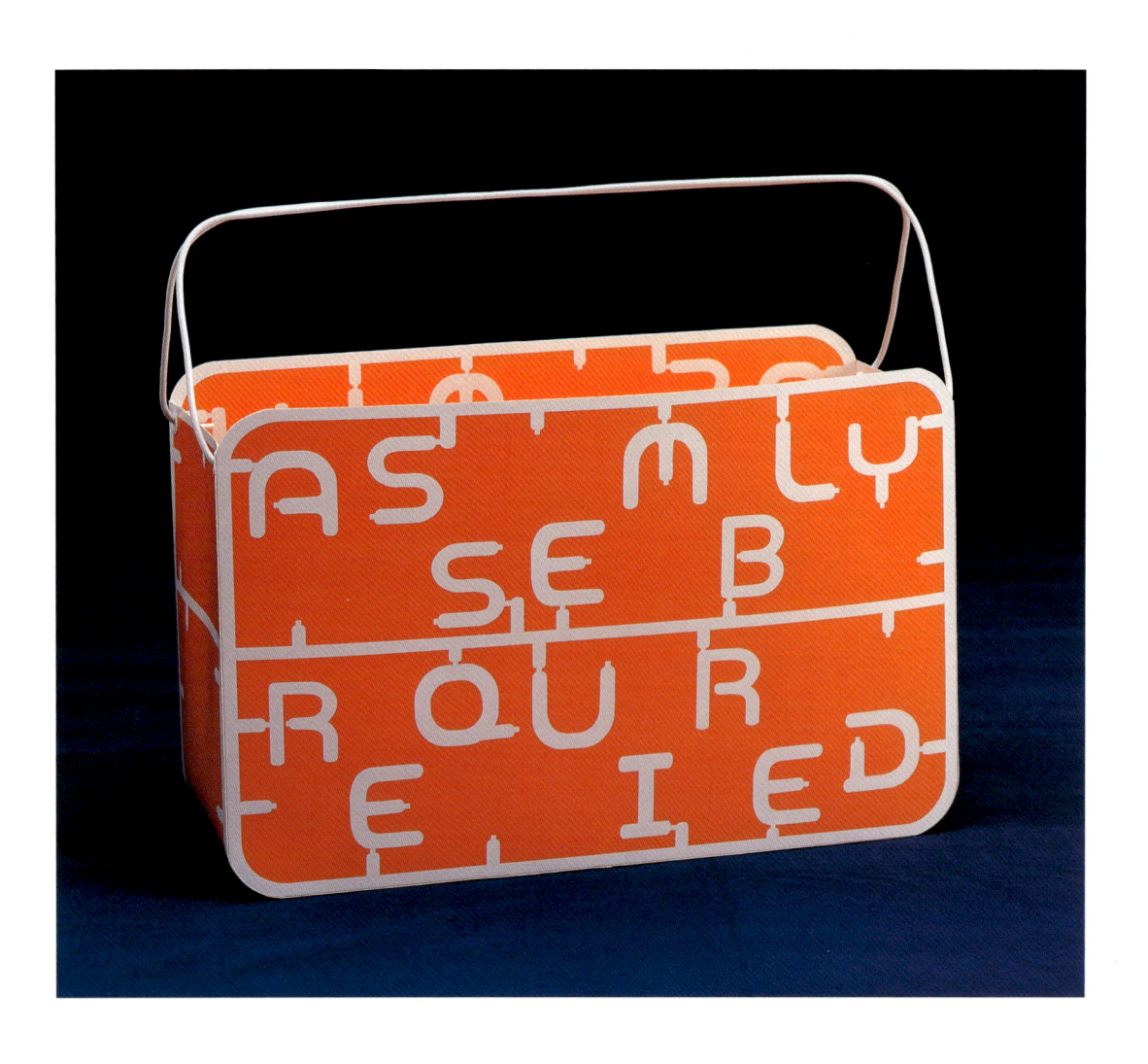

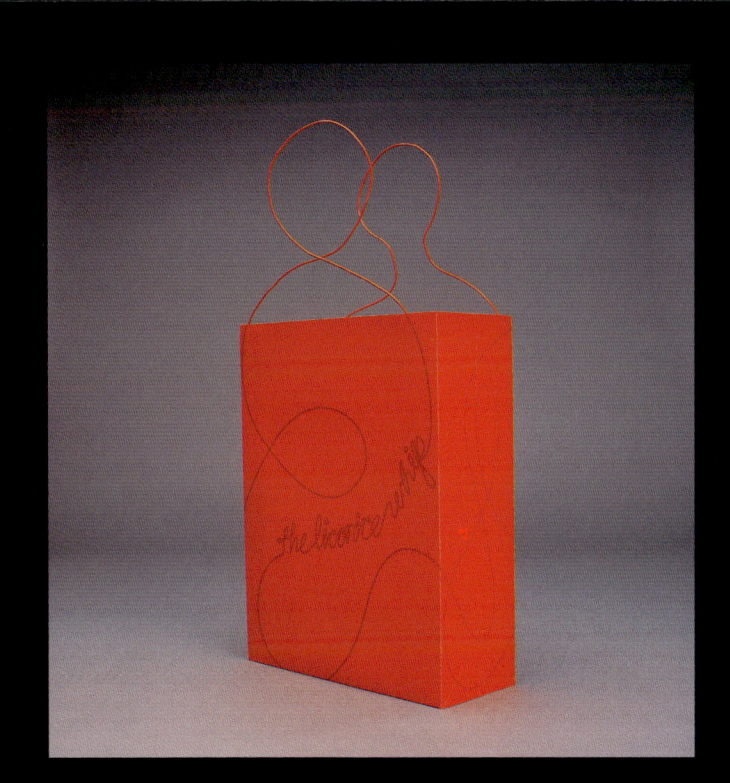

(top) **Brian McCall** Penn State University (middle) **Janet O'Neil** Penn State University (bottom) **Lindsay Himes** Penn State University   **Shopping Bags** 222, 223 (top) **Sarah Ferretti** Penn State University (middle) **Becky Berkheimer** Penn State University (bottom) **Trisha Paurelsky** Penn State University

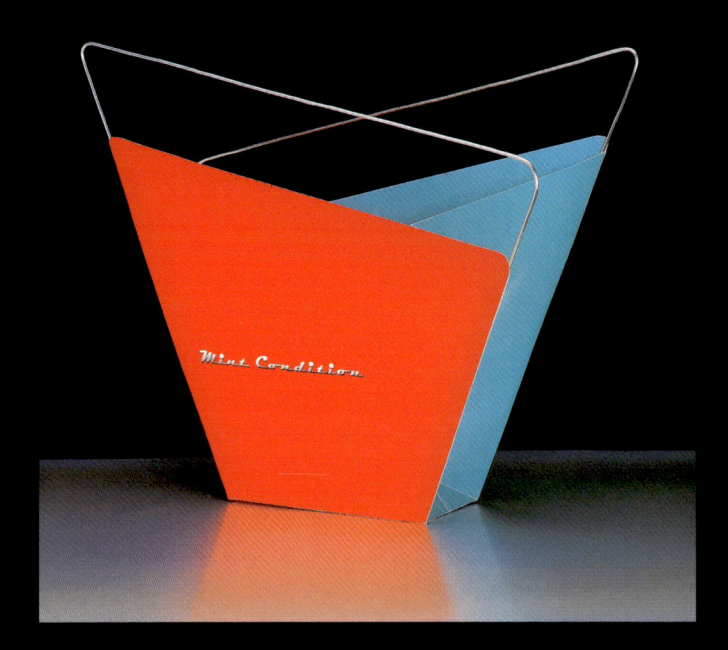

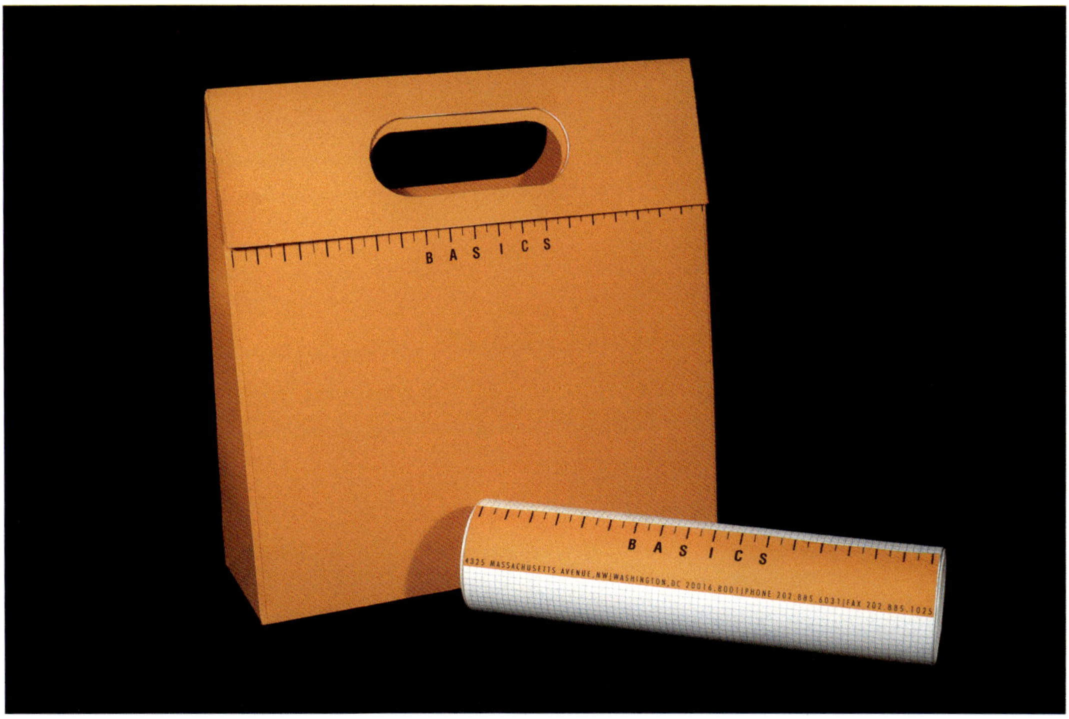

Carmen Santa-Cruz American University

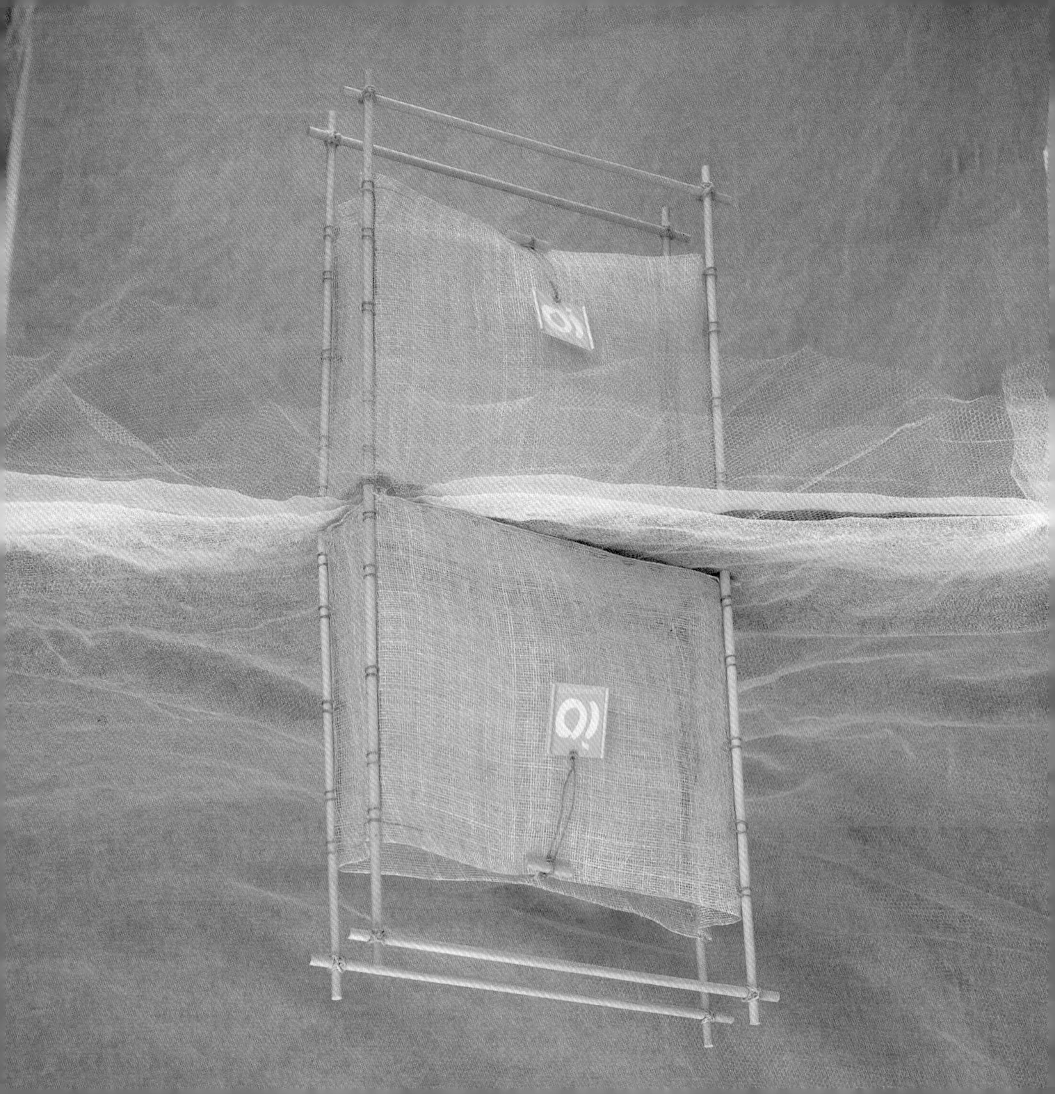

toronto 2008

toronto 2008

toronto 2008

toronto 2008

toronto 2008

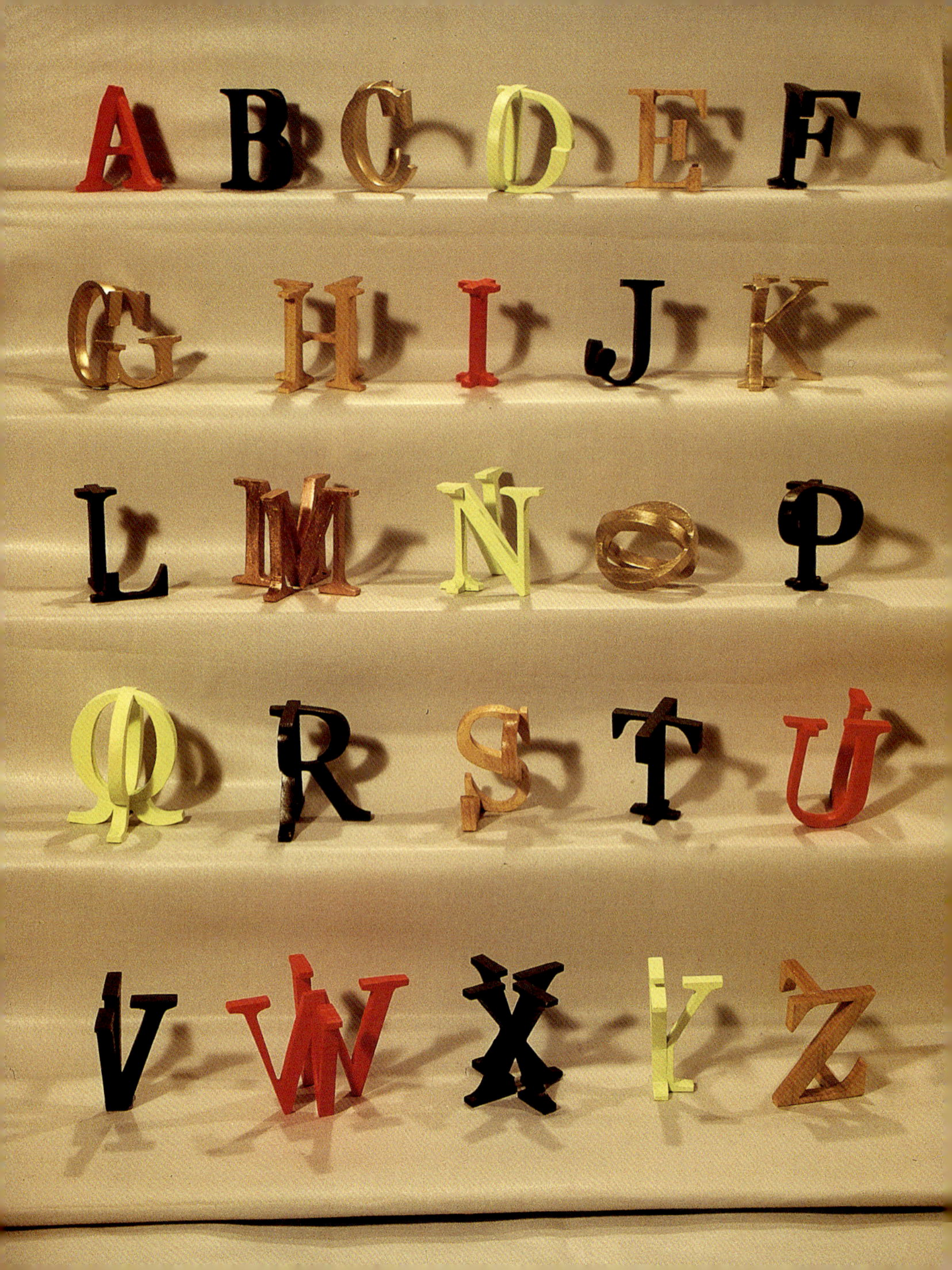
A B C D E F
G H I J K
L M N O P
Q R S T U
V W X Y Z

METAL SLUT

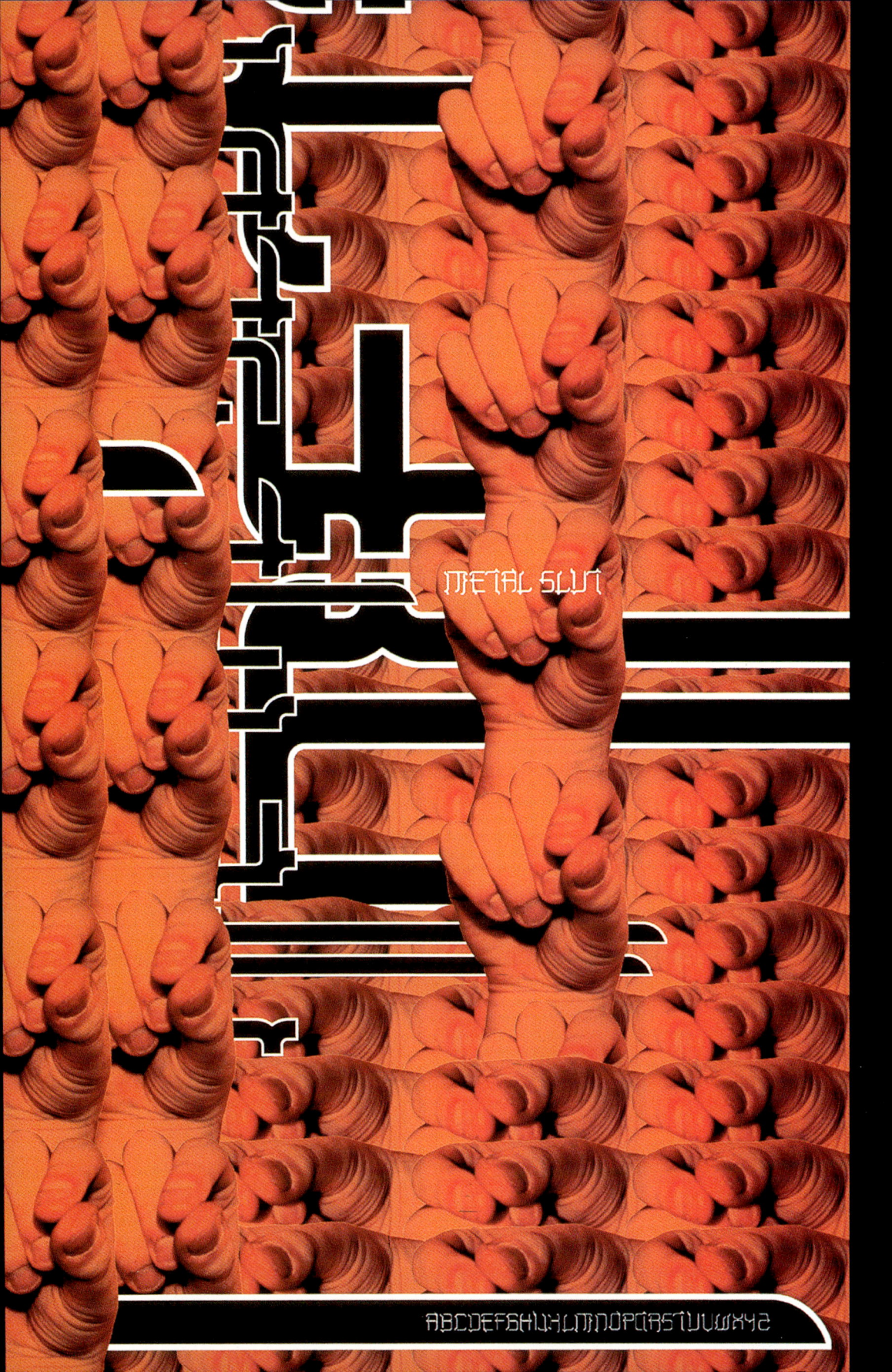

ABCDEFGHIJKLMNOPQRSTUVWXYZ

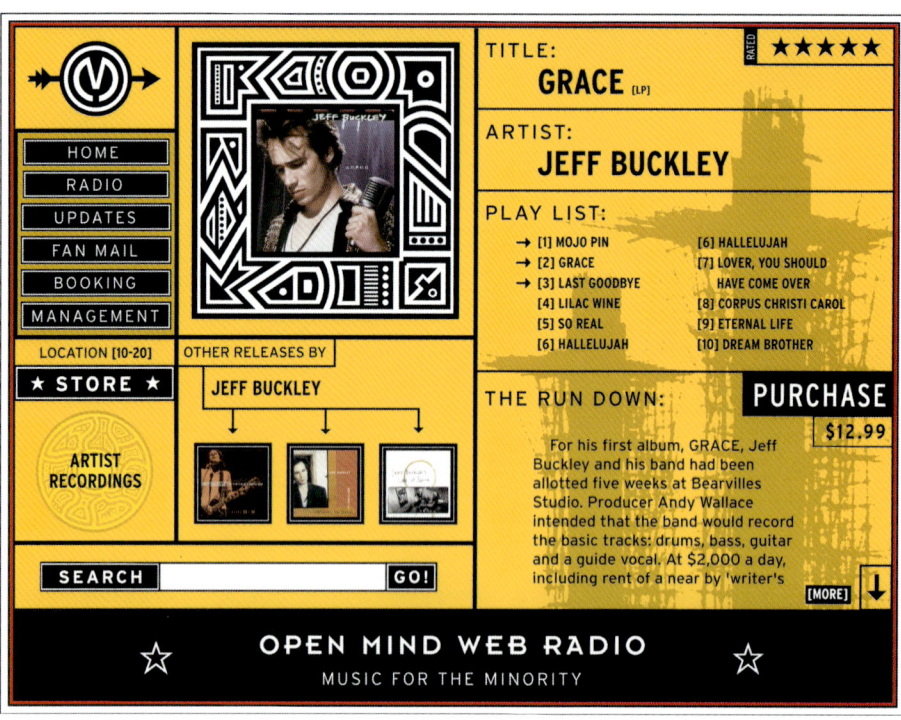

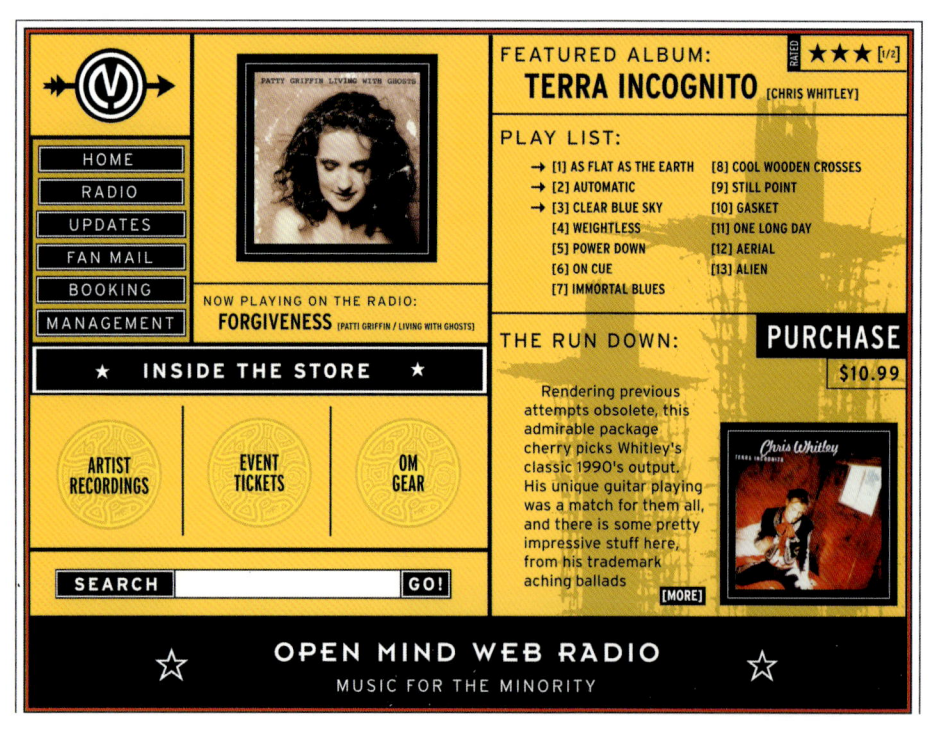

OPEN MIND WEB RADIO
MUSIC FOR THE MINORITY

- RADIO
- STORE
- UPDATES
- FAN MAIL
- BOOKING
- MANAGEMENT

TITLE: GRACE [LP]
ARTIST: JEFF BUCKLEY
RATED ★★★★★

PLAY LIST:
- [1] MOJO PIN
- [2] GRACE
- [3] LAST GOODBYE
- [4] LILAC WINE
- [5] SO REAL
- [6] HALLELUJAH
- [7] LOVER, YOU SHOULD HAVE COME OVER
- [8] CORPUS CHRISTI CAROL
- [9] ETERNAL LIFE
- [10] DREAM BROTHER

- HOME
- RADIO
- UPDATES
- FAN MAIL
- BOOKING
- MANAGEMENT

LOCATION [10-20]
★ STORE ★
ARTIST RECORDINGS

OTHER RELEASES BY JEFF BUCKLEY

SEARCH [ ] GO!

THE RUN DOWN:

PURCHASE $12.99

For his first album, GRACE, Jeff Buckley and his band had been allotted five weeks at Bearvilles Studio. Producer Andy Wallace intended that the band would record the basic tracks: drums, bass, guitar and a guide vocal. At $2,000 a day, including rent of a near by 'writer's [MORE]

OPEN MIND WEB RADIO
MUSIC FOR THE MINORITY

FEATURED ALBUM: TERRA INCOGNITO [CHRIS WHITLEY]
RATED ★★★ [1/2]

PLAY LIST:
- [1] AS FLAT AS THE EARTH
- [2] AUTOMATIC
- [3] CLEAR BLUE SKY
- [4] WEIGHTLESS
- [5] POWER DOWN
- [6] ON CUE
- [7] IMMORTAL BLUES
- [8] COOL WOODEN CROSSES
- [9] STILL POINT
- [10] GASKET
- [11] ONE LONG DAY
- [12] AERIAL
- [13] ALIEN

- HOME
- RADIO
- UPDATES
- FAN MAIL
- BOOKING
- MANAGEMENT

NOW PLAYING ON THE RADIO:
FORGIVENESS [PATTY GRIFFIN / LIVING WITH GHOSTS]

★ INSIDE THE STORE ★

- ARTIST RECORDINGS
- EVENT TICKETS
- OM GEAR

SEARCH [ ] GO!

THE RUN DOWN:

PURCHASE $10.99

Rendering previous attempts obsolete, this admirable package cherry picks Whitley's classic 1990's output. His unique guitar playing was a match for them all, and there is some pretty impressive stuff here, from his trademark aching ballads [MORE]

OPEN MIND WEB RADIO
MUSIC FOR THE MINORITY

rico poon *

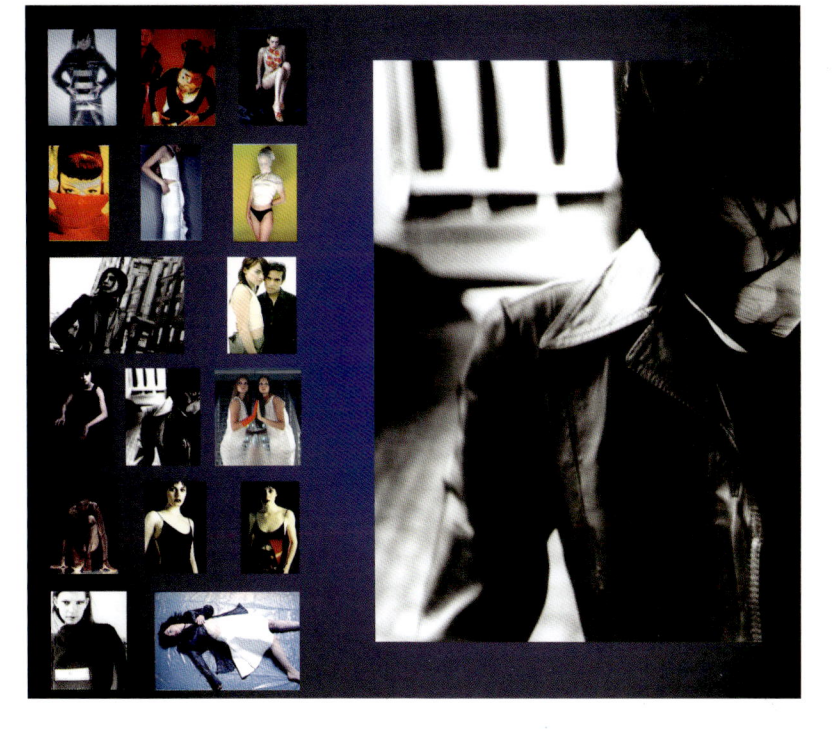

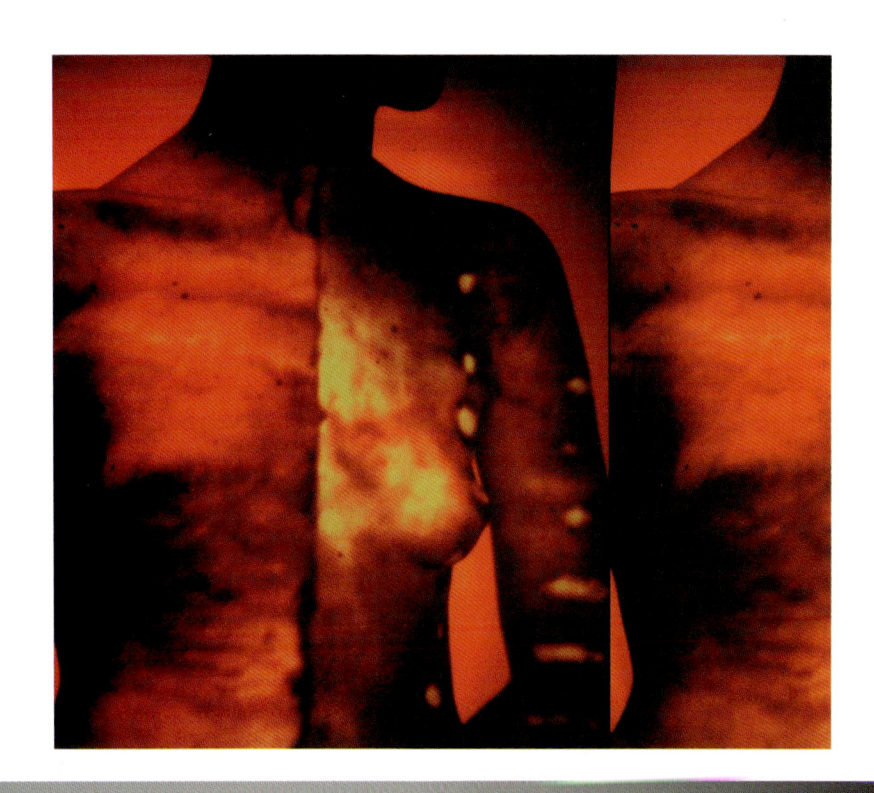

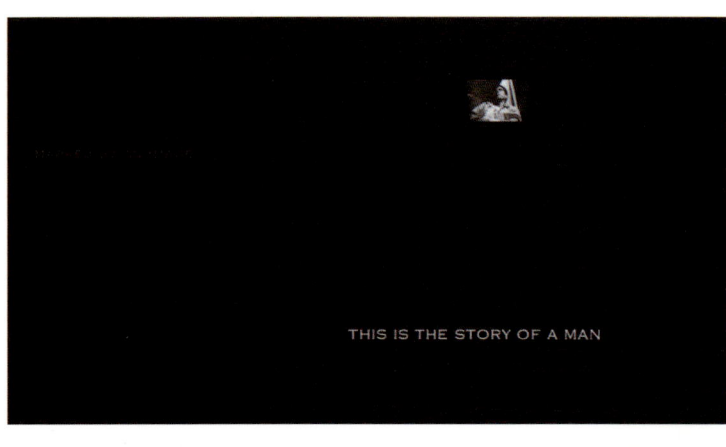

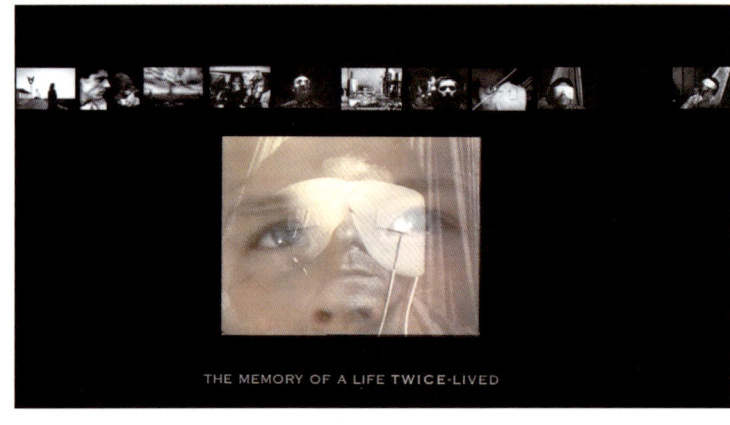

THIS IS THE STORY OF A MAN

THE SCIENTISTS SENT
EMISSARIES INTO TIME

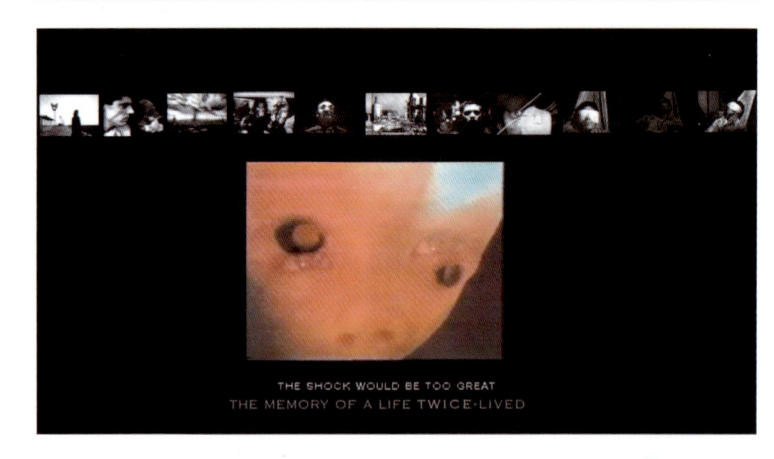

FOR HIS OBSESSION WITH AN IMAGE FROM THE PAST

THE SHOCK WOULD BE TOO GREAT
THE MEMORY OF A LIFE TWICE-LIVED

THE MEMORY OF A LIFE TWICE-LIVED

LA JETEE

Michelle Solodyna University of Illinois at Urbana-Champaign

Text is all around us. | Proposal Thesis Writings Images Experiments Tidbits | Email

Text is all around us.
ConTEXT: A Study of our Information (Textual) Landscape

ConTEXT: A Study of our Information (Textual) Landscape
Emily Carr Institute of Art + Design | Graduation Thesis Project | Fall 2000

1 November 2000

This web site is intended to be an electronic sketch/composition book for my grad thesis project - ConTEXT. I created this web site to guide and inspire my visual exploration and also to document my process. The accumulation of material here will in turn be part of the content for the "final product" (a book and this web site) of my project, which will be presented in December.

This web site is, and always will be, a work in progress. This is akin to what I propose vernacular communication might be about - change. The experiments done here will, strangely enough, inform how the print publication will take shape in the end. This interplay of the transient and the (supposedly) more permanent, and the switching of the role of the media, I think, is fascinating and may help us designers to clarify

---

Serendipity
Chance/Choice
↓

Serendipity [n.]
(talent of) making fortunate and unexpected discoveries by chance.

Whilst I walked past a wall full of handbills at UBC a few weeks ago, I thought to myself, why would anyone even bother posting anything after there were so many layers upon layers of bills, one layer obscuring other layers underneath, partially or

---

01 Serendipity
02 Vancouver Museum of Natural History
03 Sale
04 Flourishes No.1 (Airport)
05 Flourishes No.2 (Design)
06 Inscriptions and Perspective

IMAGES

Video Grabs
Vancouver
Toronto
Hong Kong

IMAGES

Sofa Rd | Hong Kong

At merely the cost of a thick black marker, this freelance sofa repairman went around the city and designed his unique advertising campaign, all on street car transformer boxes.

Gill Autrey Portfolio Center